Plug & Play
Programming

An Object-Oriented Construction Kit

An in-depth guide to building Plugs — a new object class for
connecting software components

- Create and use plugs to enhance object-oriented programming
- Use plugs to design simple controls and create class libraries
- Companion disk includes sample C++ code and a library of reusable plugs

 M&T BOOKS

William Wong

M&T Books
A Division of MIS:Press
A Subsidiary of Henry Holt and Company, Inc.
115 West 18th Street
New York, New York 10011

© 1993 by M&T Books

Printed in the United States of America

Library of Congress Cataloging-Publication Data

Wong, William, 1941–
Plug and play programming: an object-oriented construction kit / William Wong.
p. cm.
Includes index.
ISBN 1-55851-302-7: $39.95
1. Object-oriented programming (Computer science) I. Title.
QA76.64.W663 1993
005.1'1--dc20   93-20877
                    CIP

Publisher: Steve Berkowitz
Associate Publisher: Brenda McLaughlin
Development Editor: Margot Owens Pagan
Production Editor: Mark Masuelli
Assistant Production Editor: Joseph McPartland
Copy Editor: Judith Brown
Technical Editor: Michael Swaine

96   95   94   93   4   3   2   1

This book is dedicated to my children Jennifer, Robert and Laura, and to my wife Ann without whom this book would never have been completed.

Table of Contents

Acknowledgments

I would like to thank the editors at M&T Books for their help and encouragement. I would also like to thank everyone at Nu-Mega Technologies for allowing me to try out the plugs programming principles in my programming projects with them.

Why This Book is For You

This book is for if you're a C++ programmer who is gearing up to tackle a large project. *Plug & Play Programming* is for you, if you're tired of rewriting routines to implement standard features in a program, or, most important of all, if you want to write program code once and be able to use it again and again.

This book presents a new program construction technique based on a concept known as *plugs*. Plugs are objects that perform specific tasks and are designed to be reusable. They are also designed to connect to each other in a standard way, so that a series of plugs can be assembled into a functional program. This technique also makes it possible for you to remove one plug and replace it with another—no re-programming required.

In programming terminology, software plugs are *"...objects with associated class definitions."*

Plug & Play Programming shows you:

❍ How to build and use plugs

❍ How to design programs using plugs

❍ How to construct objects with plugs

❍ How to design your own plugs

❍ How to *debug* with plugs

One of the big advantages of programming with plugs is that the final application programmer does not need a high level of expertise in a broad number of areas. A programmer can use plugs, designed by experts in their field, without having to be fully versed in all the fine detail required by the designer of the plug. The overall end result is an increase in the quality of all programs that use *plug and play programming* techniques.

To help you get a running start in the use of software plugs, the book and accompanying disk contain sample C++ code and a library of reusable plugs you can work with immediately. For those of you who have not moved to C++ programming, but are using other object-oriented programming languages such as Pascal or Smalltalk, fear not. Appendix D shows you how to implement plugs in these languages too.

Introduction

This book presents a new programming method called *software plugs*. Plugs are an extension, and in some ways an alternative, to object-oriented programming. Plug-based programming attempts to deliver on the promise of object-oriented programming; the promise that programmers would be able to build programs from reusable software components.

In this introduction I explain the concept of software plugs and review the relevant object-oriented programming concepts.

Cookie Cutters

I have used a number of languages in my programming career. My introduction to object-oriented programming was through two early object-oriented languages: Simula and Smalltalk. Both are still around, and interest in Smalltalk has been growing along with the popularity of graphical environments such as Microsoft Windows and OS/2 Presentation Manager, both of which owe a lot to the Smalltalk interface. However, it is C++, an object-oriented extension of C, that is the most popular object-oriented programming language, due chiefly to the popularity of the C language.

Although each object-oriented language has its own syntax and semantics, they all share certain basic class, inheritance, and object building-block concepts.

A *class* is a description of a data structure and a set of functions that work with it. A class can be based upon another class, the *superclass*, meaning that the former can make use of the functions and data structure of the latter without having to define them for itself. In this case, the new class *inherits* the data structure and functions associated with its superclass. A class can inherit from more than one class if multiple inheritance is supported by the language.

Classes themselves don't do anything; the real action in object-oriented programming is in the objects. An *object* is an instance of a class. An object has the structure specified by the class definition, and any object of a class can use the functions defined with the class.

Object-oriented languages are a great advance in programming. Good programming practices of encapsulation and modularization, which had to be done manually using non-object-oriented languages like C, are built into object-oriented languages. Object-oriented languages also support the concept of polymorphism, which is a kind of interchangeability of software parts.

The benefits of object-oriented programming don't come automatically from using a particular language. Object-oriented programming is also a style or method of programming. Good object-oriented practices are important to good program construction and to the reuse of program code.

Think of it this way: Objects are the components used to construct a program, while classes are cookie cutters used to stamp out objects. Portions of a program can be reused by using the cookie cutter in another program or by modifying the cookie cutter so the objects will work in another program. Object-oriented programming makes the creation and manipulation of cookie cutters significantly easier than does conventional programming. Some people say that object-oriented programming ought to be called class-based programming. It is at its best in bringing order and ease to the development of cookie cutters.

Unfortunately, that's only part of the job. The overall design of a program still needs to be done, and this design must be implemented by connecting the various objects together. Object-oriented languages provide no better support for this aspect of program construction than do conventional programming languages. This is where plugs come in.

Software Plugs

The design and implementation of a computer program, particularly in an object-oriented framework, is similar in many ways to the design and implementation of a computer. Hardware can be a model for software. In software design, classes are effectively design specifications for objects. In computer design there are design specifications for integrated circuits, or chips. A class corresponds to a design specification; an object to a chip. A class can be used to instantiate any number of objects, and new classes can easily be produced as slight modifications of existing classes, from which new "lines" of objects can be cranked out. It's the same with chip design. A chip manufacturer uses the chip design specification to stamp out chips to be used in computers and other products. Designs can be changed incrementally but they remain somewhat compatible; consider the Intel 80386 and the 80386SX. Both use the same basic internal components but they have been customized. The 80386 has a 32-bit external interface, while the 80386SX has a 16-bit external interface. Chips can even exhibit polymorphism; take a simple quad 2 input NAND gate chip. This particular chip is available from a number of sources and some have different characteristics — faster, low-power, and so on. But you can unplug one chip and plug in another.

You can push this analogy between hardware and software design and implementation pretty far. Computers have higher level component structure, too. There are design specifications for circuit boards and peripherals, as well as for chips. Some people make a living plugging together components at this level. Likewise, there are different levels of design and implementation in software construction; more levels, in fact, in a large program. And the design analogy holds.

Where the analogy doesn't hold up well is in the implementation phase. The process of building a program from objects doesn't follow a nice clean parallel with the process of building a computer from components. In a computer, chips and higher level components are connected with wires. Completing a computer design is done by wiring the chips together. Connecting a PC with its keyboard and monitor is done using cables. Wires, connections, and cables are all relatively standard. This standardization of connection is extremely powerful, and is something everyone takes for granted, as you know if you have taken an electrical appliance to Europe.

Unfortunately, this powerful standardization of connection does not show up in program construction. Conventional program construction, even with classes and objects, is based on custom code written by a programmer that connects modules and objects. The closest program construction concept to wires—and it's not all that close— is probably the various interprocess communication (IPC) techniques. The plug-compatible approach in hardware design and construction, and the degree of standardization that it allows, just did not exist in software development. Until now.

Plugs are objects with associated class definitions. They are designed to provide a standard way to make connections between components. The program construction concept presented in this book shows: How to build and use plugs, How to design programs using plugs, and How to design your own plugs.

The chip analogy that broke down in the implementation phase in object-oriented programming can be carried further with this plug model.

Here's the hardware division of labor: Chip designers design chips, and computer designers design computers using chips. The chip designer supplies the computer designer with information about the chips and what connections may be made. The computer designer implements a computer by plugging the chips together. The chip designer works at a low level, while the computer designer works at a high level.

Now imagine a software component designer who designs plug classes for use by a programmer. The component designer supplies information about the component classes and what connections can be made. The programmer uses the components and connects them to make programs. The programmer works at a low level, while the component designer works at a high level.

I don't want to get carried away with this analogy. It breaks down in the distinction between the two levels of designers. It is a natural distinction in the hardware case. Chip designers typically use different tools and have different limitations and different goals than computer designers. Few computer designers have the resources to design a complete CPU like the Intel 80486. On the other hand, you use the same tools to build components as you do to build programs.

The analogy has served its purpose, because it makes it possible to see where the idea of plugs fits into the program construction process.

These plugs I'm introducing are objects. Like plugs or wires in hardware systems, these software plugs can be used in low-level portions of a software system (think of connections within a chip), up through higher level portions of a software system (think of connecting chips together or connecting the computer to peripherals).

An Example Using Plugs

Plugs have three major functions (two implemented as operators), which are used with any plug: a connection operator, <=; a disconnection operator, - and - -; and a function to check if a connection has been made, connected(). To see how these work, consider the following contrived example of a model computer system and its high-level interface. The software components include the computer, a keyboard, a display, and a printer. The computer, display, and printer will be plugged into a power connector, which will be the fifth component. The code to declare, connect, and start up the system looks like this:

```
PowerOutlet power ;
Computer computer ;
Display display ;
Printer printer ;

power.socket1 <= computer.power ;
power.socket2 <= display.power ;
power.socket3 <= printer.power ;
```

```
computer.keyboard <= keyboard ;
computer.display <= display.computer ;
computer.printer <= printer.computer ;

printer.poweron () ;
display .poweron () ;
computer.poweron () ;
```

The example assumes that each of the components has or is a plug. The computer is a component with four plugs: power, keyboard, display, and printer. The display and printer are each components with two plugs: computer and power. The keyboard is a simple component that is itself just a plug. The power outlet is a component with three plugs, here called sockets. The system is connected just like a real computer system would be connected and would be operational just like a real computer system would be, after it is connected and turned on. The high-level documentation for the components would describe what they are; what plugs are available (for example, the four just mentioned for the computer component); what each is used for, and what public functions are available (*poweron ()*). The amount and type of knowledge needed to build this system is significantly different from that required to build any of the components. The consistent connection mechanism, using <=, greatly simplifies the high-level description.

The other aspect of this high-level design approach is the way components can be built from other components.

Building components with plugs and components is an object-based construction method, as opposed to the inheritance-based construction technique normally employed with classes. Inheritance-based construction starts with a class similar to what you want. You then define a subclass and add to it or extend or change the superclass definition. Object-based construction starts with a set of components (objects) that are connected together to form a new component. This book is, in a sense, about object-based construction, as opposed to class-based design. Object-based construction can be accomplished using class definitions or some sort of template definition. The plug designs presented in this book use the class definition method. A template definition method works like this: A function is called to return an instance of the requested component. This function constructs the component by allocating the parts used to build the component and connecting them together. The interface to the component is through one of the parts, because a function cannot be used to define a new interface to an object as can a class definition. The component creation function can be simplified if a generic, table-driven component creation is available.

Class-based component definition is easier to extend and essentially includes the template definition method. In this case, a new class is defined, often with no superclass. The object structure contains the components or references to the components used to build the object. The initialization function for the class allocates any referenced components and connects the components together. In the computer model example, the computer component has four plug components, which would be connected internally. Additional functions, such as *poweron* () in the example, can be included with the class definition to manipulate the internal components. A template version of the class-based definition method is one that only includes the initialization function.

Compound Plugs and Megaprogramming
Some other plug-related issues covered in this book include compound plugs and megaprogramming. Warning: the next two paragraphs get into more detail than is absolutely necessary at this point, but compound plugs and megaprogramming are such important concepts that I want to introduce them here, at the risk of causing your eyes to glaze over. Don't get bogged down in these paragraphs; the topics of compound plugs and megaprogramming will be covered later. However, you shouldn't skip these two paragraphs altogether.

Compound plugs are analogous to physical connections with multiple wires, such as an AC power connection or a printer connection. The AC power cable contains three wires (two power wires and a ground). The printer cable contains dozens of wires. However, in both cases, all connections are made at once when the cable is plugged in. Likewise, all connections are broken when a cable is unplugged. A description of plugging in one of these cables is the same for each but always deals with the connection of the cable, not the connection of the individual wires. Compound plugs work the same way. You connect one compound plug to another, and all the internal connections between the two plugs are made for you. As a programmer, you specify only the compound connection. All the connections in our computer/keyboard/display/printer example could work in this fashion. Essentially, the inner workings are hidden.

Megaprogramming is a word coined to describe the creation of very large programs using large components. *Programming-in-the-large* is another term used to describe megaprogramming. *Programming-in-the-small* is a comparative term used to describe programming at the detailed level. Plugs are designed to work at all levels using the same syntax and semantics. This book also addresses efficiency issues that often crop up in megaprogramming discussions. This involves special plugs called *redirectors*. Redirectors are covered in more detail later in the book, but essentially they forward connection operations to the appropriate internal plugs so the real connection is made directly between two plugs, not through the redirectors. This aspect of plugs becomes very important when the number of levels of internal components becomes large. Redirectors allow one connection to cause one internal plug within one component to be connected directly to another internal plug in the other component. This can all be done without the designer's knowing about the internal construction of the internal components. The next chapter covers how plugs and redirectors operate and provides a more detailed description on how redirectors work and how they should be used.

Just as object-oriented programming is not only a matter of using an object-oriented language, plug-based programming is not only a matter of using plugs to build your programs. There is a plug-based style or design method. It's component-based design. The key to using plugs is to have a supply of components that use standard plugs. This book shows how to build plugs and use them. Some plugs are presented for use, but they are general in nature. You can build new components from scratch or use the ones presented as a basis for new components.

Plugs are not specific to C++, but this book and its examples are. It is simply a good language for implementing them. Appendix E provides a brief introduction to C++ and describes those parts of C++ used in this book. It should be a sufficient introduction if you are familiar with C. You can probably scan it quickly if you are already using C++. You can cover most of the material in this book without an understanding of C, but you may want to pick up a C++ book for reference if you are not familiar with C or C++. Appendix D addresses plugs in other languages, including Smalltalk and Pascal.

1 Program Construction: An Overview

Many issues are raised when discussing object-oriented programming environments. For instance, you've probably heard these promises before:

○ Interchangeable parts

○ Software integrated circuits

○ Reusable software

○ Enhancing software

○ Easier program construction

○ Megaprogramming

Some of these issues are addressed by using object-oriented languages such as C++ or Smalltalk, but most object-oriented languages, as they exist now, don't deliver on these promises.

This chapter addresses the advantages of using object-oriented programming languages, including the use of inheritance and classes, and the deficiencies in existing environments. The plug class is also introduced. Plugs? Yes, plugs. This whole book is based upon this one simple idea. So what are plugs, and how are they going to revolutionize object-oriented programming?

Plugs are a mechanism for connecting programs and parts of programs using a single syntax and protocol. This is similar to using files at the program level and pointers at the program code level. Before going into a more detailed discussion of plugs, let's take a look at how a conventional program is constructed.

Conventional Program Construction

Conventional program construction, including current object-oriented program construction, starts with a central module. (You can also read "central module" as the C *main()* function or the main object in some object-oriented environments.) The central module ordinarily accepts the initial input parameters for the program. It also usually uses other programmer- or system-provided modules. System modules provide support for operating system features like file system access, as well as general support routines like math libraries. These modules are associated with the main module using a linker to create a single program, or a dynamic linking mechanism, such as the one in Microsoft's Dynamic Link Libraries (DLL), which links modules together at runtime. The program interfaces with other programs, the user, and the file system through the system modules, which provide interprocess communication (IPC) support in the form of files, queues, pipes, and other system features. A structure diagram of a simple program might look like the one shown in Figure 1-1. Changes can be made by changing the code in a module and linking the program again. Program operation can be changed by altering the IPC input and output. For example, the results from a sorting program change when you give it a different file to sort.

This type of program is constructed as one monolithic piece. DLLs and IPC connections make the program adaptable but at a rather coarse level. For example, programs can be used as components at this level and have proven useful in environments such as UNIX, where the output of one command-line program can be linked to another. Program options can often be specified using command-line options or through a configuration file. This is considered a coarse level of adaptability because it is done in respect to the program, which itself is not modified. The connections between programs tend to be few in number and simple in nature, such as a stream of bytes. UNIX programs, for example, can be connected using a syntax like the following:

```
cat | sort | more
```

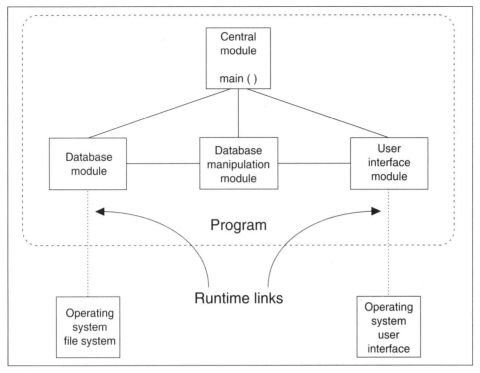

Figure 1-1. Structure of a simple database program

The vertical bars (pipes) indicate that the default output stream of the program on the left is to be connected to the default input stream of the program on the right. The same **cat** program generates an output byte stream that is a list of filenames found in the current directory, with one filename per line. The **sort** program reads this output stream, sorts it alphabetically by line, and sends it to its output stream. In the example, this output stream is connected to the input stream of the **more** program. The **more** program displays the stream a page at a time on the user's display (typically around 24 lines) and waits for input from the user. The user presses a key to see each subsequent page. In a multitasking environment like UNIX, all three programs are running at one time. Figure 1-2 shows how these programs would be connected when they are running.

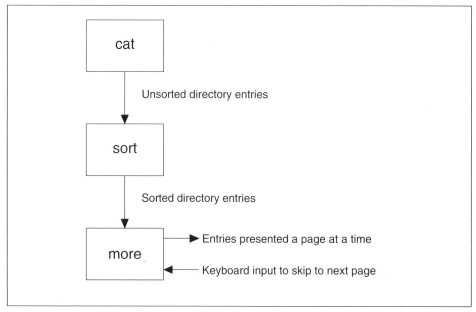

Figure 1-2.UNIX pipes

The combination of these programs can also be viewed as a program written in a higher level user interface shell script language. The operation of the program can be altered by changing the modules or the program code. For example, you could replace the **more** program with a fancier list program or text editor, or you could rewrite the program.

Changing the module is a coarse level of change. Understanding how a module change will affect a program requires a good understanding of the other modules used in the program and how they relate to the replacement module. In the simple UNIX example, the use and the relationship between modules is very apparent. Unfortunately, modules used in more complex applications tend to be used from anywhere within an application. The dependencies are often difficult to describe and often undocumented. For example, a math library may be used by a number of different modules. Some modules may use one set of functions, while another module may use a different set. Some functions provided by the library may not be used at all. Replacing the math module requires a knowledge of what is used, where it is used, and why.

Compared to changing modules, changing program code requires an even more detailed knowledge of both the program and the programming language. With modules, the assumption is that they are already written and it is simply a matter of choosing the appropriate one. Writing or modifying code is a different matter. Unfortunately, it is often the only alternative to modifying or using a portion of a program.

Code modification is a very fine level of change. For example, the **sort** program sorts the input in ascending order. The UNIX and DOS versions of this program may use additional command-line parameters to change this order, but for the example used here, assume that no parameters can be used. However, the source code is available. To make this **sort** program sort in descending order, you could make a minor change to the comparison used when sorting. To do this you must have a knowledge of the programming language, the layout of the program, and the algorithm being used.

Object-oriented programming adds the idea of classes and inheritance to program construction. A class is a way to encapsulate data and data structures along with the associated code. An object is an instance of a class that has the specified data structure and uses the associated code. A simple C++ class definition looks like the following:

```
class SimpleClass
{
  public:
    int i ;
    long l ;
    long SampleFunction () { return i + l ; }
} ;
```

An object of type *SimpleClass* is a structure with two variables: *i* and *l*. The *SampleFunction* can only be used with objects of this type or objects of classes that are built from this class. A class definition that inherits another class looks like the following:

```
class SimpleInheritedClass : public SimpleClass
{
  public:
    char c ;
    long SampleFunction2 () { return SampleFunction () + c; }
} ;
```

Objects of type *SimpleInheritedClass* contain the two variables defined for *SimpleClass* objects, as well as an additional *char* variable defined in the new class. *SampleFunction* is still applicable to this new class, and a new function has been added. This new function can be used with objects of this type but not with objects of type *SimpleClass*. The next section in this chapter describes some of the class syntax and semantics for C++ used in examples in this book.

The class and inheritance mechanisms provide a low-level (fine) mechanism for modular program construction as compared to the high-level (coarse) mechanism of module replacement. Portions of a program can be used again by using the classes, with possible modification through inheritance. These mechanisms are well defined and very useful, but they require a working knowledge of object-oriented programming, the programming language, and the class definition.

The coarse level of detail of a program leads to limited interaction between programs. Most applications tend to be monolithic, with features added at the fine level of detail, which requires a good deal of programming skill and knowledge. Microsoft Windows Dynamic Data Exchange (DDE) and Object Linking and Embedding (OLE) are two very important ways under Microsoft Windows where programs are being reused by other programs at a coarse level. DDE is a mechanism whereby two Windows programs can exchange data. OLE is a more complex scheme that allows a server program to provide services to a client program for manipulating and displaying data in a window that is part of the client program. The problem is that the techniques do not translate into tools for constructing a program. Using the techniques involved in DDE and OLE is also very different from using the programming techniques to implement the interfaces used within a program.

For example, both DDE and OLE have a set of functions and a low-level protocol for connecting two programs together. These functions and protocol must be implemented using fine level changes by writing code in a programming language like C or C++. The user of the program is expected to make the connections between programs using features provided by the application, which might include a menu/dialog box interaction, or using the drag-and-drop technique. An example of an OLE drag-and-drop operation involves a word processor and a file manager program. The mouse is used to select a file in the directory list provided by the file manager and to drag the entry to the word processor window containing a document. The file is then imbedded in the document. The word processor is the client, and it creates the window for the imbedded file to be displayed. The program associated with the imbedded file is run to provide the proper display of the imbedded file.

The details and features of DDE and OLE are beyond the scope of this book, but the example should give you an idea of the power and complexity involved. However, the difference between this type of coarse interconnection and the fine interconnection used within a program should be apparent.

Unfortunately, there is little middle ground within an application. For example, a programmer typically starts with building blocks that include the primitive operations and data structures provided by the programming language, such as numbers, strings, and arrays. The operating system and libraries provide additional building blocks such as files, window objects, and so on. The programmer creates additional structures and code to tie the basic building blocks together. These structures and code tend to be specific to the application program. The names and semantics of the functions and pointers used within the program also tend to be specific to the program or programmer.

This middle ground is where the plug class comes in. Program components can be viewed as having a set of well-defined connections called plugs. The programmer uses these components by connecting the plug of one component to a matching plug. Simpler components are used to build more complex components by plugging the simple components together. A class defines each type of component, and a component is an object that is an instance of that class. The complex component object is built from instances of other objects of other classes. This form of construction concentrates on connection instances of objects to extend functionality. On the other hand, conventional object-oriented design recommends extension by inheritance or composition. Extension by inheritance is accomplished by defining a new class, which inherits characteristics from another class. Composition uses other objects or pointers to objects when defining a new class. Connecting objects is a job left to the programmer. The problem with letting the programmer define the connection process is the number of methods available and the variety of names, syntax, and semantics that may be used. The ability of one programmer to read, understand, and possibly change or reuse all or a portion of another programmer's work will be based upon how well this variety of items is defined and understood.

The following example shows how different function names can be used to make a connection using conventional program design. The choice of names can make the operation being performed apparent to anyone reading the code. Unfortunately, the choice may not always be obvious to everyone.

```
A.setFile ( B ) ;
A.foobar ( C ) ;
A.OpenBuffer ( D ) ;
A.setup ( E, F ) ;
```

The first line looks more like a connection operation than any of the others. The second line could do anything, while the last two might perform any operation. Within a program using arbitrary name conventions, the specific nature of the connecting process makes it more difficult to understand and recognize. Plugs address this issue by using a consistent syntax for connection and disconnection.

Plugs are designed to standardize the connection and disconnection process and to provide a middle ground between internal construction of specific components and the external interface of the program. The three public member functions used by a plug class for making or breaking a connection include the following:

```
A <= B ;
-A ;
--A ;
```

Figure 1-3 shows how these operations are related to the objects involved. The first is used to connect plug A to socket B. After the operation is completed, both objects have a reference to each other, hence the use of arrowheads at both ends of the connecting line. The other two code examples disconnect plug A from whatever it is plugged into. In the figure, this happens to be plug B. The reason for two disconnect functions is that -A will return a pointer to the plug that A was plugged into, while the other does not. The operator - -A also tells the other end that it is no longer needed. This is important for dynamically created plugs because they will normally delete themselves at this point. The operator -A indicates that the other end will be used again.

Referring to everything as a plug can be somewhat confusing, so to avoid confusion, one end of a connection is called a plug, and the other end is called the socket. There is no differentiation in connection operations with respect to a plug or socket. All plugs are objects that have an associated class definition. Connections are defined using a pair of plug classes. One is referred to as the plug and the other the socket. A plug can be connected to a socket of the matching type. Plugs cannot be connected to other plugs or sockets of types that do not match. This is analogous to having a set of connectors on a video monitor. One socket is for the power and the other is for the video. You cannot plug a power cord into the video socket or a video cable into the power socket. However, plugs can be polymorphic. For example, a basic plug class can be inherited by another class, and the objects from this new class can be used in place of a basic plug class object. This is analogous to having a video monitor plug that can connect to a monochrome monitor or a color monitor.

All of the discussion in this book regarding plugs applies equally to sockets. Operationally, there is no difference between plugs and sockets, so a given con-

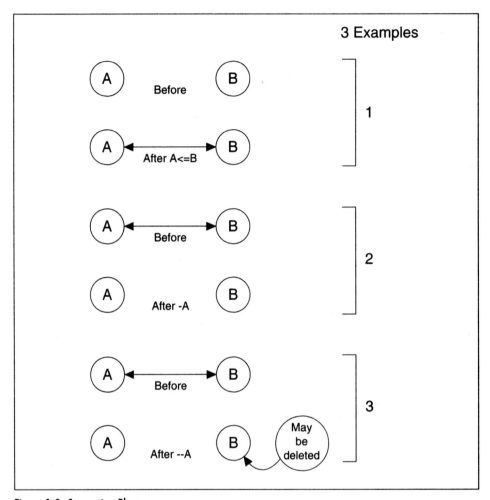

Figure 1-3. Connecting Plugs

figuration will work equally well if you define one end to be a socket or a plug. The only requirement is that the other end be of the corresponding type.

C++ allows C operators like -, - -, and <= to be defined specifically for any class. The choice of C operators instead of function names is made to illustrate the operation and to reduce the amount of typing. The alternative looks like *A.connect(B)* or *A.disconnect()*. The following example shows how both operators and normally named functions are defined in a class definition:

```
class SampleOperators
{
  public;
    void operator - () ;
    void disconnect () ;
} ;
```

Note that the connect and permanent disconnect operators return no value
and cannot be included as part of assignment or arithmetic operations. This
should prevent them from accidentally being used in expressions. For example, the following would not be allowed:

```
A <= B <= C ;
R = A <= B ;
if ( A <= B ) {}
```

Plugs have two status functions: connected and usable. The former returns
an indication as to whether a plug is connected to another plug. The latter
always returns a non-zero value for a plug, but may return a zero value for a
redirector.

A redirector is an object that works like a plug, but it really forwards operations to a plug that it points to. Although a redirector may sound like a simple pointer, it is much more. A redirector can point to another redirector,
which in turn points to a plug. Plug operations used with either redirector are
forwarded to the plug.

The redirector does not get involved with other interactions that occur once
a plug is connected. The redirector's connected and usable functions return a
zero value if the redirector does not point to a plug and a non-zero value if it
does. Redirectors have one additional function that is not provided with a
plug; the *redirect* function used to assign a plug reference to the redirector.
For example:

```
R.redirect ( A ) ;
```

Here, R is a redirector and A is a plug. A redirector is connected if it is usable and the plug at the end is connected. A simple example showing redirected plugs follows:

```
R1a.redirect ( A ) ;
R2a.redirect ( R1a ) ;
R1b.redirect ( B ) ;
R2b.redirect ( R1b ) ;
R2a <= R2b ;
```

Figure 1-4 shows the structure created by this code. Normally these statements would not appear within the same section of code, but it gives an idea of how

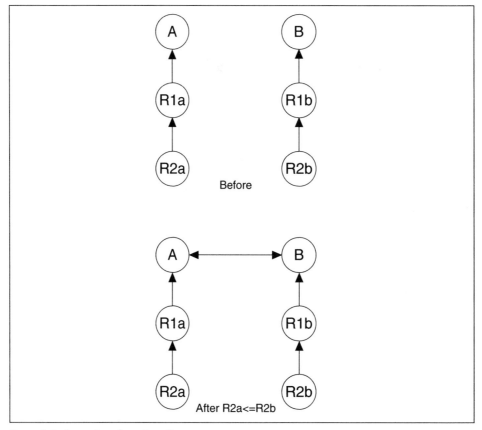

Figure 1-4. Connecting plugs via redirectors

the plugs and redirectors work. The first four statements set up four redirectors. The figure shows these connections with a single arrow indicating the direction of operations. In terms of implementation, a plug will normally have a pointer back to its redirector. This pointer is used for internal operations only. The last statement connects A to B. Note that the redirectors are not connected in any way, and the end result is the same as doing A <= B. Operations between A and B are done as efficiently as always because the redirectors are not in the way. Plug operations can still be performed using the redirectors. This means that a disconnect operation can be performed with A if you have access to A, R1a, or R2a. A redirector is reset by assigning it a zero value.

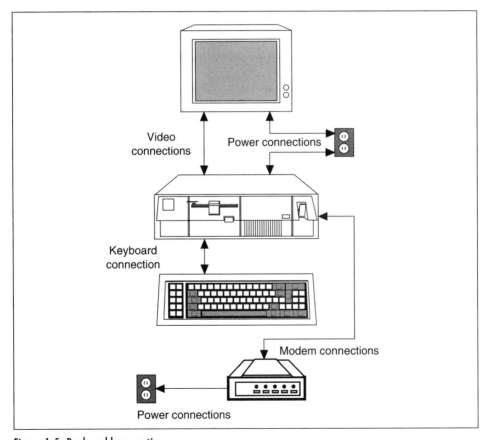

Figure 1-5. Real world connections

The concept of plugs and connections can be illustrated by analogy to a standard PC with its collection of cords and plugs, as shown in Figure 1-5. There may be a dozen connections on a single system, but you cannot plug the power cord into the modem port or the monitor into the keyboard. Each connection is keyed, and it does not matter which end gets plugged in first. Likewise, disconnecting either end of a cord effectively breaks the connection for both ends. The number of interchangeable components for the various parts of a computer system show the power of this approach.

Two questions you might have come up with are: How do you know what kind of plug can be used with another? Which plug should be on the left or right? The answer to the first question is that a connection definition defines a pair of plug classes (one plug and one socket class), and all classes based upon these classes will work with each other. The answer to the second question is, it doesn't matter. The following two statements are identical:

```
A <= B ;
B <= A ;
```

This example also shows off the two-sided nature of plugs. Conventional program construction uses single-sided pointers. That is, an object such as a stream or a buffer can be referenced by another object, but the stream object does not know how or if it is being referenced. Plugs do. Likewise, it does not matter which side of a plug is disconnected since both ends of a connection have references to each other, and both ends are disconnected regardless of which side was disconnected first. The use of - and - - may affect how the other end will respond, but the connection will always be closed. The - operator indicates that the disconnect is temporary and the plug will eventually be reconnected. The - - operator indicates that the disconnect is permanent and that the plug will no longer be needed. This information can be used by dynamic plugs to delete themselves when they are no longer needed.

A dynamic plug works like a normal plug with two differences. The first is that it is allocated from the heap (free space). The second is that it will delete itself. It does so when it is permanently disconnected. This provides a simple form of garbage collection. Dynamic plugs are important when constructing systems built from components using plugs because the builder should not have to worry about what happens when a connection is broken. Dynamic component design is more complex because the dynamic component should delete itself when all connections have been broken. A number of components could be deleted in response to a single dynamic plug connection being broken. An entire chapter is dedicated to dynamic plug design and use.

So far, the discussion has been about connections and disconnections. But another piece of the puzzle concerns what occurs after a connection is made and before it is broken. A plug can be used to access the object at the other end of the connection using the standard C indirect component selector operator, ->. This operator is normally used with a pointer to access the object it points to. C++ allows any class to define what the operator does. In this case, the plug's -> operator is used to access elements defined within the plug at the other end of the connection. The elements are specific to the class of the plug at the other end, but the operation and definition of the operator is the same for all plugs. Given a reference to a connected plug, you can access the plug's elements and the elements of the plug at the other end of the connection using ->. A plug must be connected before using ->, and the plug should be checked to see if it is connected before using the -> operator if there is a possibility that the plug has been disconnected. An error checking mechanism is described in Appendix A.

The use of the -> operator, and what elements or functions can be accessed through it, are specific to a connection definition. For example, using a plug that contains an output stream might look like the following:

```
A -> OutputStream << Hello world\n ;
```

Here, *OutputStream* is a stream located in the plug connected to A. It is more efficient to obtain a pointer to the stream if it will be used repeatedly. Plugs do not obviate the need for pointers or efficient programming practices. For example, many operations are inherently one-sided and do not require the complexity of plugs. Scanning a string of characters is more efficiently done with a simple pointer. It is important that the programmer choose the appropriate tool for the job. Plugs are just another tool to use.

Declaring Plugs and Connections

Plugs and sockets are always declared in pairs and associated with a single connection. Defining a connection is relatively simple. C macros are used to simplify the process, as shown in the next example. This approach allows the connection definitions to be customized for a particular compiler. Refer to the appendixes for details on which definition will work with your compiler.

A connection definition requires two base classes to be defined after the connection is defined. These base classes are used as the basis for the plug and socket classes of the connection. The two base classes in the next example are *plugBaseA* and *socketBaseA*. They are used in conjunction with the *DECLARE_CONNECTION* macro. The *DECLARE_CONNECTION* macro defines a connection class that contains eight classes, including an abstract plug and socket class, a plug and socket class, normal redirector classes for the latter, and dynamic redirector classes. Abstract classes are classes having at least one function that is defined but not implemented. A class that inherits from an abstract class is also an abstract class if it does not implement all of the unimplemented functions.

Objects cannot be allocated using abstract classes. Abstract classes are used to implement polymorphic objects or interchangeable parts. For example, you start with an abstract class A with a function *foo* that is not implemented. You then define classes A1 and A2 based upon A. Objects of type A1 and A2 can be used interchangeably wherever a reference to an object of type A is required. You can have pointers or references to an object of class A, but you cannot create an object of class A, only objects of classes that inherit from class A.

All plug classes are based upon the Plug class, which defines a minimum set of functions provided by all plug classes. This class and other definitions required for plugs and connections is contained in the *PLUGS.HPP* file. The protocols defined by the classes in this file are covered in the next chapter. The contents of the file are presented in Appendix A. The Plug class definition looks like the following:

```
class Plug
{
  public:
    virtual ~Plug () {}
    virtual BOOL usable        () {return TRUE;}
    virtual BOOL isRedirector  () {return FALSE;}
    virtual BOOL connected     () = 0 ;
    virtual void operator --   () = 0 ;
    virtual void connectFailed (){}
} ;
```

You will be looking at these functions and others in the rest of the book.

The first example of a connection definition uses two macros: *DECLARE_CONNECTION* and *DECLARE_PLUG*. These macros are used throughout the book and define the plug and connection classes that allow objects and subclasses to be defined. The first connection definition looks like the following:

```
DECLARE_CONNECTION ( connectionA, plugBaseA,
  socketbaseA )
class plugBaseA : public connectionA::plug
{
  public:
    DECLARE_PLUG ()
    int inPlugA ;
} ;
class socketBaseA : public connectionA::socket
{
  public:
    DECLARE_PLUG ()
    int inSocketA ;
} ;
```

The macro is expanded by the compiler at compile time and compiled. The macro expands into the class definitions. These classes provide the basis for other class definitions that can be used to allocate class objects. This approach makes it easier to use polymorphic plug objects from different classes that inherit from the same base connection class, or more simply, interchangeable parts.

The plug classes are defined so objects of class *connectionA::plug* can only be connected to objects of class *connectionA::socket*.

The classes defined at this point provide all the members for making, maintaining, and breaking a single connection. Additional classes must be defined using these classes if the base classes contain pure virtual members.

The following code shows how to create a connection using the plug and socket classes defined in the sample code:

```
void sample ()
{
   plugA A ;
   socketA B2, B1 ;
   A <= B1 ;
   A -> inSocketA = 1 ;
   B1 -> inPlugA = 2 ;
   A <= B2 ;
   B2 -> inPlugA = 3 ;
}
```

The preceding function doesn't do anything useful, but it does show how plugs can be created, connected, and accessed. Figure 1-6 shows how plugs *A*, *B1*, and *B2* are connected during the operation of this function. The first connection is made by statement *A <= B1*. A second connection is made by statement *A <= B2*. Note that A and B1 are first disconnected when A is connected to B2. B1 can no longer be used to access *inPlugA* in *plug A* after *B1* is disconnected from *A*.

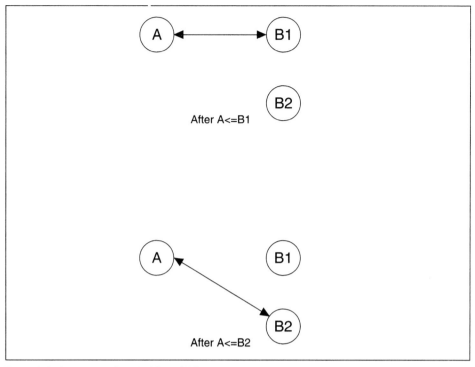

Figure 1-6. Connecting plugs A, B1, and B2

The three plugs (okay, a plug and two sockets, but they are both really plugs) are defined as locals to the sample function, and they will be disconnected and then freed when the function exits. Automatic cleanup is one of the advantages of C++. Plugs may be dynamically allocated using *new* just like any other object. Chapter 8 shows how to create dynamic plugs and components using various techniques.

The *DECLARE_CONNECTION* macro defines redirector classes implicitly. Two types of redirector classes are defined for the plug and socket classes for a connection. The first type is a basic redirector class. The second type is a dynamic redirector class. (Dynamic redirector classes are described in more detail in Chapter 8.) The following example defines a pair of redirectors:

```
connection::plugRedirector MyPlugRedirector ;
connection::socketRedirector MySocketRedirector ;
```

Redirectors can be defined immediately after a connection is defined using the *DECLARE_CONNECTION* macro. The classes are not abstract and are typically used as is instead of being subclassed. *DECLARE_CONNEC-TION* expands to a rather large amount of text that is on the order of 2K to 4K, depending upon the length of the parameters. The Microsoft C 7.0 & C 8.0 compiler is the only compiler that I have encountered with respect to the *DECLARE_CONNECTION* macro due to its small, fixed-size macro expansion buffer. The problem was only encountered when the class name parameters were lengthy; on the order of 25 characters each. Reducing the size of the connection name by a few characters usually eliminates the problem. I discovered the problem while writing a sample program with some rather verbose class names. The complete source for the macro is given in Appendix A, along with a description of its contents. You can refer to Appendix A if you encounter any problems using the macro. The macro is defined in the file *PLUGS.HPP.*

Megaprogramming, Programming-in-the-Large, and Programming-in-the-Small

The terms megaprogramming and programming-in-the-large are used to describe program creation at a very high level. These terms typically imply very large programs and programming staffs, and building large systems from smaller components. Project management and CASE systems are often used in these environments. Project management software provides the coordination and documentation needed for large systems, but it does not do well at connecting the components together. CASE systems do better in this area because they are designed to generate program code. CASE systems have typically been used to connect a basic set of components together; for example, menus and dialog boxes. A program specification often involves the creation of menus and dialog boxes using screen-based editors. The CASE systems connect menu selections to dialog boxes by generating the conventional C program code to bring up a dialog box when a menu item is selected. These systems make program construction easier, but the code they generate is sometimes difficult to modify.

Plugs address the construction aspect of megaprogramming. The same protocol is used for a simple plug or a very complex plug. A connection may provide access between a buffer and a communication port driver or between a client portion and a server portion of a program. Plugs make it easy to connect or disconnect large components using a consistent mechanism.

The term *programming-in-the-small* refers to the fine details of programming ordinarily associated with writing a small program or module. All programs are eventually implemented at a low level, whether through an assembler, compiler, or interpreter.

Plugs must be discussed at both levels because they are implemented at a low level and used at a high level. Both levels are addressed in this book. At the high level, or *programming-in-the-large* level, plugs are discussed from the aspect of using the plug operations for connecting and disconnecting. Plugs and components can also have functions associated with them that invoke high-level operations using their connection. At the low level, or *programming-in-the-small* level, plugs are discussed from the aspect of plug object contents and functions at the other end of a connection. The high-level functions invoke the lower level functions. Using the high-level functions should not require the knowledge or understanding of the lower level functions.

Plugging, Unplugging, and Other Plug Ideas

Plugs are used to make connections. One aspect of plugs not readily apparent is the ability to unplug a pair of plugs and reconnect one or both of them to different plugs. This can be done for a number of reasons. You might want to insert a filter between two plugs, add a debugging or trace facility between two plugs, or replace one or both of the plugs for other purposes. An example of the latter case would be replacing an existing component such as a text editor with another component.

Unplugging and reconnecting plugs is not a difficult operation. The following example shows how to plug a pair of plugs together, unplug them, and plug them into different plugs.

```
void plugUnplugExample ( plugA & A1 )
{
  plugA A2 ;
  socketA B2, * pB1 ;
  pB1 = -A1 ;            // disconnect and save other end
  A1 <= B2 ;             // new setup
  A2 <= (* pB1 ) ;
}
```

Figure 1-7 shows how the plugs relate to each other as each statement is executed. *A1* is assumed to be already connected to another plug, called *B1*. Note that all the plugs are disconnected when the function returns because a plug automatically disconnects itself before it is destroyed. Plug *A1* will still exist, but it will not be connected to *B2* because *B2* is local to this function. This example uses the - operator to disconnect *A1* so *B1* does not get deleted. It would only be deleted if *B1* is a dynamic plug, but there is no way to determine this. Also, the - operator is the only way to obtain a reference to *B1*.

This is a contrived example, but it shows how a connected pair of plugs (assume that *A1* is connected to *B1*) can be disconnected and reconnected. *A1* is directly accessible, while a pointer is used to keep track of *B1*. In most instances a function will not have direct access to both ends of a connection, but it can obtain the reference by disconnecting the plug it does have access to. The new setup shows the two ways a plug can be reconnected.

There is no useful work done in this example because it would occur only after the connection has been made. The two plugs defined locally in the example will be deleted when the function exits, which will cause the two plugs, *A1* and *B1*, to be disconnected when the function exits. Adding the following statement to the end of the function will reconnect them:

```
A1 <= (* pB1) ;
```

The ability to disconnect and reconnect plugs is extremely important for program construction based upon existing programs. An existing program can be enhanced or changed if the appropriate plugs are available for reconnection and their types are known. The types must be known in order to make new connections to the proper type of plug.

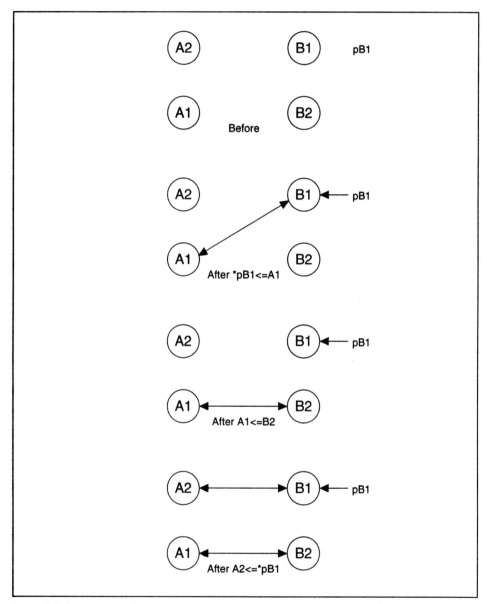

Figure 1-7. Reconnecting plugs

Most large or complex programs tend to be dynamic, both from a construction viewpoint and a data viewpoint. Plugs adapt well to this environment because they can be disconnected and then reconnected for other purposes or to other parts of the program. A plug need not be connected at all times, but a program needs to be written properly to accommodate possible disconnections. In general, this is not too different than trying not to use an unopened file.

Plug and Component Design

Connections always define a pair of plugs: one designated a plug and the other a socket. Plugs may have public data and functions, also called members and member functions, included as part of their definition, or they may be more complex. Access to public data and functions is straightforward. The public functions are considered the high-level plug interface. However, the purpose and implications of the public data and function need to be well defined if others are to use a particular pair of plugs. Data that are objects or pointers to objects require more description. This description should include answers to questions like these: What is the pointer used for? Where is the object referenced by the pointer located? What can be done with the referenced object?

The way each object is to be used must also be made clear. In general, data and pointers associated with plugs should be kept to a minimum, especially if redirectors will be used. Redirectors can only be used to make and break connections, but they inherit any data items defined in the plug base classes. Functions incur no or almost no overhead, but data members can incur overhead. This overhead will be wasted with a redirector object.

Another consideration is the use of plugs within plugs, called compound plugs. These are analogous to a physical connector with multiple wires, such as the keyboard plug and cable on a PC. One large plug causes many smaller connections to be made when the large plug is connected. The way to accomplish this with plug classes is to include public pointers to additional plugs. The connection methods must also be redefined for the class so the additional plugs can be connected whenever the outer plug is connected. Disconnection support is also required. The details on how this is done internally are covered later in the book.

Compound plugs are connected to the corresponding plug types using the same protocols as simple plugs. For example:

```
void compoundPlugExample
  ( compoundPlugA & cpA, simplePlugA & spA )
{
  compoundSocketA cpB ;
  simpleSocketA spB ;
  cpA <= cpB ;
  spA <= spB ;
}
```

This example assumes, of course, that the *A* and *B* plug types can be connected to each other. What has not been presented is how complex the compound plugs really are. If you are designing a plug, it is necessary to know the details of the plug protocol. You need to know about the abstract class definitions if you are creating a polymorphic plug. These details can be found in Appendix A. However, if you are using an existing plug definition, then changing the plug protocol functions may be all that is necessary to make use of the plug, whether it is internally a simple or complex plug. These details are covered in Chapter 9.

The lack of distinction between simple and complex plugs at the connection protocol level makes the plug concept a powerful tool in program design, because much of the power of a program comes from how the components are connected and used. Keep this lack of distinction in mind as you move on to the discussion of program construction considerations in the next section.

A number of different aspects of plugs and components have been covered so far. The following is a quick overview of the central terms used in this book.

○ **Plug.** A plug is an object that can be connected to a matching socket (which is also a plug object).

○ **Component.** A component is an object that contains one or more plug or redirector objects, or pointers to plug or redirector objects. You use a component by making connections with the component's plugs.

○ **Compound plug.** A compound plug is a special case of a component that is also a plug. At the high-level interface, the compound plug looks and works like a simple plug. The plugs and redirectors on either side of the connection are used by the low-level functions. Connecting a compound plug to its mate also causes these plugs to be connected to their counterparts in the mate, as shown in Figure 1-8. The corresponding disconnect operations are performed when the compound plug is disconnected. Figure 1-9 shows the same type of operation as Figure 1-8, but the low-level plugs on one side are replaced with redirectors to externally defined plugs.

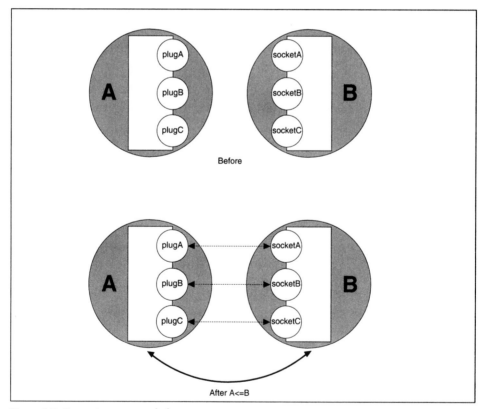

Figure 1-8. Connecting compound plugs

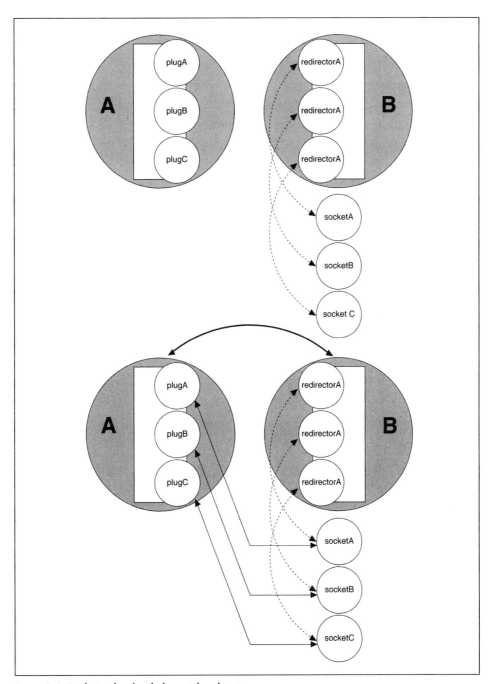

Figure 1-9. Replacing low-level plugs with redirectors

Component design is usually easier than plug design because the plugs and redirectors used within a component are already designed and available. Building a component is a matter of designing and implementing a class using the appropriate mix of public plugs and additional methods or variables necessary to get the job done. A program is then constructed by allocating the necessary components and plugging them together. Typically, at least one component will have a member function to start things going. For example:

```
DECLARE_CONNECTION
   ( StartupConnect
   , StartupPlug
   , StartupSocket
   )
class StartupPlug : public StartupConnect::plug
{
  public:
    DECLARE_PLUG ()
    void Startup () ;
} ;
class StartupSocket : public StartupConnect::socket
{
  public:
    DECLARE_PLUG ()
    void LowLevelFunction () ;
} ;
void main ()
{
  StartupPlug plug ;
  StartupSocket socket ;
  plug <= socket ;
  plug.Startup () ;
}
```

All this just to show the *Startup* function. In theory, this is how plugs should be used at the high level. The appropriate objects are defined, connected, and then a high-level function is used to start things rolling. Additional high-level functions may be called while everything is still connected.

Using Plugs in Program Construction

Program construction can be viewed from a number of different levels. At the low end you have the syntax of the programming language and the options for compilers and linkers. At the high end you have CASE tools, program generators, and project management tools. The middle area, where plugs are used, is discussed here.

For purposes of discussion in this section, assume that most or all of the plugs to be used in a program are already implemented, and constructing a program is a matter of plugging them together. Likewise, the majority of the components used within a program will already be defined. In the simplest case, everything is done within the main function. The main function is whatever function is initially called when a program starts up. This is *main()* for a standard C program for environments like DOS or UNIX, but it may be another function in environments like Windows or the OS/2 Presentation Manager. An example under DOS follows:

```
void main ()
{
  plugA A ;
  plugB B ;
  componentC C ;
  A <= C.mySocketA ;
  B <= C.mySocketB ;
  C.startup () ;
}
```

The initial overall construction for this program should be readily apparent. Figure 1-10 shows the structure built up by the connection statements. There are three components. The central component, *C,* is connected to a pair of simple plugs, *A* and *B*. The entire operation is started up by the component method *C.startup ()*.

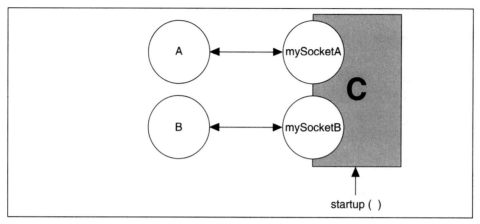

Figure 1-10. A basic component

A more complex construction example is shown in Figure 1-11. The different line styles are used to make them easier to follow--the style does not indicate anything special. The code to build this structure looks like the following:

```
void main ()
{
    componentA A1, A2 ;
    componentB B1, B2 ;
    componentC C ;
    A1.plugA <= C.matchingSocketA ;
    B1.plugB <= C.matchingSocketB ;
    A1.matchingSocketD <= A2.plugD ;
    B2.matchingSocketA <= A2.plugA ;
    C.matchingSocketC <= A2.plugC ;
    A1.setup () ;
    A2.setup () ;
    C.startup () ;
}
```

Again, the purpose of the program has not been defined, but the high-level connections are rather evident from the statements in the main function. Additional setup methods have been invoked, which would seem to perform some required operations.

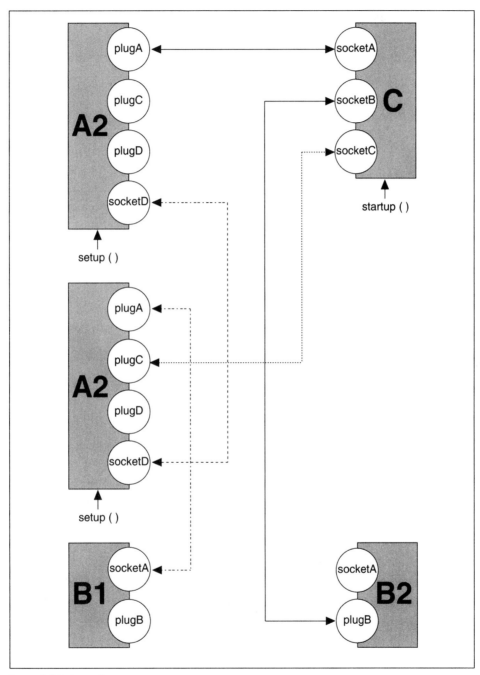

Figure 1-11. A set of components

How does this method of program construction differ from conventional modular program construction? The difference becomes apparent if you compare the prior example with a more conventional program example, albeit a contrived program:

```
void main ()
{
   componentA A1, A2 ;
   componentB B1, B2 ;
   componentC C ;
   A1.plugA.setFile ( C.matchingSocketA ) ;
   B1.plugB.setWidget ( C.matchingSocketB ) ;
   A2.plugD.marginObject ( C1.matchingSocketD ) ;
   A2.plugA.setFile ( B2.matchingSocketA ) ;
   A2.plugC.assignHandler ( C.matchingSocketC ) ;
   A1.setup () ;
   A2.setup () ;
   C.startup () ;
}
```

The names of the components remain the same, and the logical names of the plugs remain the same. The setup and startup methods remain the same. Two major changes have taken place. First, the connection between the components is not obvious and, due to the unidirectional nature of pointers, there may not necessarily be an associated linkage between components. Second, the method of connection is component specific. Note how the *setFile* method must be used to connect *plugA* to *matchingSocketA*. Again, due to the unidirectional nature of pointers, *matchingSocketA* must be connected to *plugA* using the *setFile method*.

On the plus side, the connecting method names may enhance the readability of the sample program and give some insight into the purpose of the components, assuming you know what a file or widget is. However, descriptive method names are not a replacement for good documentation or comments. In this example the file or widget could be anything, but it is hoped that the documentation or comments would describe them adequately.

On the minus side, all sense of interconnection between the components has been lost, and you must now know the unique methods used to connect one part of a component with another. Also, it is not apparent that a connection is actually made. There are four different function names used to make connections. It is assumed that this version of the program does the same thing as the prior plug-based example. Changing the method name from *setFile* to *useFile* or *setupResponse* may make the purpose of the operation very obscure. There is also a propensity to include a number of other setup parameters when defining methods, to either simplify the setup/connection procedure or to perform additional operations based upon the other parameters. In this case, the actual connection parameter might be mixed up in the parameter list, or multiple connections may be made using multiple parameters. Just to confuse the issue, a programmer might require some connections using references, while another programmer might use pointers. C++ allows both types of parameters, so the choice is arbitrary. A programmer might have a preference one way or the other, and library code may use a different preference than that of the programmer. In any case, the lack of consistency is due to the lack of a standard protocol. The plug protocol is consistent in both syntax and semantics.

The use of plugs and components does not totally eliminate the requirement for methods of this type nor the use of pointers or references. In fact, to be simple and useful, a plug may contain all of these and more. What plugs and components do is make the connection process consistent, easy, and apparent.

In general, a program is constructed by allocating the initial set of components, connecting them together, and then invoking the necessary methods to start up one or more of the components. Additional components and plugs may need to be built depending upon the available components and the requirements of the application. There is also the consideration of dynamically allocated components and additional and dynamic connections that may occur while a program is operating.

Making connections is not the only thing that can be done with components. There is also the issue of modification of internal component connections.

These connections would normally be set up by the component when it is created. However, the application using the component may need to modify these connections for a variety of reasons. For example, the programmer may wish to filter the information going across a connection. The programmer can insert a component between the two plugs involved in the connection. The component would have to include two plugs of the appropriate type to be plugged into the two plugs involved in the connection. Another reason for altering a connection is to replace the component on one side of the connection with a new component.

Replacement of internal components or the addition of new internal components can be easily accomplished if the component being modified makes one or more internally used plugs available in some fashion. This can be done by making them public object variables in the component's class definition, or by providing access to them through method return values. The actual mechanism is application specific, but the preferred method is public variables. This replacement mechanism is one way a component can be customized before use. For example, a component X may be the basis for a component called Y. There would be a class definition for each. An instance of class Y would allocate an instance of class X and modify the internal connections accordingly. Class Y would be a subclass of X, and the constructor for class Y would perform the change of connections after an instance was allocated and initialized by the methods associated with class X. Examples on how this is done can be found in later chapters of this book.

Finally, I would like to reiterate an important detail about plugs and components. They have a two-level nature to them. The low level requires an understanding of how to use the variables and methods at the other end of a plug; but this is not necessary at the high level, where connections and possibly some high-level methods associated with a component are important. This is analogous to the PC keyboard connection/cable/motherboard interface. A designer is concerned with the signals on the wires, the timing, and other minute details. The implementer is interested in the number of connections, the physical plugs, and wire. A user is interested in the keyboard and getting it to work with the PC. They all know about how a connection is made, and because of the keying of the plug, there is no way to mix things up. A user is unconcerned with the low-level details, and the designer knows that the keyboard design can be used with different computers with the appropriate changes in cable connectors, and so on.

So is it safe to let anyone build complex programs using plugs? Essentially, it is as safe and easy as it is to let someone put together a PC or a stereo system. Of course, the resulting application will be based upon the available components and the expertise, time, and desire of the person plugging them together. Having the appropriate components and documentation can make this possible.

The key to making this happen is limiting the number of methods available for use with plugs. Programmers typically learn a good deal about the programming language they use and the libraries they employ. Users are more concerned with components and how they fit together. Programmers want this too. Making it easy to do is important to constructing large programs.

Summary

Plugs are a simple class that can be defined in almost any object-oriented language. Components utilize plugs for building modular programs that can easily be enhanced as well as described and understood; they can be powerful tools in initial program construction and reconstruction. The rest of this book presents examples of plugs and components and addresses the internal details of building plugs and components, debugging with plugs, and other related design details.

The use of plugs and components, as described in this book, is still in its infancy. Plugs and components can be readily utilized in any program, but the big change will occur when they are part of commercially available libraries, and when debugging tools provide support for plugs, redirectors, and components in much the same way as some debuggers currently do for objects and pointers. Some debuggers can move from one displayed structure to another by following a pointer. Some debuggers can even display tree structures found within the program. Unfortunately, these tend to be limited to viewing an object class hierarchy. What will be interesting is when debuggers determine what components are in a program and how to traverse the connections to other parts of the program. Without a standard mechanism like plugs and components, such a debugger will be very hard to create, let alone operate.

2 Implementation of Plugs and Redirectors

This chapter deals with the general implementation of plugs, sockets, and redirectors using the macros described in the first chapter. It also takes a detailed look at the internal implementation of a key macro, DECLARE_CONNECTION. Full details of the internal implementations of plug and redirector macros can be found in Appendix A.

The first section of the chapter takes a look at the class hierarchy for plugs and connections. The next part examines the use of the DECLARE_CONNECTION macro and what classes it defines. Subsequent sections examine the plug and redirector functions used to implement the plug classes and the associated protocols. Sections on multiple connections and multiple inheritance wrap up the chapter.

Plugs, at a first approximation, are essentially bidirectional pointers. Here, as in the previous chapter, most references to plugs also refer to sockets. A socket is just the plug at the other end of a connection. All the member functions described in this chapter are applicable to both plugs and sockets. Where plugs and sockets differ is in the definitions of the base class and the classes that use the plug classes as base classes.

Redirectors look and act like plugs. They also share a common abstract superclass. Redirectors are used to rechannel the connection of a plug. That said, an improved definition of a plug is: a plug is essentially a bidirectional pointer that knows about redirectors.

To begin learning about plugs, let's examine the member functions of the plug class. All plugs have a common set of member functions, which can be divided into three groups: operational, connection, and internal. In brief, operational members are used to manipulate the plug, connection members are used when a connection is made or broken, and internal members are rarely modified functions that are internal to the definition of a plug.

First take a look at the class hierarchy for plugs, sockets, and connections.

Plug Class Hierarchy

The class hierarchy for plugs is a bit more complicated than most class libraries because of the required relationships among the various plug classes. Figure 2-1 shows the class hierarchy for a single connection. The top class is the *Plug* class. It is the superclass for all plug classes. Also notice the use of nested classes. The connection class contains eight nested classes. The connection class itself contains no functions or variables. It is not an abstract class so you could, in theory, allocate a connection object, but the program could not do anything with it. The purpose of the connection class is to provide a name space for the nested classes.

A *name space* is a way to isolate the names used in one space from another space. A C++ program contains a number of name spaces, among them a global name space, which includes all global classes, global functions, global variables, and global type definitions. Each class and structure is a name space. This is what allows you to use a name for a variable in one class or structure and to use it again in a different class or structure. In this case, the reused names in each connection class are the names of the nested classes: *plugA, socketA, plug, socket, plugRedirector, socketRedirector, dynamicPlugRedirector,* and *dynamicSocketRedirector.* Currently, few class libraries use nested classes.

Nested classes are used for two reasons: The first, already mentioned, is the ability to use the same names for more than one connection. The second is to keep the related classes together. The alternative is to use a prefix or suffix to each class name. Using nested classes allows you to use a class name like *Connection::plug* (the kind used in this book) instead of *Connectionplug.*

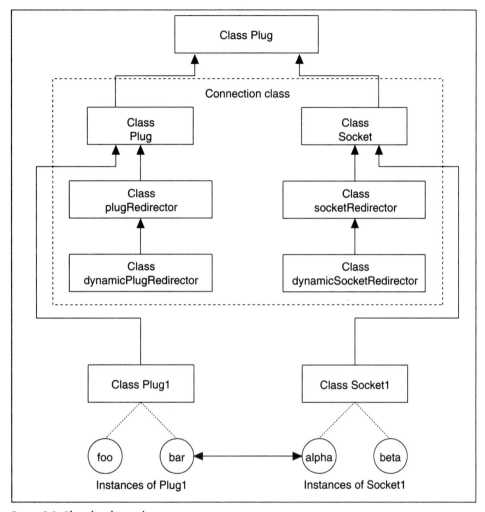

Figure 2-1. Plug class hierarchy

A connection definition includes the connection class, its eight nested classes, and a pair of global plug classes. The *Plug* class at the top of the hierarchy is shared by all plug classes and is not considered part of a connection definition. The connection class and its nested classes are defined using the DECLARE_CONNECTION macro. All that is needed for the macro is the name of the connection class and the names of the global plug classes. The nested classes are referred to as inner plug classes, while the global plug classes are referred to as outer plug classes. Inner plug classes define the functions that support the plug connection protocol. Outer plug classes are used to define plug-specific functions, which are divided into two types: internal protocol functions and external protocol functions. Internal protocol functions are usually protected functions that can be used only by the plug classes; external functions are usually public functions that can be used by any part of the program that can reference a plug object.

Now back to the matter at hand. The classes contained in the connection class are divided into two groups, one for the plug side of a connection and the other for the socket. Each side contains the same kind of classes with different names, so only the plug side will be dealt with here. Each class group uses pointers to objects of the other group. The top of the hierarchy within the connection class is the abstract plug class, *plugA*. You will never be able to create an object from this class, but you can have pointers of this type. This common pointer type allows you to use the two subclasses interchangeably.

The subclasses are *plug* and *plugRedirector*. The functions in the abstract class include all the *plug* protocol functions, and the two subclasses implement these functions. The *plug* class is an abstract class, which must have the *getPlug* function implemented by a subclass. The outer plug class is a subclass of the plug class. Objects can be created from the outer plug class, unless it is an abstract class, because it includes at least one pure virtual function definition. The *plugRedirector* class is not an abstract class, and objects can be defined. Objects of either of the last two classes can be used in making a connection to a corresponding object from the socket class group.

The last class in the group is the *dynamicPlugRedirector*. It is used to assist in the implementation of dynamic plugs. Chapter 8, on dynamic plugs, covers the use of objects from this class. Ordinarily, this is the only subclass of *plugRedirector* needed. The exception is redirector classes for debugging.

Subclasses can be defined using any of the classes in a connection definition, and objects can be defined from some of the classes. Objects are usually defined from the redirector classes and possibly the outer plug classes. Subclasses are usually defined from the outer plug classes. The subclasses typically implement plugs for different purposes.

Each connection definition, regardless of the definition of either outer plug class, creates a class hierarchy identical to the one presented in this section. The structure of the class hierarchy is a bit more complicated than the one found in a conventional class library, but it is consistent, and the definition is completely hidden by the *DECLARE_CONNECTION* macro.

Understanding the class hierarchy is not necessary to be able to use plugs, but it does help if you are defining new connections or doing something special like dynamic plugs. It also helps to understand the class hierarchy if you want to understand how the plug connection functions work internally. Luckily, it is not necessary to know all these details to make connections. All you really need to know are the functions like *connected* and operators like <= and -. The next section describes how the *DECLARE_CONNECTION* macro works.

Plug Class Definition

A connection definition consists of three parts: the connection class definition, the outer plug class definition, and the outer socket class definition. All three are required, and the minimal version is very simple. The simplest version looks like the following:

```
DECLARE_CONNECTION
  ( ConnectionClass
  , ConnectionPlug
  , ConnectionSocket
  )
class ConnectionPlug : public ConnectionClass::plug
{
  public:
    DECLARE_PLUG ()
} ;
class ConnectionSocket : public ConnectionClass::socket
{
```

```
public:
    DECLARE_PLUG ()
} ;
```

The classes *ConnectionPlug* and *ConnectionSocket* can be used to declare plug objects because they are not abstract classes. They would be if a *pure virtual function* were included in their declaration. This example declares the class hierarchy described in the previous section. The only difference between this definition and another connection definition will be the names of the connection and plug classes and any additional declarations in the outer plug classes.

There are a few syntactic requirements when defining a connection. The first is the order. The *DECLARE_CONNECTION* macro must occur before the outer plug definitions. The order of the outer plug declarations is irrelevant and can occur in different source files. The superclass declaration must include the connection class and nested class specification, as in *ConnectionClass:plug*. Multiple inheritance can be used with the outer plug class definitions, and the inheritance is usually *public* for the nested connection class. Visibility can be restricted by using *protected* or *private* instead of *public*, but this will restrict the use of the plug functions and operators like *connected* and <=. The superclass definition can use the *virtual* keyword, but be very careful when doing so. Virtual superclasses are useful but not always easy to understand.

The *DECLARE_PLUG* macro defines the *getPlug* function. The outer plug class declarations do not have to include this macro or a definition for *getPlug*, but the outer plug class will then be an abstract class, because *getPlug* is defined as a pure virtual function in the inner plug class declaration. Any outer plug class or subclass that is not an abstract class must have *getPlug* defined for it.

One thing to keep in mind when using connections is the type definition of pointers and references. There are a number of possibilities because of the number of classes. The most general definitions use the abstract plug and socket classes. These can be obtained using either of the following:

```
ConnectionClass:plugA & Plug1 ;
ConnectionClass:socketA & Socket1 ;
Plug1 <= Socket1 ;
ConnectionClass:plug::myEnd & Plug2 ; ConnectionClass:socket::myEnd
& Socket2 ;
Plug2 <= Socket2 ;
```

The *plugA* and *socketA* are the abstract plug classes. They allow a pointer or reference of this type to refer to either a plug or a redirector. This type can be used with the connection operators like <= and -. The former is shown in the last example. The plug and redirector classes also contain a *typedef* for *myEnd*, which refers to the same type. The myEnd and its associated *typedef* names are normally used within subclass definitions. A step down the class hierarchy ladder lets you specify a particular class, as in:

```
ConnectionPlug & Plug3 ;
ConnectionClass:socketRedirector & Socket3 ;
Plug3 <= Socket3 ;
```

In this case, *Plug3* must refer to an outer plug class or subclass object. *Socket3* must refer to a redirector.

The most general version, shown first, is usually best. It lets you assign a value that refers to any kind of plug object for that connection. The pointer or reference can be used with any of the plug functions, but if you want to use functions declared in the outer plug classes, you will need a pointer of the appropriate type. A pointer to the abstract plug class or redirector class will not give you access to these functions.

Plug Protocol

The code used to implement the plug protocols is presented in the section, "Connection Member Function Descriptions," later in this chapter, along with the details on how it works. This is the same code found in the PLUGS.HPP file. You will find a list of this file and a description of its contents in Appendix A. Here, a short overview of the plug protocol for the three main plug class operators is provided. The three main operators are <=, -, and --. The connection operator, <=, works as follows:

1. Disconnect using the - operator if a connection exists.

2. Free the plug at the other end of the old connection using the - operator.

3. Get pointers to both sides of the new connection using getEnd.

4. Get pointers to both plugs using *getPlug*.

5. Call *connectFailed* if *getPlug* fails.

6. Call *connectto* for both sides.

7. Call *afterConnect* for both sides.

The disconnect operators are a little simpler. The - operator does nothing if there is no connection, but if there is, then it works as follows:

1. Call *beforeDisconnect* for both sides.

2. Call disconnected for both sides.

The - operator calls the - operator to remove the connection and then calls disconnectedFree to allow a dynamic plug to delete itself.

Plug Member Functions

The next three sections present the plug protocol functions. Each plug class supports these functions. They are divided into three groups: operational, connection, and internal. These sections present the functions, their purpose, and their use and are followed by three more sections covering the same groups from an implementation point of view.

Operational member functions

Operational members are used by programmers who merely use the plugs, as one might use hardware components, to put together a computer system. In general, it is unnecessary for such programmers to know about any of the other members. The following is a list of the operational members.

```
Plug.connected ()
Plug.usable ()
Plug.isRedirector ()
Plug <= Socket
-Plug
- -Plug
Plug.addBefore ( pSocket, pPlug )
Plug.addAfter ( pSocket, pPlug )
Plug -> element
(* Plug).element
pOther
```

The connected, usable, and isRedirector functions each return a Boolean value that indicates the state of the plug used in conjunction with the function. The -> operator can only be used with a connected plug. A plug is always usable, or rather connectable, via the <= operator. A redirector is usable only when it has a plug associated with it. A redirector with no plug associated with it is considered unusable.

The remaining six functions implement the plug protocol. The protocol for the connection operator, <=, is shown in Figure 2-2. It connects a plug and matching socket together. First, both the plug and socket are disconnected if they are initially already connected. The disconnection is performed using the internal *disconnectedFree* function. Next, the plug and socket pointers are obtained using the *getEnd* and *getPlug* functions. Then both ends are notified of the connection using the internal connectto function. Finally, each end is allowed to complete the connection when the afterConnect function is called. The *afterConnect* function is normally used with compound plugs to make additional internal connections.

The - and -- operator functions disconnect a plug if it is already connected. They do nothing if the plug is not connected. The difference between the two is that - calls the internal disconnected function, while - calls the internal *dis-*

connectedFree function. Both call the *beforeDisconnect* function for both ends of a connection before disconnecting them. Figures 2-3 and 2-4 show how these operators work.

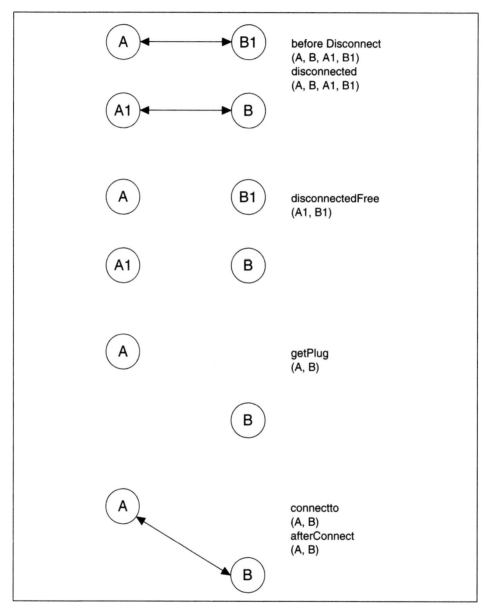

Figure 2-2. Plug connect protocol

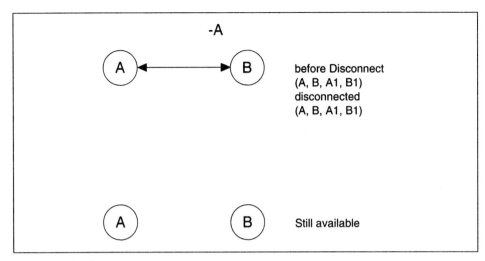

Figure 2-3. Plug disconnect protocol

The -> operator is used once a connection is made. It provides access to any public members (variables or functions) available through the plug at the other end of a connection. Private or protected members cannot be accessed using this operator. The * operator does the same type of thing as the -> operator, except that it returns the address of the other end of the connection. The

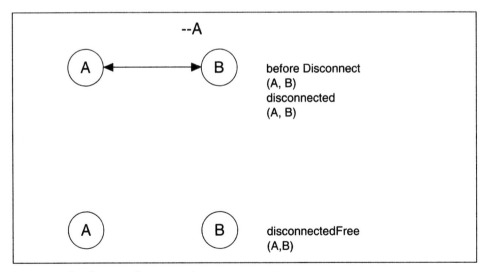

Figure 2-4. Plug disconnect free protocol

pOther variable provides access to the other end of the connection but only for functions defined by the class.

Redirectors support the same functions as plugs, plus an additional operational member function, shown here:

```
Redirector.redirect ( Plug ) ;
```

Figure 2-5 shows the protocol associated with a plug and redirector. Normally a plug will have at most one redirector associated with it. A redirector can reference a plug or another redirector. Assigning a plug to a redirector causes any previous redirector associated with the plug to be reset and performs a similar operation with the redirector if it was pointing to a plug.

Figures 2-6, 2-7, and 2-8 show how the protocol changes for the <=, -, and - operators when used with redirectors. Essentially the operations are forwarded to the plug at the end of a redirector chain.

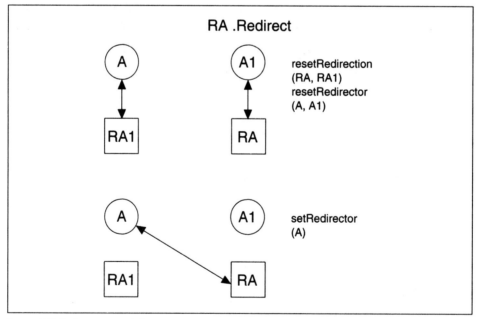

Figure 2-5. Redirector protocol

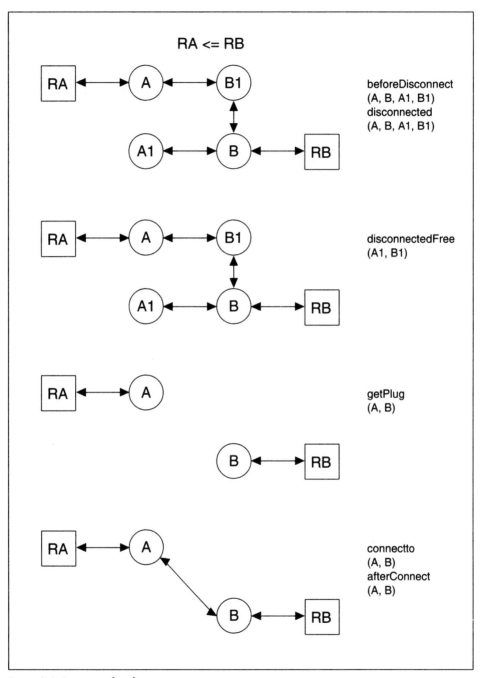

Figure 2-6. Connect with redirectors

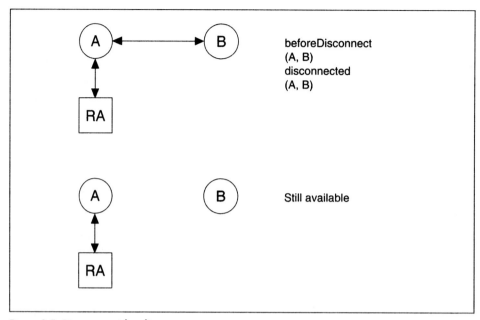

Figure 2-7. Disconnect with redirectors

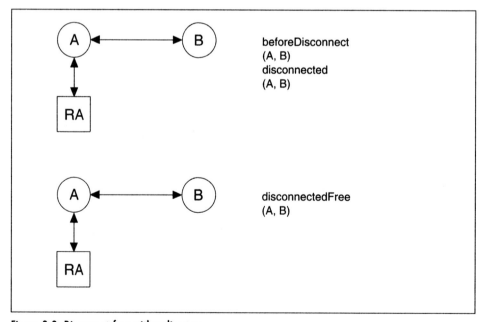

Figure 2-8. Disconnect free with redirectors

The *addBefore* and *addAfter* functions insert a socket/plug pair in between a connection, creating two new connections. The reason for two functions becomes apparent when redirectors are considered. Figures 2-9 and 2-10 show examples of before and after views of the plugs and connections when used with these functions. The functions utilize the - and <= operators already discussed.

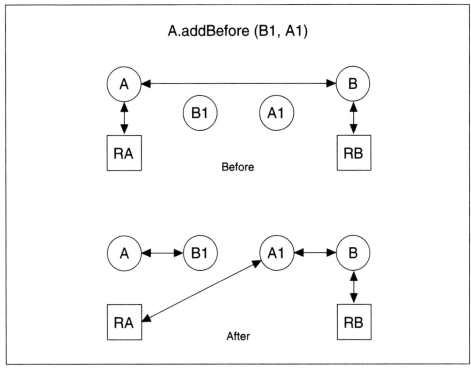

Figure 2-9. The addBefore protocol

Connection member functions

Connection members are involved in the connection process, which will be described later in this chapter. You don't have to know about these members if you are merely using plugs. You do need to know about them if you want to create your own types of plugs. Connection members can be redefined to implement special kinds of plugs. For example, compound plugs, discussed in Chapter 9, typically redefine the *afterConnect* and *beforeDisconnect* members. The following lists the connection members.

```
getPlug ()
getEnd ()
afterConnect ( pOtherPlug )
beforeDisconnect ( pOtherPlug )
connectFailed ()
disconnected ( pOtherPlug )
disconnectedFree ( pOtherPlug )
```

The *getPlug* and *getEnd* functions are used when making a new connection using the <= operator. A simple plug returns *this,* a pointer to the plug itself. A redirector or specialized plug returns a pointer to a plug, but not a pointer to itself. Two functions are provided for different purposes. The *getEnd* function should only be called by the <= operator when making a connection. It is used by dynamic generator plugs (see Chapter 8 on dynamic plugs for more details) to provide a new instance of a plug. The *getPlug* function is used to obtain a pointer to a plug regardless of the type of object being used to call the function. In particular, it can be used with a redirector to obtain a pointer

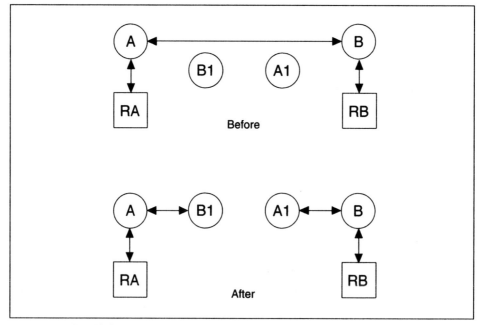

Figure 2-10. The addAfter protocol

to the plug at the end of a redirector chain. The *getPlug* function will not allocate a new object as *getEnd* might.

The *afterConnect* and *beforeDisconnect* functions are called after a connection is made and before a connection is broken to allow setup or cleanup to be performed while a connection is in place. The pointer to the other end allows access to the plug at the other end of the connection without having to determine this internally and makes it possible to have a plug that can maintain multiple connections simultaneously. The same is true for the disconnected and *disconnectedFree* functions.

The default *connectFailed* function does nothing, but it can be redefined so that a plug can clean up after itself. For example, dynamic plugs can free themselves. Other plugs may perform initialization in preparation for a subsequent connection.

All of the functions, except *getEnd* and *getPlug,* also notify each redirector in a plug's redirector chain if there are redirectors associated with the plug. The redirector functions have the same name, but the parameter is different. The redirector functions are called with a pointer to the plug instead of a pointer to the other plug. This is done because the redirector functions normally need the pointer to the plug and can obtain the pointer to the other plug through the redirected plug.

Internal member functions

Internal members are rarely redefined, although even they can be redefined by a plug designer. Internal members are used in the connection process and in conjunction with redirectors. The following is a list of the internal members.

```
connectto ( pOther )
getRedirector ()
setRedirector ( pRedirector )
setMyEnd ( pMyEnd )
```

The *connectto* function is called when a connection is made and before the *afterConnect* function. The *connectto* function normally saves the pointer to the other end for later use by the -> operator. The *getRedirector* and *setRedirector* functions are used by a redirector to tell a plug that it is being redirected. The *getRedirector* function can also be used to determine if a plug is redirected and to get a pointer to the redirector. A redirector uses the *setMyEnd* function when adjusting the redirector chain.

Redefining Plug Member Functions

Keep in mind the plug class inheritance tree, shown in Figure 2-11, when defining subclasses that redefine the plug base class and plug member functions. The base class should include only virtual functions to allow redefini-

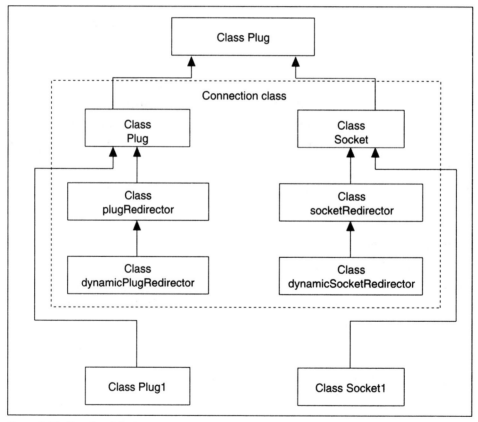

Figure 2-11. Plug class inheritance

tion by subclasses. Likewise, subclasses usually need to call superclass functions, which they redefine to allow the superclass function to complete the work required for the superclass.

Whether you are simply using plugs to build programs or designing your own plug types, you need to know how to redefine the plug member functions. For this, you use the C++ inheritance mechanism. An additional class must be defined with the appropriate member functions defined by the class. An additional class will be required if the base plug class is an abstract class. For example:

```
DECLARE_CONNECTION
  ( connectionA
  , plugAA
  , socketA
  )
class PlugAA : public connectionA::plug
{
  public:
    DECLARE_PLUG ()
    virtual int sample () = 0 ;
} ;
class socketA : public connectionA::socket
{
  public:
    DECLARE_PLUG ()
} ;
```

plugAA is an abstract class. The socket, *socketA,* is not an abstract class and therefore can be used to define objects. You can use the following:

```
class PlugA1: public PlugAA
{
  public:
    int sample () { return 1 ; }
} ;
```

The sample function definition takes care of the abstract class definition. Objects of type *PlugA1* can be allocated and connected to socketA objects.

Redefining base class functions can be a useful way to extend a plug—or it may be a requirement, as with *BaseA*. The functions must be virtual for this redefinition to be useful because most plugs are used with generic plug references. That is, the only functions available across a connection are those defined in the base class and by inherent plug functions described in this chapter. The next example defines a plug class that can also be plugged into a socketA object. The difference between this class and the prior example is that this class redefines one of the inherent plug functions, *afterConnect*.

This new class, *PlugA2*, keeps track of the number of successful connections made with the plug. It does this by redefining the *afterConnect* function to increment a counter, *connections*. For example:

```
class PlugA2 : public PlugAA
{
  public:
    int connections ;
    PlugA2 ()
      : connections ( 0 )
      {}
    int sample () { return 1 ; }
    void afterConnect ( otherPlug * pOther )
    {
      ++ connections ;
      PlugAA::afterConnect ( pOther ) ;
    }
} ;
```

The constructor function, *PlugA2*, initializes the counter to 0. The sample function is included for completeness; it must be defined if *PlugA2* objects can be defined. The *afterConnect* function is called every time a connection is made. It increments the *connections* variable and also calls *PlugAA's* after-Connect function.

Now for a detailed examination of the purpose and operation of the plug-specific member functions, starting with the operational member functions.

Operational Member Function Descriptions

The function definitions presented in this section are extracted from the PLUGS.HPP file described in Appendix A. The function descriptions are with respect to standard plug class definitions instead of the connection class plug definitions. Most of the function definitions within the connection class definitions are pure virtual functions and hence have no function body associated with them. Comments are made with regard to considerations for specialized plugs that are also discussed in this book, such as compound and dynamic plugs.

The plug operational members include the following:

```
BOOL connected () ;
BOOL usable () ;
BOOL isRedirector () ;
void addBefore ( otherEnd * inner, myEnd * newEnd ) ;
void addAfter  ( otherEnd * inner, myEnd * newEnd ) ;
void operator <= ( otherEnd & plug ) ;
otherEnd * operator -> () ;
otherEnd & operator * () ;
otherEnd * operator - () ;
void operator - - () ;
pOther
```

The *myEnd* and *otherEnd* types are specific to the plug or socket being defined. *myEnd* is the abstract class for the plug or socket being defined. The *otherEnd* is the abstract class for the socket or plug (note the reversal). The types are defined in the abstract class, so any plug inheriting from these classes will be able to use the appropriate definitions regardless of whether the class was the plug or socket within a connection. A redirector type definition is also included, which is associated with the abstract redirector class for the *myEnd* class.

The standard plug is implemented with a pair of pointers: *pOther* and *pRedirector*. They are initially *0*, indicating no connection. Making a connection with the <= operator sets the *pOther* pointer, and assigning a plug P to a redirector R points the plug's *pRedirector* to R. Specialized plug implementations may implement these pointers in a different way, which will be noted when a particular function is discussed.

The first three member functions are used to test the status of a plug or redirector. You can tell a plug from a redirector using *isRedirector*. A plug returns *FALSE*, while a redirector returns *TRUE*. In general, there is no need to distinguish between the two types, but the function is there just in case it is needed. A *FALSE* value indicates *pRedirector* is *0*.

The usable function is also used in conjunction with redirectors and will normally be used instead of *isRedirector*. A plug is always usable, so *usable* will return *TRUE*. (There may be special cases where it will not return *TRUE*, but I haven't thought of any yet.) A redirector's *usable* function returns *FALSE* if the redirector does not reference a plug; otherwise, it returns the value of the plug's usable function. A redirector does nothing if it is not usable.

For example, using the <= connection operator on a redirector that is not usable will not cause an error, but it will also not result in a connection. The redirector's usable function is actually forwarded to its reference, if there is one, because a redirector can point to another redirector. All the redirectors in this type of chain will return the same value for the usable function: *FALSE* if there is no plug at the end of the chain and *TRUE* if there is one.

The connected function returns *TRUE* or *FALSE* depending on whether the plug is connected to something. It has some obvious uses. Here's one: The reference function, ->, should not be used unless a plug is connected. The *connected* function can (and should) be used before -> whenever there is a possibility that a plug might be disconnected arbitrarily.

The connection class is usually required if you build a class that inherits from a plug or a socket. This is where the type definitions come into play. For example:

```
DECLARE_CONNECTION
  ( nothing                               // connection class
  , nothingPlugA                          // plug definition
  , nothingSocketA                 // socket definition
  )
class nothingPlugA : public nothing::plug
{
  public:
    DECLARE_PLUG ()
} ;
class nothingSocketA : public nothing::socket
{
  public:
    DECLARE_PLUG ()
} ;
class nPlugA : public nothingPlugA
{
  public:
    otherEnd * operator - () ;
} ;
```

The *addBefore* and *addAfter* functions require — and deserve — some further explanation. Both temporarily break an existing connection. They then connect the plug to one parameter and connect the other end, which has just been disconnected, to the other parameter. The difference between the two functions is more apparent with respect to redirectors. No change is made if *addAfter* is used. However, the redirector (if any), which references the plug in question, will be changed to the newly added plug.

This distinction allows a redirector to always point to the appropriate plug. For example, you have a component that has public redirector members. You want to modify the component by adding new connections such that the component is altered but the change is not apparent to anyone using the object.

Don't worry about freeing objects added in this way. They should be dynamically allocated, and they will be freed when the component object is freed because all connections are supposed to be broken before a plug object is freed. If not, the objects should be defined in the same allocation scope of the connection. For example, if the other objects are allocated as locals, then these objects may also be defined in the same function or one that calls the function containing the other objects, and each will be freed automatically when the functions return.

The following definition is used for the *addBefore* function:

```
void addBefore ( otherEnd * inner, myEnd * newEnd )
{
  redirector * old = pRedirector ;
  addAfter ( inner, newEnd ) ;
  if ( pRedirector )
  {
    pRedirector -> redirectBefore ( newEnd ) ;
  }
}
```

The *addBefore* function lets the *addAfter* function do the work of inserting inner and *newEnd* plugs into the connection. The *addBefore* function then changes the old redirector, if it exists, so it now points to the *newEnd*. Note that inner and *newEnd* may be 0, which will not create a new connection with them. Likewise, the plug need not be connected for this function to be usable. This case even makes sense because the redirector is being changed. It will point to the *newEnd*, which will be used in subsequent connections initiated using the redirector.

The *addAfter* function is simple but uses some rather convoluted C-style idioms. The following definition is used for the *addAfter* function:

```
void addAfter ( otherEnd * inner, myEnd * newEnd )
{
  if ( pOther && newEnd )
```

```
    {
      ( * newEnd ) <= ( * - * this ) ;
    }
    ( * this ) <= ( * inner ) ;
}
```

A new connection with *newEnd* is made only if *newEnd* is not 0 and the plug is connected, in which case *pOther* is also not 0. The * - * *this* idiom can be read right to left and works as follows: start with a pointer to the current object, *this;* get its address so the object functions can be used; use the - *operator* that disconnects both ends of the connection, which has already been determined to exist; take the result from the operator that is a pointer to the other end of the connection; and get its address so it can be used to create a new connection with the <= operator. This sequence has different results than simply using the following:

```
      ( * newEnd ) <= ( * pOther ) ;
```

In this case, when the code is executed, the current plug would be disconnected and freed using the *disconnectedFree* function. The overall effect would be nil if the current plug is not a dynamic plug, but the effect with a dynamic plug would be catastrophic. Essentially, the current plug would be freed before the second connection was made, causing the second connection to be made with something in free space. The *this* pointer would essentially be a dangling pointer. Not a fun thing to have around in any program.

The * and -> operators provide access to the other end of a connection. They do not check to see if the plug is connected. This makes the functions as fast as possible. However, you might want to redefine the function to perform this check for debugging purposes or when a plug may be prematurely disconnected. Unfortunately, the normal way out will be to use exception handling support, which can be added by defining the *plugCheck* macro. This macro is used in the following definitions for the * and -> functions.

```
otherEnd * operator -> ()
{
  plugCheck(pOther);
  return pOther;
}
otherEnd & operator * ()
{
  plugCheck(pOther);
  return*pOther;
}
```

The *plugCheck* macro is defined to do nothing by default. It is defined in the *PLUGS.HPP* file only if it has not been defined before. It can also be redefined after the file is included and before a plug definition is used. Furthermore, the *plugCheck* macro can be changed more than once within a file to allow some plug types to be checked while others are not. A possible definition for *plugCheck* is as follows:

```
#define plugCheck(p) if (p)\
  { error ( "Illegal use of disconnected plug ) ; }
```

This assumes that the error function accepts an error message string as a parameter. This type of function would normally display the error and then terminate the program. Another alternative would be to generate an *INT 3* interrupt. This is the normal way to bring up a debugger and would allow the program to be run from a debugger to catch such errors.

The advantage of this approach is that no code is generated by default, but error checking can easily be added. An example of plug definitions with different *plugCheck* values is as follows:

```
#include "Plugs.HPP"
// -- default null plugCheck used here --
DECLARE_CONNECTION
  ( connection1
  , plug1
  , socket1
```

```
  )
class plug1 : public connection1::plug
{
  public:
    DECLARE_PLUG ()
} ;
class socket1 : public connection1::socket
{
  public:
    DECLARE_PLUG ()
} ;
// -- error() plugCheck used here --
#define plugCheck(p) if (p)\
  { error ( "Illegal use of disconnected plug ) ; }
DECLARE_CONNECTION
  ( connection2
  , plug2
  , socket2
  )
class plug2 : public connection2::plug
{
  public:
    DECLARE_PLUG ()
} ;
class socket2 : public connection2::socket
{
  public:
    DECLARE_PLUG ()
} ;
// -- default null plugCheck used here --
#define plugCheck(p)
DECLARE_CONNECTION
  ( connection3
  , plug3
  , socket3
  )
class plug3 : public connection3::plug
{
  public:
    DECLARE_PLUG ()
```

```
} ;
class socket3 : public connection3::socket
{
  public:
    DECLARE_PLUG ()
} ;
```

It is even possible to use different error handlers for different plug definitions. It is not possible to use different handlers for different objects declared from the same class, though, without adding more functions to the plug's base class.

The disconnect operators, - and --, break a connection if they exist. The difference between the two is that the - operator assumes the plugs will be used again after the connection is broken. The -- operator assumes the plugs are no longer needed. Dynamic plugs should free themselves when the -- operator is used, even if there is no connection. The differences between the two operators will be more apparent after looking at the following definitions:

```
otherEnd * operator - ()
{
  otherEnd * prior = pOther ;
  if ( prior )
  {
    beforeDisconnect ( prior ) ;
    prior -> beforeDisconnect ( this ) ;
    disconnected ( prior ) ;
    prior -> disconnected ( this ) ;
  }
  return prior ;
}
void operator - - ()
{
  otherEnd * prior = - * this ;
  if ( prior )
  {
    - - * prior ;
  }
```

```
        disconnectedFree ( prior ) ;
    }
```

The -- operator uses the - operator to perform the actual disconnection. The - operator returns the pointer to the plug at the other end of the connection. The *beforeDisconnect* function is called for both plugs before a connection is broken. Both disconnected functions are then called. The *disconnectedFree* function will be called if the - - operator is used after the *disconnected* functions are called. Dynamic plugs normally free themselves when *disconnectedFree* is called. Any connection level cleanup should be done within the *beforeDisconnect* function. Any other cleanup should be done in the *disconnected* function, with freeing of a dynamic plug done by the *disconnectedFree* function. The *disconnectedFree* function can free any other resources used by the plug that were also dynamically allocated. By default, all three functions do nothing. This is all that is necessary for a simple global or stack defined plug.

The connection function, <=, uses the disconnect function, --, to break an existing connection before making a connection. This will normally cause a plug at the other end to be freed if it was a dynamic plug created from free space using *new*. This freeing of plugs via -- is why the temporary disconnect function, -, is used. In general, if a plug is to be reused, it should be disconnected using -. The returned pointer can be used to connect the plug at a later time. The definition for the => operator is as follows:

```
    void operator <= ( otherEnd & p )
    {
      otherEnd * prior = - * this ;
      if ( prior )
      {
        - - * prior ;
      }
      if(&p)
      {
        myEnd * el = getEnd() ;
        if (el)
        {
```

```
            otherEnd * e2 = p.getEnd() ;
            if (e2)
            {
              myPlug    * p1 = e1 -> getPlug () ;
              otherPlug * p2 = e2 -> getPlug () ;
              e1->connectto(p2);
              e2->connectto(p1);
              e1->afterConnect(p2);
              e2->afterConnect(p1);
            }
            else e1->connectFailed();
          }
        }
      else
        connectFailed() ;
      }
```

The first thing done is to disconnect the plug. This is accomplished using the
- operator so that the plug will not be freed, but the other end, if there is a
connection, will; or at least its *disconnectedFree* function will be called. This
version of the <= operator does not assume that the connection is maintained
using pOther. The next thing is to get the pointer to a new plug for this end
of the connection. This is done by calling *getEnd*. If this fails, or there is nothing at the other end, then the *connectFailed* function for the plug is called.
Assuming that a pointer to a plug is obtained, then the pointer for a plug at
the other end is obtained by calling *getEnd* with *p*. As you can see, both ends
are obtained using *getEnd* instead of using *this* and the address of *p*. With
simple plugs, the values are the same, but they do not have to be. For example, a plug that generates dynamic plugs will normally redefine the *getEnd*
function. All connections will be initiated with the generator plug, which allocates new plugs for each *getEnd* call. In this case, the newly allocated plug
will be used to complete the connection, not the generator plug.

The *connectFailed* function is called if the *p* is allocated but a plug for the
other end cannot be obtained. The main plug's *connectFailed* function is called

if a new plug cannot be allocated. This situation could occur if the *getEnd* function generates new plugs from a limited supply of plugs.

If all goes well, you wind up with valid pointers in *e1* and *e2*. The *getPlug* function is then called using both pointers to obtain the plugs to be connected. This is done because the ends referenced by *e1* and *e2* may be redirectors, and the connection must be made directly between two plugs. Note the type differences for the pointers *e1* and *e2* and *p1* and *p2*.

The *connectto* functions are called after the plug pointers are obtained. This lets each side record the connection. The *afterConnect* functions are then called. Any additional processing, such as making connections in a compound connection or other initialization, should be relegated to the *afterConnect* function. Any initialization that needs to occur before the *afterConnect* function is called can be placed in the connectto function, but the function cannot use the connection because it may not exist in both directions. There is no guaranteed ordering of the connectto and *afterConnect* functions with respect to the plug and socket. That is, the plug functions are not guaranteed to be called before the socket's version. The only guarantee is that both connectto functions will be called before the *afterConnect* functions. There is no equivalent *afterAfterConnect* function, although something like this can be implemented by redefining the <= operator. However, note that the <= operator must be redefined for both the plug and socket because there is no guarantee which one will be used.

The functions listed in this section are the ones that tend to be redefined the least. They have been defined to utilize functions defined in the next section, and they include functions such as *afterConnect*.

Connection Member Function Descriptions

Connection members are involved in the creation and termination of connections between plugs. They control what goes on underneath the <= function and the disconnect functions, - and - -. You can use plugs with the operational member functions without ever needing to use or know about the connection member functions. Even so, it is a good idea to know what is going on when you use <=. The functions defined in this section should not be used outside of the plug-specific functions. Any use outside of these functions can cause significant problems. For example, half a connection might be broken, leading to a dangling pointer problem.

You will need to know and often modify the definitions for the connection member functions when creating compound or dynamic plug classes (discussed in Chapters 7 and 8). Compound plugs are more complex entities containing one or more plugs, redirectors, or references to plugs and redirectors. Dynamic plugs are plugs created from the heap and freed when they are no longer connected.

The following is a list of the connection members.

```
void afterConnect ( otherPlug * ) ;
void beforeDisconnect ( otherPlug * ) ;
void connectFailed () ;
void disconnected ( otherPlug * ) ;
void disconnectFree ( otherPlug * ) ;
myEnd * getEnd () ;
myPlug * getPlug () ;
```

These functions are used in conjunction with the connection function, <=, and disconnect functions, - and --. The default definition for all of these functions, except *getPlug,* is an empty function. The *afterConnect* is called for each plug after a successful connection is made, and *beforeDisconnect* is called before a connection is broken due to a <=, -, or - - function. There is no guaranteed order to which plug's *afterConnect* or *beforeDisconnect* is called, so be sure to define which plug is going to make which connections. Likewise, take care when implementing the functions, since there is no guarantee that specific connections will be made or broken before these functions are called.

The *disconnected* function is called for both plugs after both plugs have been called with the *beforeDisconnect* function. The *disconnected* function can perform any necessary cleanup, possibly in preparation for a subsequent connection.

The *connectFailed* and *disconnectFree* functions can be redefined to handle dynamic plugs. Dynamic plugs are normally allocated from the heap and free themselves when they are no longer referenced. This is the case when either *connectFailed* or *disconnectFree* is called. These two functions are provided so that special action can be taken, depending upon when a connection is broken. Both indicate the plug is no longer referenced through a previous connection. The *connectFailed* function is called when a => function fails to make a connection. The *disconnectFree* function is called by the -- function.

Each of the functions just discussed calls a function of the same name for the first redirector in a plug's redirector chain, if it exists. The parameter to this function call is *this,* which is a pointer to the plug itself. In this way, the redirectors can follow the connection operations as they occur. That is why it is very important to call the superclass version of these functions if you redefine them in a plug subclass.

Now let's examine the *getEnd* and *getPlug* functions, where you will see how connections are really made and broken. The *getEnd* function is used to obtain a pointer to a plug during a connection function call, <=. It is used to obtain pointers for both sides. For a simple plug, the *getEnd* function returns *this,* a pointer to the plug itself. For a more complex plug, one that generates dynamic plugs, for example, the *getEnd* function would not return *this* but rather a pointer to a plug object created with *new.* The *getPlug* complements the *getEnd* function by providing access to the plugs to be connected using the result returned by the *getEnd* function. The *getPlug* function may be used independent of the <= operator, but *getEnd* should only be used by this operator. Review the <= operator function definition in the previous section to see how *getEnd* and *getPlug* are used.

Although this may sound like a lot of work for the *getEnd* and *getPlug* functions, it allows some kinds of dynamic plugs to be built that could not otherwise be built.

Redefinition of these functions typically occurs in plug subclasses. For example, a simple dynamic plug definition is as follows:

```
DECLARE_CONNECTION
  ( connectX
  , PlugX
  , PlugY
  )
class PlugX : public connectX::plug
{
  public:
    DECLARE_PLUG ()
} ;
class PlugY : public connectX::socket
{
  public:
    DECLARE_PLUG ()
} ;
class DynamicPlugX : public PlugX
{
  public:
    void connectFailed ()
    {
      PlugX::connectFailed () ;
      delete this ;
    }
    void disconnectedFree ( otherPlug * pOther )
    {
      PlugX::disconnectedFree ( pOther ) ;
      delete this ;
    }
} ;
class DynamicPlugXGenerator : public PlugX
{
```

```
public:
   myEnd * getEnd () { return new DynamicPlugX ; }
} ;
```

The *DynamicPlugX* plugs will free themselves using *delete* when they are disconnected using the -- operator, or if a connection initiated using the => operator fails. The initial connections are made to an object of type *DynamicPlugXGenerator.* This is a very simple example of a dynamic plug. No tracking of newly created plugs is done. An object of type *DynamicPlugXGenerator* will always return *FALSE* when the connected function is called, even though the <= operator may have been used on it, because the *getEnd* function will return a pointer to a newly created object of type *DynamicPlugX.*

Internal Member Function Descriptions

You'll need to know about the internal member functions if you want to design a new plug, particularly if you are defining a plug along the lines of a compound or dynamic plug. Another possible reason for redefining internal member functions is for debugging purposes. In general, though, these functions are not redefined. The following is a list of the internal members.

```
connectto ( pNewPlug
getRedirector ()
setRedirector ( pRedirector )
setMyEnd ( pMyEnd )
```

The *connectto* function is called for both plugs after a successful connection and before the *afterConnect* functions are called. This means that both plugs know about each other, but additional operations may not have been performed. In a normal plug, the *pNewPlug* parameter is assigned to the *pOther* pointer variable, which is part of the plug. It is possible for one plug to make and track more than one connection because the connections are made via connectto, and disconnections are made using *disconnected* and *disconnectedFree,* which all include a parameter that is a pointer to the other end for the connection.

The redirector functions are used in conjunction with a redirector. A plug keeps track of what redirector, if any, is pointing to it. Only a single conventional redirector may point to a plug. The pointer to the redirector is used in conjunction with the *addBefore* and *addAfter* functions. The redirection functions also include a parameter that points to the redirector involved in the operation. This allows more than one redirector to be used in conjunction with a single plug if so implemented. The normal plug only allows one redirector per plug, just as a normal plug only allows one connection per plug. Like a connection, a subsequent redirection will reset the prior one, if it exists.

Redirector Implementation

Redirectors, so far alluded to but not explained in detail, perform the same set of operations as a plug. The difference is that a redirector forwards the functions to its plug if one is assigned to the redirector. In general, a redirector can only reference one plug, and a plug can have at most one redirector. Redirector classes are declared when a connection is declared.

Redirectors are important because they provide structure to a system without imposing undue overhead on a connection. Connections may be initiated using redirectors, but the final connection is always made between the plugs referenced by the redirectors regardless of the number of redirectors within the reference chain.

In general, a redirector should only be used for getting status and making connections and disconnections. The -> operator can be used to access the member functions and elements of the other plug if a connection is made. However, the redirector does not contain the elements, and non-virtual functions of the redirected plug cannot be accessed. A pointer to a redirected plug can be obtained using the *getPlug* function. The *getPlug* function is supported by both the redirector and the plug and returns a pointer to the plug, which can then be used to access the member functions and elements.

Redirectors forward most plug-specific functions to their reference, which may also be a redirector. Functions like *connected* return a value that is based upon the available reference. In this case, a *FALSE* value is returned if the redirector has no reference associated with it; otherwise, the result of the reference's connected function is returned. This works properly regardless of the number of redirectors involved. The disadvantage of using the redirector is that all functions wind up following the redirector chain when they are called, which is rather inefficient, especially for long chains. On the other hand, most function calls and information exchange should occur across the connection from one plug to the other, which always occurs directly and ignores any redirector chain on either side.

The interaction between plugs and redirectors is why redirectors must be used instead of pointers. It is the same reason simple pointers are not the same as using a plug connection. Redirectors handle the connections and references automatically using a well-defined protocol.

Three functions are involved in the redirection protocol: *remove, redirect,* and *redirectBefore.* Only the *redirect* function is called externally. The other two functions are used internally. The *remove* function removes a redirector from a redirector chain if it is in one. It is called before a redirector is destroyed and when a new redirection is performed. The redirect function first removes the redirector from its current chain by calling *remove,* and then adds itself to the new chain. The *redirectBefore* function is called by a plug's *addBefore* function. It allows a redirector to move itself from the redirector chain of its original plug to the new plug specified by the *addBefore* function. The default case is to move to the new chain. Some special redirectors may not move themselves from one chain to the other. This is occasionally done for dynamic redirectors, discussed in Chapter 8. The function definitions for these functions are as follows:

```
void remove ()
{
  if (pMyEnd)
    pMyEnd->setRedirector(pRedirector);
  if (pRedirector)
    pRedirector->setMyEnd(pMyEnd);
```

```
    }
    void redirect(myEnd*pNew)\
    {
      remove();
      if (pNew)
      {
        pMyEnd=pNew;
        pRedirector = pNew->setRedirector(this);
        if ( pRedirector )
          pRedirector -> setMyEnd ( this ) ;
      }
    }
    void redirectBefore(myEnd*pNew)
    {
      redirector*pOld=pRedirector;
      redirect(pNew);
      if (pOld)
        pOld->redirectBefore(pNew);
    }
```

The *remove* function takes a redirector out of its redirector chain, which is a doubly linked list. Adjustment of both ends of the linked list are conditional because a redirector can be at either end. It can be at the top end if there is no plug being redirected. The *redirect* function first removes itself from its redirector chain by calling *remove*. The *setRedirector* call adds the redirector to the chain and returns the redirector that was at the head of the chain before the call. The prior head is notified of the change by the *setMyEnd* call. The *redirectBefore* function is called by a plug after it has made changes for its *addBefore* function. The default case is to change redirection chains using the redirect function. The *redirectBefore* function also calls the *redirectBefore* function for the next redirector in its original chain, if one exists. This lets the other redirectors move to the new chain.

Redirectors have a very simple protocol. They also receive status function calls for plug operations like *disconnected* and *afterConnect*. The default redirector class for a plug is defined when a connection is defined. Objects of this type can be used to redirect connections, and the class can be subclassed to create objects that monitor connections.

Inside Plugs

Appendix A gives the contents of *PLUGS.HPP,* the file that must be included as part of every C++ source file that uses or defines plugs. In this file various necessary or useful macros are defined. One of these is the *DECLARE_CONNECTION* macro, which is where the plug protocol is implemented. A description of this macro is given here. If you want to follow along in the actual code, you'll find the *DECLARE_CONNECTION* macro near the start of the *PLUGS.HPP* listing in Appendix A.

The plug class definition in the *DECLARE_CONNECTION* macro starts by declaring two protected variables, *pRedirector* and *pOther.* These are the two crucial pointers that make the whole concept of plugs work, making it possible to refer to a redirector and to the other end of a plug connection. Both are initialized to *0* in the next section of the macro, in the public portion of the class definition.

Next, the destructor resets the redirector and breaks the connection, if this has not already been done.

The definition of the connection operator, <=, comes next in the code. Used like A <= B, the connection operator connects *A* to *B,* performing a - -*A* and a - -*B* first. Here, in its defining code, is where the plug connection protocol is laid out.

Next come the definitions of the -> and * operators. The -> operator, used like *A* -> *V,* accesses a member of the object at the other end of *A,* normally assuming that there is something there. As the code shows, these operators simply return the *pOther* pointer value after using the *plugCheck* macro/function. *PlugCheck* is an optional macro/function; it checks for invalid access in the case of an unconnected plug.

Then come the definitions of the disconnect operators, - and --. Their syntax is -*A* or --*A.* The former disconnects *A,* does not free the other end, and returns a pointer to the other end. The latter disconnects *A* and frees the other end, calling its *disconnectedFree* function. Note that the -- operator uses the - *operator* to handle the actual disconnection, so it doesn't have to do everything for itself; in particular, it doesn't have to call *beforeDisconnect*.

The *addBefore* and *addAfter* functions handle adjustments to the plug connections and redirector connections when adjustments are necessary. They are not often needed. The syntax of *addBefore* is *A.addBefore(B,C)* to connect *A* to *B* and connect *C* to what *A* was connected to. If *A* has a redirector, then it ends up pointing to *C*. The syntax of *addAfter* is similar.

Definitions of the special redirector functions follow *addBefore* and *addAfter*. There are three of them: *getRedirector, setRedirector,* and *setMyEnd*. They are very simple; their inclusion just allows for a consistent interface to that protected *pRedirector* pointer defined at the top of this class definition. Another purpose for them is to allow for implementations that differ from the basic implementation; for example, when there are multiple redirectors or no redirectors.

Multiple Connections to a Single Plug

As you've seen in this chapter, it is possible to build a plug that provides public members to more than one plug at the same time. This type of plug uses the counter mechanism described for dynamic plugs. However, it does not alter the *getPlug* function and change the *connectto* function, so it does not remember what plugs are connected to it. The counter is incremented for each call to *afterConnect* and is decremented by *beforeDisconnect*. If the plug is dynamic, then it can free itself when *disconnectedFree* is called and the counter is *0*.

Another approach is to track not only the number of connections but each plug at the other end of each connection. This requires a plug to use a list, array, or other mechanism to save the connection pointers supplied by the connectto function. The disconnected function removes the entry from the list.

Multiple connections to a single plug are useful when it does not matter when or which connection uses a particular plug function. For example, a plug that supplies information could operate this way, but connections that require sequencing could not. An example of the latter would be a database that could be updated using a commit-style update. In this case, a transaction is started with a function call, and subsequent operations are performed, followed by a commit function call. The connection is dedicated to the transaction and the requestor, and the database plug providing the service must track all these calls sequentially. In this case, the database plug is better implemented in a generator/dynamic plug configuration, where the initial connection causes the main database/generator plug to create a dynamic server plug, which will field the requests from the connection.

Both types of plugs can operate transparently to the user. Figure 2-12 shows the similarities and differences between the two approaches.

Multiple Inheritance

Multiple inheritance is a powerful part of C++. It can be used with plugs, but be careful when using various combinations. For example, including multiple plugs in the inheritance list is possible, and connection to the appropriate plug is handled by the C++ inheritance mechanism. The problem occurs when trying to use functions like -> and *usable* with a plug object that inherits from multiple plugs. In this case, the function must be explicitly specified using ::, as in *foo::usable ()* or *foo::operator -> ()*.

In general, multiple inheritance is not something you want to use with plugs, at least not multiple plugs. Instead, you might want to use compound plugs. If you do use multiple inheritance, you should determine if you want separate components or a single plug that looks like multiple plugs. In the latter case you need to redefine the connection and disconnection functions accordingly.

It is possible to redefine individual plug protocol functions for individual superclasses when using multiple inheritance because of function overloading and because the parameter types are different. For example, let's say you have two plug classes, *A* and *B*. You have a class *C*, which inherits from both, but you want to redefine the *afterConnect* of both classes in the new class. The parameter type for the *afterConnect* function for class A is different than

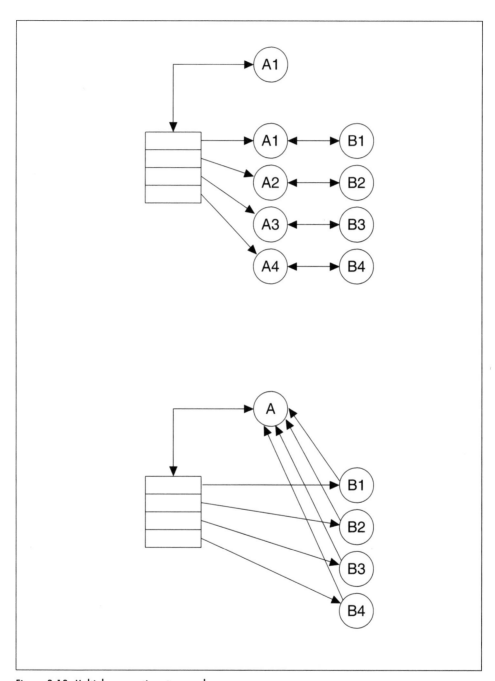

Figure 2-12. Multiple connections to one plug

the *afterConnect* function parameter for *B*. You will have a problem if you want to redefine a function that has no parameter, such as connected. Luckily, this type of function is not usually redefined, although it may be used within other function redefinitions. A superclass function can be expressly called using the syntax, *A::connected* () and *B::connected* ().

Remember, multiple inheritance is a valid way to use plugs, but it should be the right choice. Dynamic and compound plugs are other alternatives and combinations, so look closely at what you want to do before you implement a new plug class. It is even possible to implement compound plugs and dynamic plugs using multiple inheritance. Also take care in defining redirectors. A redirector for a multiple inheritance class can be created, but it is not easy.

Enough preliminaries. In the next chapter you'll build some plugs.

3 Simple C++ Plugs

In the previous chapter I gave as a working definition of plugs that they are bidirectional pointers. That's true, as far as it goes. But using plugs as simple bidirectional pointers is a lot like using C++ as a better version of C. It's a good way to get started and it works, but the real payoff comes when you start using C++ as an object-oriented development environment. Similarly, the real payoff of plugs comes when you start using plugs for what they were designed for. In this chapter you will start to see what that is.

The plug classes presented in this chapter can be used within almost any program, although some are more effective than others. The trade-offs for each implementation are discussed along with general uses for these plugs.

First, plug construction, base classes, and protocol definitions are covered. This includes how a plug is defined and allocated; how base classes are defined; what documentation needs to be included; and how, after connection, plug protocols need to be defined. Next, you are introduced to components and how plugs are used to define and build them. (A more complete discussion of components is presented in Chapter 8.)

The next section looks at trade-offs in plug implementation and presents very simple examples. In fact, these first examples are really too simple to show the applications of plugs, but they do demonstrate some important ideas about how to implement plugs. After this, you'll look at some more useful, but still simple, plugs and components; for example, string stream plugs, which employ C strings, are presented. This section is followed by a discussion of basic components, such as filters, tees, and merges using the string stream plugs. A more complex example using a transaction-oriented buffer protocol is presented last.

Plug Construction, Base Classes, and Protocol Definitions

Plugs are defined in pairs as a connection. Base classes are required for each plug class. The base class defines the functions and variables that will be available to the other plug once a connection is made. The base class can be any C++ class, but it is typically defined specifically for the plug definition. In general, it is best to include only pure virtual functions in a base class definition, as shown in the "Trade-offs" section later in this chapter. The base classes are defined after the connection definition, which is done using the *DECLARE_CON-NECTION* macro. The base class superclass is either the plug or socket class defined in the connection class. The base class must also include a definition for the getPlug function. This is normally done using the *DECLARE_PLUG* macro. This method is used in the following base class definition.

```
DECLARE_CONNECTION
  ( StopLight1
  , StopLight1Plug
  , StopLight1Socket
  )
class StopLight1Plug : public Connection::plug
{
  public:
    DECLARE_PLUG ()
    virtual void RedLight ( int nOn ) = 0 ;
    virtual void YellowLight ( int nOn ) = 0 ;
    virtual void GreenLight ( int nOn ) = 0 ;
} ;
class StopLight1Socket : public Connection::socket
{
  public:
    DECLARE_PLUG ()
} ;
```

StopLight1Plug is an abstract class. It defines the interface via the three virtual functions but does not implement the functions. An *internal* plug-to-plug protocol is where the invocation of a function at one plug causes functions at the other plug to be called. The public functions can provide an *external* plug-to-

plug protocol. In this case, there are what appear to be three independent functions. Associated documentation or comments would verify this. For example:

```
/*
Connection: StopLight1
External Interface Description:
  A StopLight1 provides access to a StopLight1Plug that
  controls three lights: red, yellow, and green. They can be
  independently set (a non-zero parameter to the associated
  function) or reset with a 0 parameter value. The functions are
  accessed from a StopLight1Socket.
*/
```

These comments indicate that the functions operate independently of each
other and can be accessed externally. External accesses can be made by a reference to the plug or across a connection, using the plug at the other end in
conjunction with the access operator, ->. The difference between internal and
external protocols becomes more apparent when looking at an external protocol example, as follows:

```
DECLARE_CONNECTION
  ( StopLight2
  , StopLight2Plug
  , StopLight2Socket
  )
class StopLight2Plug : public StopLight2::plug
{
  protected:
    DECLARE_PLUG ()
    friend StopLight2Socket
    virtual void RedLight ( int nOn ) = 0 ;
    virtual void YellowLight ( int nOn ) = 0 ;
    virtual void GreenLight ( int nOn ) = 0 ;
} ;
class StopLight2Socket : public StopLight2::socket
{
  public:
    DECLARE_PLUG ()
```

```
        virtual void RedLight ( int nOn ) ;
        virtual void YellowLight ( int nOn ) ;
        virtual void GreenLight ( int nOn ) ;
} ;
// —— This normally goes in a .CPP file  —-
void StopLight2Socket::RedLight ( int nOn )
{
  pOther->RedLight ( nOn ) ;
}
void StopLight2Socket::YellowLight ( int nOn )
{
  pOther->YellowLight ( nOn ) ;
}
void StopLight2Socket::GreenLight ( int nOn )
{
  pOther->GreenLight ( nOn ) ;
}
```

The connection class in the preceding example uses a very simple internal connection. Each function on the *StopLight2Socket* calls a matching function at
the other end of the connection. It does this using the *pOther* pointer, which
references the plug at the other end of the connection. Note that the current
implementation of *StopLight2Socket* assumes a connection is in place and
will cause an error if there is no connection.

The difference between the *StopLight1* and *StopLight2* connection class definitions is that *StopLight2* uses a different external protocol and an internal
protocol. The functions of a *StopLight2Socket* can be accessed externally; the
functions of a *StopLight2Plug* cannot, because they are protected. They cannot be accessed externally either through the plug or via the *StopLight2Socket*
and the -> operator.

In this particular example socket class, *StopLight2Socket* is not abstract and
can be used to define objects; the plug class cannot. A sample plug class definition follows:

```
class SimpleStopLight2Plug : public StopLight2Plug
```

```
   {
     public:
       int nRedLight ;
       int nYellowLight ;
       int nGreenLight ;
     protected:
       void RedLight ( int nOn ) { nRedLight = nOn ; }
       void YellowLight ( int nOn ) { nYellowLight = nOn ; }
       void GreenLight ( int nOn ) { nGreenLight = nOn ; }
   } ;
```

The protected functions save their parameters in public variables, but these
will not be accessible across a connection. Only the base class functions can
be used, and they all are protected for internal use. A function or class that
includes a *SimpleStopLight2Plug* object, or pointer to one, can access the public variables. These objects can be used in connections to *StopLight2Socket*
objects, but the socket objects cannot access the public variables.

So far, examples have been of connections with no internal protocol, *Stop-
Light1*, and with a one-sided protocol, *StopLight2*. Now let's look at a two-
sided internal protocol example.

```
DECLARE_CONNECTION
  ( CopyConnection
  , CopyPlug
  , CopySocket
  )
class CopyPlug : public CopyConnection::plug
{
  public:
    DECLARE_PLUG ()
  protected:
    friend CopySocket ;
    virtual void DoCopy () ;
    virtual int ProcessData ( const char * buffer, int nSize ) = 0
;
} ;
class CopySocket : public CopyConnection::socket
```

```
  {
    public:
      DECLARE_PLUG ()
    protected:
      friend CopyPlug ;
      virtual void BeginCopy () = 0 ;
      virtual int GetData ( const char * buffer, int nSize ) = 0 ;
      virtual void EndCopy () = 0 ;
      virtual void Error ( int n ) = 0 ;
    public:
      virtual void DoCopy () ;
  } ;
  // —  The following is normally in a .CPP file  —-
  void CopySocket::DoCopy ()
  {
    pOther->DoCopy ()
  }
  void CopyPlug::DoCopy ()
  {
    char buffer [ 256 ] ;
    pOther->BeginCopy () ;
    for ( ; ; )
    {
      int nSize = pOther->GetData ( buffer, sizeof ( buffer )) ;
      if ( nSize == 0 )
        break ;
      if ( ProcessData ( buffer, nSize ) != nSize )
      {
        pOther->Error ( nSize ) ;
        break ;
      }
    }
    pOther->EndCopy () ;
  }
```

The internal protocol can be defined in the comments and documentation, but in this example it is shown in the code. In some cases, this is not possible or desirable; for example, it is not desirable when you want to specify the functions involved but not an actual implementation. In this example the

ProcessData function is used to handle data obtained via *GetData* from the other end of the connection.

The external protocol is on the socket side with the *DoCopy* function. This initiates a copy operation on the plug side, which invokes the following internal protocol:

```
Socket side                      Plug side
1. DoCopy
                                 2. DoCopy
3. BeginCopy
4. GetData
                                 5. ProcessData
x. Repeat 4 and 5 until all data copied
6. EndCopy
```

This is the protocol spelled out in the code for *CopySocket::DoCopy* and *CopyPlug::DoCopy*. The problem with defining some or all of the protocol in a function is that it locks in the operation as well as the intent. Supplying the basic functions with the documentation is a way to provide the protocol and intent without locking in the way the protocol is implemented. Figure 3-1 shows how the protocol timing diagram looks. It looks just like a timing diagram for an integrated circuit. Each line represents a Boolean indicator of when each function is called.

In the previous example both *CopyPlug* and *CopySocket* are abstract classes. A subclass of *CopyPlug* needs to define *ProcessData*, while *CopySocket* subclasses need to define *BeginCopy*, *GetData*, and *EndCopy*. The following shows an implementation of a *CopySocket* utilizing a standard C file:

```cpp
#include <stdio.h>
class FileCopySocket : public CopySocket
{
  protected:
    char FileName [ 256 ] ;
    int FileHandle ;
```

```
        void Error ( int nSize ) {}
        void BeginCopy ()
        {
          FileHandle = open ( FileName, "r" ) ;
        }
        int GetData ( char * buffer, int nSize )
        {
          return fread ( FileHandle, buffer, nSize ) ;
        }
        void EndCopy ()
        {
          close ( FileHandle ) ;
        }
    public:
        void SetFileName ( const char * pName )
        {
          strcpy ( FileName, pName ) ;
        }
  } ;
```

The added external protocol with this plug is the *SetFileName* function, which must be called before the connection can be used. It ignores any errors by defining an *Error* function that does nothing.

Defining base functions and protocols can be done in a straightforward manner, but be careful not to try to include all the functionality in the base class when what is really necessary is a function that returns a pointer or reference to another object. For example, you might need a base class that can support a C file as part of its protocol. Supplying the C file can be done in one of three ways: inheriting the file into the base class, making a file a member of the class, or defining a function that returns a reference to a file. The last way is the preferred mechanism because it allows the other two approaches to be used to actually implement a subclass of the plug, but does not require one particular method. In fact, the file does not have to be part of the plug. The function only needs to be able to obtain a pointer to the file object.

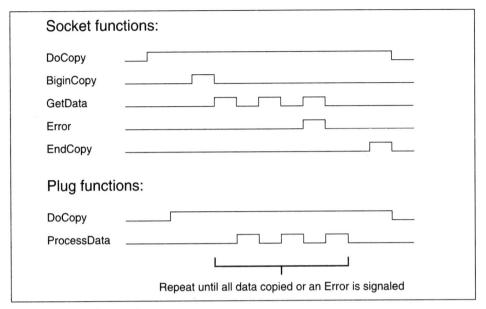

Figure 3-1. Protocol timing diagram

The main idea to get from this section is that there are two plug protocols that may be defined for a connection, internal and external. Implementers of a plug subclass must understand both, and often implement both, if they are not implemented by the base class. Users of a plug need only know about the external protocols and functions. The external protocol and functions tend to be simpler and at a logically higher level than the internal protocol and functions.

Introduction to Components

Components are objects that contain one or more plugs. "Contain" can mean various things: components can contain plugs via inheritance, plugs as members, or both. Simple plugs are contained via inheritance. Normally, components with more than one plug implement the references to plugs as functions, as in the following example:

```
class SimpleComponent
{
  public:
```

```
      virtual PlugX & MyPlug () = 0 ;
      virtual SocketX & MySocket () = 0 ;
  } ;
```

As you can see, the components can also be implemented as abstract classes. One way to implement this component is to include the corresponding plugs as members or pointers to members, as follows:

```
class SimpleComponent1 : public SimpleComponent
{
  protected:
    PlugX Plug1 ;
    SocketX Socket1 ;
  public:
    virtual PlugX & MyPlug () { return Plug1 ; }
    virtual SocketX & MySocket () { return Socket1 ; }
} ;
```

The other alternative is to implement the plugs via inheritance. The following example does so, hiding the inherited plugs but making them available through the virtual functions. The advantage of this approach is that the plug member functions can be redefined within the class, thereby having access to the members of *SimpleComponent2*.

```
class SimpleComponent2
    : public SimpleComponent
    , protected PlugX
    , protected SocketX
{
  public:
    virtual PlugX & MyPlug () { return this ; }
    virtual SocketX & MySocket () { return this ; }
    // PlugX or SocketX functions can be redefined here.
} ;
```

Simple components include simple plugs and slightly more complex plugs with a specific purpose, such as adapters, filters, tees, and 2 to 1 (2:1) merges, as shown in Figure 3-2.

Adapters and filters contain two plugs. Adapters contain plugs from different kinds of connections and are designed to convert one connection to another. An example, shown later, is an adapter that converts a string stream to a buffered stream. Filters contain a plug and a socket from the same type of connection. Tees contain three plugs, normally for the same type of connection. Two are

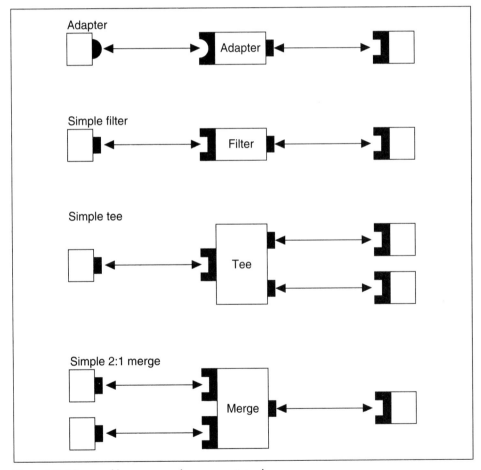

Figure 3-2. Adapters, filters, tees, and merges contain plugs

of one type, plugs or sockets, while the third is the opposite type, socket or plug. Tees are normally associated with connections that have a data flow in one direction, usually from the single type of plug to the other two. Tees are therefore a way to increase the number of destination plugs. Merge components essentially serve the opposite function of tees. Merge components also contain three plugs, two of one type and one of the other, but the purpose is to merge two data flows from the two plugs of the same type to the single plug. A sample tee and merge component definition looks like this:

```
class GenericTee
{
  public:
    virtual SocketX & Source () = 0 ;
    virtual PlugX & Plug1() = 0 ;
    virtual PlugX & Plug2() = 0 ;
} ;
class GenericMerge
{
  public:
    virtual SocketX & Source1 () = 0 ;
    virtual SocketX & Source2 () = 0 ;
    virtual PlugX & Plug1() = 0 ;
} ;
```

More complex tees and merges can be built by combining multiple tees or merge components of the same type. Alternatively, a multiple connection tee or merge component can be created.

Notice that the kind of connections involved in the components are not specified. The examples use generic *PlugX* and *SocketX* class names, but these must be replaced by real plug class names to define a function that returns a reference to this type of object.

Another type of component that contains multiple plugs is the compound plug. A compound plug is one side of a compound connection. A compound plug operates like a normal plug and is defined as such. The difference between a compound plug and a simple plug is that after a compound plug is connected, it immediately makes more connections using the plug at the other end of its connection. Likewise, it breaks these connections when the compound connection is broken. It is analogous to plugging in a power cord for a computer. The compound plug is the power cord. The subsequent connections are the two power lines contained in the power cord. A typical compound connection definition looks like this:

```
DECLARE_CONNECTION
  ( CompoundConnection
  , CPlug
  , CSocket
  )
class CPlug : public CompoundConnection::plug
{
  protected:
    virtual PlugX & Plug1 () = 0 ;
    virtual SocketX & Socket2 () = 0 ;
    virtual void afterConnect ( otherPlug * ) = 0 ;
    virtual void beforeDisconnect ( otherPlug * ) = 0 ;
  public:
    friend CSocket ;
    DECLARE_PLUG ()
} ;
class CSocket : public CompoundConnection::socket
{
  protected:
    virtual PlugX & Plug2 () = 0 ;
    virtual SocketX & Socket1 () = 0 ;
    virtual void afterConnect ( otherPlug * ) = 0 ;
    virtual void beforeDisconnect ( otherPlug * ) = 0 ;
  public:
    friend CPlug ;
    DECLARE_PLUG ()
} ;
void CPlug::afterConnect ( otherPlug * pOtherEnd )
{
  Plug1 () <= pOtherEnd -> Socket1 () ;
```

```
    }
    void CSocket::beforeDisconnect ( otherPlug * pOtherEnd )
    {
      -- Plug1() ;
    }
    void CSocket::afterConnect ( otherPlug * pOtherEnd )
    {
      Plug2 () <= pOtherEnd -> Socket2 () ;
    }
    void CSocket::beforeDisconnect ( otherPlug * pOtherEnd )
    {
      -- Plug2() ;
    }
```

The example compound plug contains two internal connections. One is made and broken when the plug side of the compound connection is made; the other is made by the socket side. The choice may make no difference and therefore is up to the connection designer. On the other hand, a specific sequence to either the connection or disconnection may be required, in which case these operations must be done by one side of the compound connection.

You will notice that the definitions of the base classes for the compound plugs look a lot like those for the other components discussed in this section. The main difference is that the compound plug base classes hide the virtual functions used to access the other plugs by making them protected.

The component and plug definitions shown in this section are all pure virtual functions. Trade-offs to using this approach are addressed in the next section.

Trade-offs

The simplest case is a pair of plugs where one has a base class with a public member. For example:

```
DECLARE_CONNECTION
    ( Int1Connection
    , Int1Plug
    , Int1Socket
```

```
      )
    class Int1Plug : public Int1Connection::plug
    {
      public:
        int i ;
        DECLARE_PLUG ()
    };
    class Int1Socket : public Int1Connection::socket
    {
      public:
        DECLARE_PLUG ()
    };
```

Int1Plug objects are used by themselves or within other structures. The part of the program that defines these objects can update the variable directly, while an *Int1Socket* object must reference the variable as though the plug were a pointer, using ->. The only advantage to using this pair of plugs instead of a single pointer is that the *Int1Plug* objects can be used to break the connection.

One disadvantage of this approach is that the object is imbedded in the object and any derivatives. There is not much overhead for simple elements like integers, but other objects can take up a significant amount of space. Another disadvantage occurs when the element is an object where the methods are not virtual. In this case, the operation of the object can only be altered within the limitations of the initial class definition.

One way around the space problem is to use pointers or references in the plug base definitions, as in this example:

```
    DECLARE_CONNECTION
      ( Int2Connection
      , Int2Plug
      , Int2Socket
      )
    class Int2Plug : public Int2Connection::plug
    {
      public:
```

```
        int * i ;
        DECLARE_PLUG ()
    } ;
    class Int2Socket : public Int2Connection::socket
    {
      public:
        DECLARE_PLUG ()
    } ;
```

The overhead within a plug is now only an additional pointer for each object referenced. A pointer does add overhead for each access in addition to a reference through the plug, but this can be eliminated by copying the pointer into a local variable that is used directly. This approach can be used with plugs in general, assuming the pointers are not changed by the plug during the connection. If this does occur, then the protocol for notification of such changes should be part of the plug base class interface definition.

Using pointers does not overcome the disadvantage of using an object that does not use virtual member functions. One of the key ideas about using plugs is that replacement should be easy. The only way to make this possible is to make creation of interchangeable plugs possible. Virtual functions and abstract classes make this possible.

There are two ways to use abstract classes with plugs. Each has its trade-offs. The first method is to make the plug base an abstract class. For example:

```
    DECLARE_CONNECTION
        ( Int3Connection
        , Int3Plug
        , Int3Socket
        )
    class Int3Plug : public Int3Connection::plug
    {
      public:
        virtual int Get () = 0 ;
        virtual void Set ( int i ) = 0 ;
        DECLARE_PLUG ()
```

```
};
class Int3Socket : public Int3Connection::socket
{
  public:
    DECLARE_PLUG ()
};
```

In this case, all operations are virtual functions, and an abstract class allows any implementation to be used interchangeably. The overhead is minimal because an abstract class, without additional members, only incurs a pointer to the table that contains the address for the virtual functions. The other alternative is to use pointers or references to instances of abstract classes. You cannot build an object out of abstract class objects because you cannot instantiate an abstract class, hence the use of pointers and references. Copying the pointers to local variables once a connection is made can reduce the calling overhead.

The following is an example of a plug using pointers to abstract classes:

```
DECLARE_CONNECTION
  ( Int4Connection
  , Int4Plug
  , Int4Socket
  )
class AnAbstractClass
{
  public:
    virtual int Get () = 0 ;
    virtual void Set ( int i ) = 0 ;
} ;
class Int4Plug : public Int4Connection::plug
{
  public:
    AnAbstractClass * i :
    DECLARE_PLUG ()
};
class Int4Socket : public Int4Connection::socket
{
  public:
```

```
        DECLARE_PLUG ()
    } ;
```

The advantage of this approach is that members can be easily added with min-imal overhead. They can also all be easily replaced by interchangeable instances. For example, the following shows how the previous definition can be used to build an actual instance of *Int4Plug*:

```
    class AnInstanceClass : public AnAbstractClass
    {
      protected:
        int value ;
      public:
        virtual int Get ()  return value ;
        virtual void Set ( int i )  value = i ;
    } ;
    class Plug4Version1 : public Int4Plug
    {
      protected:
        AnInstanceClass myValue ;
      public:
        Plug4Version1 ()
        {
          i = & myValue ;
        }
    } ;
```

An additional plug connection declaration is not required. Instances of this type of plug include the object within itself, but this is not a requirement. In any case, creating the classes is not a difficult procedure. Consider one more option:

```
    DECLARE_CONNECTION
      ( Int5Connection
      , Int5Plug
      , Int5Socket
      )
    class Int5Plug : public Int5Connection::plug
    {
```

```
  public:
    AnAbstractClass const * i () = 0 ;
    DECLARE_PLUG ()
} ;
class Int5Socket : public Int5Connection::socket
{
  public:
    DECLARE_PLUG ()
} ;
```

This final approach is the preferred method of implementing plugs. Abstract classes can clearly define the interface, and obtaining the pointer through a member function prevents the pointer from being modified. A reference provides the same feature but prevents the pointer from being updated by the class that defines the object. You can use references or various combinations of *const* to control access to the objects being referenced.

In this last approach, the space overhead is minimal for the plug definition because the base definition for an abstract plug is a single hidden pointer. Adding object references only increases the size of the member pointer table. References to the objects are normally saved locally and used as needed.

This trade-off discussion may seem obvious if you have been using C++ for a while, but it is important to stress the ability to build interchangeable parts. Defining a plug using one approach uses fewer statements, but it will lock subsequent users of the plug into a particular implementation.

The general rules for defining plugs are, first, define base plug classes as abstract classes (that is, all members are virtual and pure) and, second, any pointers to internal objects should also be to abstract classes. Just don't take things to extremes. If the purpose of a plug is to provide access to an array of integers, simply define a member function that returns a pointer to the array.

Some Simple, Useful Plugs

This section presents some simple abstract base classes, as well as simple plugs that incorporate these base classes. You can incorporate these plugs or declare new plugs that also use multiple instances of the abstract base classes.

One of the simplest and most useful abstract classes virtualizes the basic C variables: characters, integers, and so on. The following classes define an abstract class and another class based upon it, which are used like integers, at least at the source code level. Underneath it is all member functions.

```
class virtualInt
{
  public:
    virtual int operator = ( int i ) = 0 ;
    virtual operator int () = 0 ;
} ;
class hiddenInt : public virtualInt
{
  public:
    int value ;
    virtual int operator = ( int i )  value = i ; return i ;
    virtual operator int ()  return value ;
} ;
```

These classes provide controlled access and assignment. An alternative to an abstract *virtualInt* class is one that retains the virtual function definitions and replaces pure function indicators with simple functions. For example, the assignment operator would ignore the parameter, and the access operator would return a constant value, such as 0.

The following definitions can be used if you want to allow a pointer to the internal value. The internal value can be placed anywhere, but in the case of *hiddenIndirectInt*, it is in the same object that supports.

```
class virtualIndirectInt : public virtualInt
{
```

```
  public:
    virtual int * operator & () = 0 ;
} ;
class hiddenIndirectInt : public virtualIndirectInt
{
  public:
    int value ;
    virtual int operator = ( int i )  value = i ; return i ;
    virtual operator int ()  return value ;
    virtual int * operator & ()  return & value ;
} ;
```

Defining a base class using *virtualInt* allows an implementation using hiddenInt. However, *hiddenInt* is only one way to implement *virtualInt*. The following example shows a general plug definition using *virtualInt*:

```
DECLARE_CONNECTION
  ( VirtualIntConnection
  , VirtualIntPlug
  , VirtualIntSocket
  )
class VirtualIntPlug : public VirtualIntConnection::plug
{
  public:
    DECLARE_PLUG ()
    virtual virtualInt & foo () = 0 ;
} ;
class VirtualIntSocket : public
VirtualIntConnection::socket
?Line above s/b on one line.
{
  public:
    DECLARE_PLUG ()
} ;
A class that implements VirtualIntPlug using hiddenInt is:
class HiddenIntPlug : public VirtualIntPlug
{
  public:
    hiddenInt Hidden ;
```

```
        virtualInt & value ()  return Hidden ;
    } ;
```

This class provides controlled access to the integer value contained within Hidden, through *foo* and the member functions defined in *virtualInt*. The value can be accessed directly through the plug using *Hidden.value*.

```
    class hiddenIntPointer: public virtualInt
    {
      public:
        int * pValue ;
        virtual int operator = ( int i )  (* pValue) = i ; return i ;
         virtual operator int ()  return * pValue ;
      } ;
    class HiddenPointerIntPlug : public VirtualIntPlug
    {
      public:
        hiddenIntPointer Hidden ;
        virtualInt & value ()  return Hidden ;
      } ;
```

From the point of view of a *VirtualIntSocket*, a *HiddenIntPlug* object and *HiddenPointerIntPlug* object are identical. The obvious advantage of *HiddenPointerIntPlug* is that the pointer can be changed, and the value does not have to reside in the object containing the pointer.

However, changing the internal state of the object, such as changing the value of the pointer in a *HiddenPointerIntPlug* object, is something that the other end of the plug may want to know about. The following class can be used in place of the empty socket class in the previous *VirtualIntConnection* examples.

```
    class VirtualIntSocket : public VirtualIntConnection::socket
    {
      public:
        DECLARE_PLUG ()
        virtual void Notify () = 0 ;
      } ;
```

The *Notify* member is called when a change occurs. The class is not abstract because the simplest case is to do nothing. The *Notify* function is virtual, which allows it to be redefined arbitrarily. The type of change is plug specific but, like the *virtualInt*, it is another standard class that can be used to build more complex plugs. A simple handshake mechanism might work like this. The *Notify* member is called when a new value is available.

The *Notify* member function, referenced through the plug connection, would be called when the pointer is changed, or when the value it referred to changed, or ... (you get the idea). The actual semantics should be defined, at least within comments associated with the class definition, for a particular plug connection declaration. Note, the *Notify* function should be called only if a connection exists (that is, if *connected* returns *TRUE*).

Keep in mind that changes during a connection are the kinds of changes that need to be handled by *Notify* or a similar member function. You can redefine the plug member functions like *afterConnect* and *beforeDisconnect* to handle changes that must occur when a connection is made or broken.

Any C data type can be used in place of the integer type in the previous examples. Notification is optional but is easy to implement. The space overhead is minimal if only one notification function is used, and the performance overhead is nil if the functions are not used. Defining plugs with useful but sometimes unused functionality makes future changes easier.

Hiding Connection Support Members

In the previous chapter I explained the three categories of plug member functions: operational, connection, and internal. Another way of dividing plug members is into the following two categories: those used by programmers who merely use plugs, and those used by programmers implementing a plug. Programmers in the former group need to know about the standard plug functions and any public members required after a connection is made. Programmers in the latter group need to know all of that and more, and will often use members not used by the first group.

It's important not to burden programmers in the first group with information only needed by programmers in the second group. One way to differentiate the members to be used by the two groups is by commenting the class definition appropriately. Another alternative is to use a C++ feature, *protected members.*

C++ protected members can be accessed by the class in which they are defined, by subclasses, and by *friend* classes or functions. However, there is a problem with inheritance. Protected members can be accessed by subclasses or friend classes but not subclasses of friend classes. Plug classes fall into the latter category. It is possible to get around the limitation with a little extra work while still retaining the control of protected members. For example:

```
DECLARE_CONNECTION
  ( SimpleProtectedConnection
  , SimpleProtectedNotifyPlug
  , SimpleProtectedSocket
  )
class SimpleProtectedSocket
  : public SimpleProtectedConnection::socket
{
  public:
    DECLARE_PLUG ()
  protected:
    virtual virtualInt & Status () = 0 ;
    virtual virtualInt & Command () = 0 ;
    virtual virtualInt & Result () = 0 ;
    friend PlugSimpleProtectedNotifyBase ;
    static inline void Notify ( otherPlug * p, Change status )
      { p -> Notify ( status ) ; }
} ;
class SimpleProtectedNotifyPlug
  : public SimpleProtectedConnection::plug
{
  public:
    DECLARE_PLUG ()
    virtual void Start () = 0 ;
    enum Change { CommandDone, StatusChange } ;
```

```
  protected:
    virtual void Notify ( Change status ) = 0 ;
    friend SimpleProtectedSocket ;
    static inline virtualInt & Status ( otherPlug * p )
      { return p -> Status () ; }
    static inline virtualInt & Command ( otherPlug * p )
      { return p -> Command () ; }
    static inline virtualInt & Result ( otherPlug * p )
      { return p -> Result () ; }
} ;
```

This approach duplicates the protected members of the other plug using its
own protected members. The protected members are accessible to any subclass but still hidden from general use.

Unfortunately, this approach gets significantly more difficult to implement as
the number of protected member functions increases.

A better alternative is to use a trick. First start with the following definitions,
which look a lot like the original definitions:

```
DECLARE_CONNECTION
  ( SimpleFriendConnection
  , SimpleFriendNotifyPlug
  , SimpleFriendSocket
  )
class SimpleFriendNotifyPlug
  : public SimpleFriendConnection::plug
{
  public:
    DECLARE_PLUG ()
    virtual void Start () = 0 ;
    enum Change { CommandDone, StatusChange } ;
  protected:
    virtual void Notify ( Change status ) = 0 ;
} ;
class SimpleFriendSocket
  : public SimpleFriendConnection::socket
```

```
{
  public:
    DECLARE_PLUG ()
  protected:
    virtual virtualInt & Status () = 0 ;
    virtual virtualInt & Command () = 0 ;
    virtual virtualInt & Result () = 0 ;
} ;
```

Second, depending upon which side of the plug you are defining, declare a pair of classes similar to the following:

```
class MySimpleFriendNotifyPlug : public SimpleFriendNotifyPlug
{
  protected:
    friend MySimpleFriendSocket ;
    // These members can use SimpleFriendBase members.
} ;
class MySimpleFriendSocket : public SimpleFriendSocket
{
  protected:
    friend MySimpleFriendNotifyPlug ;
    // These members can use SimpleFriendNotifyBase members.
} ;
```

The *friend* declaration gives the other class access to the protected members, which were previously hidden. The trick here is to define the pointer to the other plug using the class defined above. A cast is required when assigning the pointer a value, because the pointer is a subclass of the type actually used by the plug operations.

If you define plugs, you have a choice of making members *public*, *protected*, or *private*. Although it is more difficult to use protected members, it does let users know what should and should not be used. In general, a user of a plug should use only public members, not members related to the operation of the connection.

Templates and Simple Plug Members

The plug member classes described in this chapter, such as *virtualInt*, are applicable to just about any data type. Most C++ compilers now support C++ templates, which make these declarations easy to build. For example:

```
template <class type>
class virtualType
{
  public:
    virtual type operator = ( type i ) = 0 ;
    virtual operator type () = 0 ;
} ;
Now, virtualInt can be defined as:
class virtualInt : public virtualType<int>  ;
```

You can also use *virtualType<int>* directly within class declarations. Template declarations can get quite complex, but most of those used with plugs should be as simple as the one just presented.

String Stream Connection

The string stream connection, *StrStream1*, is a very simple connection used in this chapter to introduce a suite of basic components. This section describes the connection, while the next chapter describes the basic components that can be used with the plugs and sockets of this connection.

The *StrStream1* connection has an extremely simple internal and external protocol. The connection is a useful but basic tool used to move C strings from one end of the connection to the other. The plug is the source and the socket is the destination. The plug contains one external function, *Process*. The socket contains one internal function, also named *Process*. The plug function calls the socket function.

You might be wondering what a *StrStream1* connection could be used for. Consider Figure 3-3, which shows a simple old-style computer terminal interface with two connections: one from the keyboard to the computer and another from the computer to the display. The keyboard interface is assumed to be one line at a time, which conforms to the C string used in the connection.

The *StrStream1* connection class is designed for simplicity. Its operation is easy to understand, while keeping the associated definitions and examples short and to the point. The connection definition is as follows:

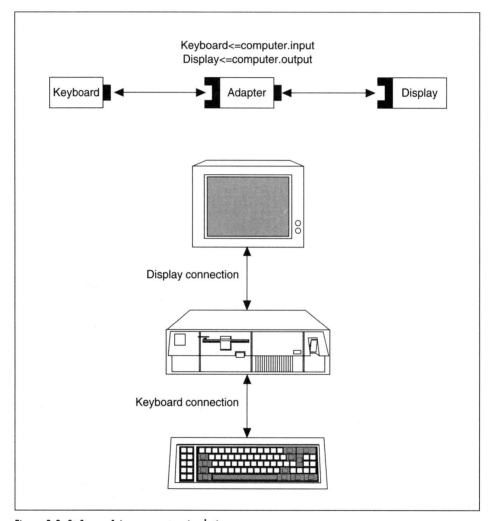

Keyboard<=computer.input
Display<=computer.output

Figure 3-3. StrStream1 in a computer simulation

```
DECLARE_CONNECTION
  ( StrStream1
  , StrStream1Plug
  , StrStream1Socket
  )
class StrStream1Plug : public StrStream1::plug
{
  public:
    DECLARE_PLUG ()
    virtual void Process ( const char * buffer ) ;
} ;
class StrStream1Socket : public StrStream1::socket
{
  public:
    DECLARE_PLUG ()
  protected:
    friend StrStreamSocket ;
    virtual void Process ( const char * buffer ) = 0 ;
} ;
void StrStream1Plug::Process ( const char * buffer )
{
  pOther->Process ( buffer ) ;
}
```

The socket base class, *StrStream1Socket,* is an abstract class that means subsequent plug class definitions must implement the *Process* function before objects can be defined. A generic plug class object can be defined using the following code:

```
StrStream1Plug MyStrStream1Plug ;
```

A plug object of this type can be used to connect to a *StrStream1Socket.* The external protocol can then be used to supply data via the *Process* function. Defining socket classes is a bit more difficult because you need to know what you are going to do with the data when you get a socket *Process* function call.

I used the connection name *StrStream1* because the connection has a one-way internal protocol. A *StrStream2* connection is the logical extension. A *StrStream2* connection is a compound connection made up of a pair of *StrStream1* connections in opposite directions. Appendix B contains a complete definition for *StrStream1* and *StrStream2* connections, including plug and socket definitions utilizing C files.

The next section looks at some simple components based upon the *StrStream1* connection definition.

Adapters, Tees, Filters, and Merges

Connections can be useful between individual sets of plugs and sockets, but program construction becomes more interesting when other building blocks are available. This section presents some basic components that use simple plugs based upon the *StrStream1* connection class presented in the previous section. The basic components include adapters, tees, filters, and merges. These types of components work well with directional internal protocol connections, such as *StrStream1*. They may not be applicable to other internal protocol connections, but then most components of this type are included as part of a connection class library definition. The types of components described in this section are designed to reflect the types of components available in electronic digital devices.

Adapters convert one type of connection to another. The number and types of adapters can be quite varied and will depend upon the internal and external protocols supported by the associated connections. There can be four types of adapters given one pair of connections. For example, given connections C1 and C2, you could have an adapter between a *C1::plug* and a *C2::plug*, a *C1::socket* and a *C2::socket*, a *C1::plug* and a *C2::socket*, and a *C1::socket* and a *C2::plug*. The number of combinations and their operation should not be restricted to these possibilities, nor required by them. The amount of information and protocol transferred through an adapter is based on the connection protocols as well as the adapter construction.

Filters, tees, and merges utilize the same type of connection with all public plugs. This is actually a restriction placed upon the examples presented in this section rather than a plug restriction or design recommendation. The filters, tees, and merges presented here are also very simplistic. They are based on the *StrStream1* connection plugs and perform no additional processing when passing the data through the components. The components are initially presented as abstract classes. This allows the definitions to be used as the basis for a whole class of implementations that are interchangeable. The class definitions are as follows:

```
class StrStream1Filter
{
  public:
    virtual StrStream1::plug & Plug () = 0 ;
    virtual StrStream1::socket & Socket () = 0 ;
} ;
class StrStream1TeeFilter : public StrStream1Filter
{
  public:
    virtual StrStream1::plug & CopyPlug () = 0 ;
} ;
class StrStream1Merge
{
  public:
    virtual StrStream1::socket & Socket1 () = 0 ;
    virtual StrStream1::socket & Socket2 () = 0 ;
    virtual StrStream1::plug & Plug () = 0 ;
} ;
```

A filter is designed to be interposed in the midst of a connection that includes plug and socket. A filter contains its own plug and socket, which are connected appropriately. The *StrStream1Filter* provides access to a *StrStream1* plug and socket. Assume for a moment that there are plug, socket, and filter classes defined that are not abstract and can be used to allocate objects. A filter could be interposed between the plug and socket using the following code:

```
SampleStrStream1Plug Plug ;
SampleStrStream1Socket Socket ;
SampleStrStream1Filter Filter ;
Plug <= Filter.Socket () ;
Socket <= Filter.Plug () ;
```

In most cases the Plug and Socket will also be parts of a component. A very simple pass-through filter is defined using the following code:

```
class StrStream1NullFilter
  : public StrStream1Filter
  , protected StrStream1Socket
{
 protected:
    StrStream1Plug MyPlug ;
    void Process ( const char * buffer ) { MyPlug.Process ( buffer
)
; }
  public:
    virtual StrStream1::plug & Plug () { return MyPlug ; }
    virtual StrStream1::socket & Socket () { return * this ; }
} ;
```

The *Process* function call for the socket is passed on to the plug, which is defined as part of the filter object via multiple inheritance. An alternative, used in Appendix B, is to define a socket that takes a pointer to a plug, where the socket passes the *Process* function parameter to the plug. In this case the filter component contains two hidden objects, the plug and the special socket. *Null* filters, or filters that do nothing, are useful because a system may require a filter to be installed between two plugs.

The *StrStream1TeeFilter* is a subclass of *StrStream1Filter;* it adds one plug. Normally a tee passes through the socket information to both plugs. A simple tee does so without any modification of the information, and it essentially acts as a replicator. This is not a requirement, and in many cases a tee actually has a different connection plug as the additional plug. The null tee filter shown in the next example utilizes the *StrStream1NullFilter* just presented. Incremental enhancement is not always this easy, but it is nice when it happens.

```
class StrStream1NullTeeFilter
  : public StrStream1NullFilter
{
  protected:
    StrStream1Plug MyCopyPlug ;
    void Process ( const char * buffer )
    {
      StrStream1NullFilter::Process ( buffer ) ;
      MyCopyPlug.Process ( buffer ) ;
    }
  public:
    virtual StrStream1::plug & CopyPlug () { return MyCopyPlug ; }
} ;
```

The tee filter redefines the *Process* function and adds one plug data member. The new *Process* function forwards input to the socket to the *StrStream1Null-Filter* function, thereby passing the information out the main plug connection. It also sends the same information to the *MyCopyPlug*, thereby replicating the connection information.

The *StrStream1Merge* is the opposite of the *StrStream1TeeFilter*. The null merge class presented next utilizes two specialized sockets and a plug. The information received by the sockets is sent to the plug. There is no special synchronization mechanism, which might be necessary in a multitasking environment. The specialized forwarding socket passes information to a corresponding plug. The socket class definition is set up so that the plug reference is specified when the socket is initialized, and the plug reference cannot be changed. This is not a requirement for our design but simply the way it was implemented for this example. A pointer, which could be changed, could be used instead. The null merge component and socket definitions are as follows:

```
class StrStream1ForwardSocket : public StrStream1Socket
{
  protected:
    Stream1::plug & Plug ;
  public:
    StrStream1ForwardSocket ( Stream1::plug & MyPlug ) ;
    void Process ( const char * buffer ) { Plug.Process ( buffer )
;
  }
} ;
class StrStream1NullMerge : public StrStream1Merge
{
  protected:
    StrStream1ForwardSocket MySocket1 ;
    StrStream1ForwardSocket MySocket2 ;
    StrStream1Plug MyPlug ;
  public:
    StrStream1NullMerge ()
      : MySocket1 ( MyPlug )
      , MySocket2 ( MyPlug )
      {}
    virtual StrStream1::socket & Socket1 () { return MySocket1 ; }
    virtual StrStream1::socket & Socket2 () { return MySocket2 ; }
    virtual StrStream1::plug & Plug () { return MyPlug ; }
} ;
```

The socket constructor requires a plug as a parameter. This initialization is done in the merge component in its constructor. Both sockets reference the same plug, *MyPlug*.

The simple components presented in this section are designed to show how such components are constructed. They are not designed to be extensive or flexible, although they can be used as the basis for new classes that implement more sophisticated components.

Transaction-Oriented Connections

The components presented in this chapter utilize very basic internal and external protocols. A transaction in these connections consists of a single function call, often with a response that is also a single function call. This is appropriate, since this chapter is dedicated to simple plugs, connections, and components. However, this simplistic presentation should not be viewed as a requirement or restriction. Many applications and connections will require significantly more complex protocols. One step up might include something along the lines of a simple external function that invokes the following internal protocol:

○ Open

○ Multiple Process calls

○ Close

Here, *Open, Process,* and *Close* are internal functions at the other end of the connection. A more complex protocol might include handshaking functions in both directions.

This last comment on transaction-oriented connections is simply to present the possibility of such connection definitions. It is not difficult to see how such protocols can be implemented. The next chapter explores more complex examples associated with the development of some software components.

4 Simple Controls Using Plugs

This chapter explores creating controls using plugs. In creating the controls, you will build software components. As explained in Chapter 1, the goal of plug-based programming is to develop components that can be plugged together by programmers, very much as hardware components can be plugged together. In Chapter 3 you saw some examples of how to construct simple plugs and components; now you'll see how to build more complex components. In the process, examples of simple useful plugs will be described.

Building components from scratch takes a good understanding of plugs, inside and out. Using components or building components from other components is much easier, but of course it requires that some components already exist. Many components are specific to a certain application or type of application, but many others are generic and can be used in most any program. This chapter presents a few generic components, and shows how to present components and their associated classes.

The connection types and components presented here include simple controls that deal with basic C data types such as integers and strings, simple file components, and some examples using these components.

A Basic Control-Controller Connection

The first example connection definition is based on a control-controller model (analogous to a simple client-server model). You can use the connection to implement control sliders or scroll bars in Windows or Macintosh applications, for example.

The connection is presented using integers, but it is applicable to any data type. The control component can be adjusted at any time after a connection is made. The controller is designed to provide an initial value after a connection is made, and a final value is saved before a connection is broken. Any change on the control side is indicated by a notification function that can indicate whether a change should be allowed.

The basic control-controller connection starts with a pair of classes similar to *virtualInt* presented in Chapter 3. The difference is that the control does not try to look like a variable, and the notification side is conditional and includes an initialization and termination section.

The basic control and controller classes utilize virtual functions, but the classes are not abstract. The default function definitions for these classes essentially ignore the parameters passed or return an appropriate value. Most implementations will redefine these functions; the example class definitions included here do just that.

```
class intControl
{
  public:
    virtual void set ( int ) {}
    virtual int get ()
    {
      return 0 ;
    }
} ;

class intController
{
  public:
    virtual void finalValue ( int ) {}
    virtual int initialValue ()
    {
      return 0 ;
    }
    virtual BOOL notify ()
```

```
    {
      return TRUE ;
    }
} ;


// ====  Variable implementations for control/controller

class intControlVariable : public intControl
{
  public:
    int value ;

    intControlVariable ( int initial = 0 ) : value(initial) {}
    virtual void set ( int i )
    {
      value = i ;
    }
    virtual int get ()
    {
       return value ;
    }
} ;


class intControllerVariable : public intController
{
  public:
    int value ;

    intControllerVariable ( int initial = 0 )
      : value (initial)
      {}
    virtual void finalValue ( int i )
    {
      value = i ;
    }
    virtual int initialValue ()
    {
      return value ;
    }
} ;
```

The variable class implementations both utilize a public variable. The controller variable will normally be set before a connection is made and used after a connection is broken. The control variable will be used during a connection. Notification is not integrated with the classes, although the controller class contains the appropriate function definition. Figure 4-1 shows what the connection looks like.

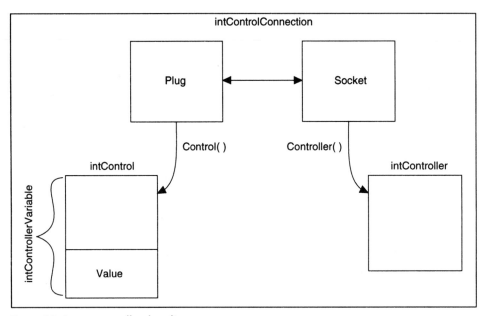

Figure 4-1. Integer controller class diagram

Source code for this example is as follows:

```
DECLARE_CONNECTION
  ( intControlConnection
  , intControlPlug
  , intControllerPlug
  )

class intControlBase : public intControlConnection::plug
{
  public:
    DECLARE_PLUG ()
```

```
        virtual intControl * control () = 0 ;
  } ;



class intControllerBase : public intControlConnection::socket
{
  public:
    DECLARE_PLUG ()
    virtual intController * controller () = 0 ;
  } ;
```

The *intControlPlug* and *intControllerPlug* classes do not provide implementations for the control and controller functions. Another pair of plugs is needed to implement these details. The sample plug definitions provided here use the previously defined control variable class definitions as well as add support that uses the connection procedures that were previously defined.

```
// ====   Implementation of intControlPlug and intControllerPlug

class intControlVariablePlug : public intControlPlug
{
  public:
    intControlVariable variable ;

    virtual intControl * control ()
    {
       return & variable ;
    }
    void afterConnect ( otherEnd * pNew )
    {
       variable.set ((pNew -> control ()) -> initialValue ());
    }
    void beforeDisconnect ( otherEnd * pOld )
    {
       (pOld -> control ()) -> finalValue ( variable.get ());
    }
    virtual BOOL change ( int i )
    {
        int old = variable.value ;
        variable.value = i ;
```

```
            if ((pOther -> control ()) -> Notify ())
                return TRUE ;
            variable.value = old ;
            return FALSE ;
        }
    } ;


class intControllerVariablePlug : public intControllerPlug
{
    public:
        intControllerVariable variable ;

        virtual intController * control ()  return & variable ;
    } ;
```

The *intControlVariablePlug* implements the connect/disconnect procedures. An additional procedure is included to change the value of the variable. It even restores the prior value if the notification fails. An alternative is to define the notification function with a parameter that is the new value so the existing value is not changed until it is validated.

C++ Streams and Plugs

Like most classes and C elements such as integers, C++ stream objects can be viewed as a single entity. Using streams in simple base classes is actually easier than setting up new classes for the controller variables described in the previous section. The simplest case would include the following:

```
    // ====  istreamConnection  ====

DECLARE_CONNECTION
    ( istreamConnection, istreamPlug, istreamSocket )

class istreamPlug : public istreamConnection::plug
{
    public:
        DECLARE_PLUG ()
        virtual istream * stream () = 0 ;
    } ;
```

```
class istreamSocket
  : public istreamConnection::socket
  , public NotifyBase
{
  public:
    DECLARE_PLUG ()
} ;


// ====  ostreamConnection  ====

DECLARE_CONNECTION
  ( ostreamConnection, ostreamPlug, ostreamSocket )

class ostreamPlug : public ostreamConnection::plug
{
  public:
    DECLARE_PLUG ()
    virtual ostream * stream () = 0 ;
} ;

class ostreamSocket
  : public ostreamConnection::socket
  , public NotifyBase
{
  public:
    DECLARE_PLUG ()
} ;



// ====  iostreamConnection  ====

DECLARE_CONNECTION
  ( iostreamConnection, iostreamPlug, iostreamSocket )

class iostreamPlug : public iostreamConnection::plug
{
  public:
    DECLARE_PLUG ()
    virtual iostream * stream () = 0 ;
```

```
} ;

class iostreamSocket
  : public iostreamConnection::socket
{
  public:
    DECLARE_PLUG ()
} ;
```

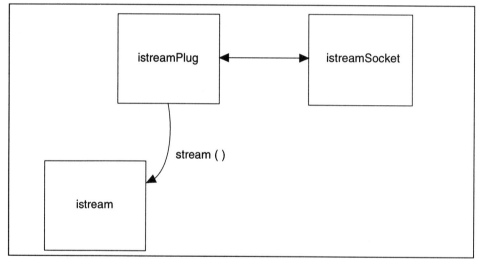

Figure 4-2. Integer control connection

The protocol is for the stream plugs to call *Notify* if the stream object changes. This allows the user of a stream plug to obtain the pointer to the stream once and use that pointer directly, without having to go through the plug connection, while still maintaining the pointer if changes should occur. This approach simplifies the interface to existing stream definitions by not changing the semantics associated with streams.

The alternative is to change the way streams interact. For example, current C++ extensions in the area of error detection and recovery use a

CATCH/THROW mechanism, which wraps the control structures with an additional control mechanism that can be invoked whenever an error occurs. However, this mechanism is usually synchronous, in that an error associated with an object only occurs when a function associated with the object is called. All errors are handled through a single control structure associated with a single thread or task. The alternative is to use a client-server approach, which requires changes in operation of a stream or file-like object. The syntax and most semantics for the stream base class remain the same. The semantics that change are related to error handling. The changes must also be reflected in the notification plug. For example:

```
class StreamNotification
{
  public:
    enum exception
      changed,
      closed,
      deleted,
      endOfFile,
      insufficientResources,
      illegalAccess,
      other  ;

    virtual void Notify ( exception why, int what )
} ;


class StreamNotificationBase
{
  public:
    virtual StreamNotifiation * Notify () = 0 ;
} ;

DECLARE_CONNECTION
    ( iostreamNotifyConnection, iostreamBase, StreamNotificationBase
    )
```

The only real difference between this example and the prior one is the notification function, which now takes two parameters. The first indicates the type of change while the latter defines why the change occurred. Why a change occurred may be environment specific. The default definition for the notification function is to ignore all errors. It is the simplest case and may be appropriate in some instances.

The main difference to note with the client-server approach is that errors are not handled using the *CATCH/THROW* mechanism but rather a notification mechanism that is ideal for plugs and more applicable to multitasking environments. For example, one task may be handling the stream while another is performing operations on it and handling the errors. The operation can be split further by allowing a third task to handle the errors or at least the reception of the errors. Yet another option is to build a notification class that sends the notification to more than one destination.

Using the Plugs

Like most classes and C elements such as integers, C++ stream objects can be viewed as a single entity. Using streams in simple base classes is actually easier than setting up new classes for the controller variables described in the previous section. The simplest case would include the following:

```
class FileCopyComponent
{
  public:
    ostreamConnection::PlugRedirector ostream ;
    istreamConnection::PlugRedirector istream ;

    virtual BOOL copy () = 0 ;
} ;
```

The redirector definitions are normally included with the stream connection definitions. Redirectors provide access to the sockets without including explicit plug definitions. The copy function is invoked after a pair of streams is connected through the redirectors. This approach could be extended to copy portions of a file or adjust to other unique requirements. Another option is to make the *FileCopyComponent* a plug and allow the two streams to be connected when the *FileCopyComponent* is connected to a matching socket (which would of course have a pair of redirectors to match the ones in the *FileCopyComponent*).

The control-controller plugs described at the beginning of the chapter can also be put to work in a variety of places. For example, control sliders or scroll bars on windows, as on the Mac or Microsoft Windows, interact in a fashion similar to the connection protocol presented here. An initial value is required when a slider is displayed, and a final value can be obtained before the window is destroyed. Likewise, changes in the value of a slider by the user via a mouse or the keyboard can be done using the notification function in a connection.

Where sliders diverge from the control plugs used here, is in their various limitations or additional controls. For example, sliders normally have a range associated with them, as well as redrawing characteristics. These can be split from the value settings into either an additional plug or function. Values can then be handled independently, making the connection for tracking a value, very simple.

The next chapter will look more closely at how plugs can be used to implement basic Windows elements.

List Box Control

This section presents two connection types that can be used as list box controls found in most graphical user interfaces. There are two connections, to both distribute the wealth and partition the problem. One connection deals with the presentation of information; the other with control information normally associated with a list box, such as selection and keyboard input. This partition allows a list box control to be built with plugs for both types of connections. Figure 4-3 shows the display connection definition, *LBDisplay*, while Figure 4-4 shows the control connection, *LBControl*. Figure 4-5 shows how these two connections can be used with a visual control. Note that the list box display interface presented here supports C text strings. Other types of list boxes could include bitmaps or mixed bitmaps and text. It's interesting to note that these other types of list boxes would probably have the same control connection.

The type of component on one side of the connections doesn't have to be a list box control. There are a number of other possibilities, including a combo box, which is a list box combined with an edit control. Later in the chapter you will see how the connections in this section can be used with other controls. The types of components that can be plugged into an *LBDisplay::socket* could include a list of strings, an array of strings, or any other collection of text. Implementation of the list box control won't be discussed until the next

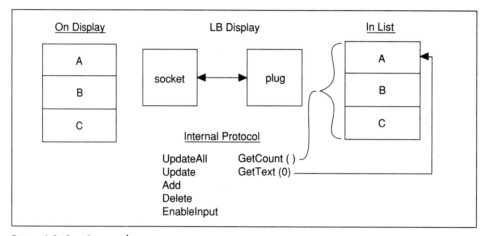

Figure 4-3. C++ Stream plugs

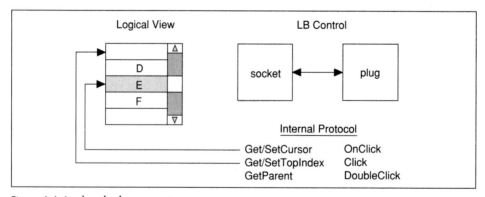

Figure 4-4. List box display connection

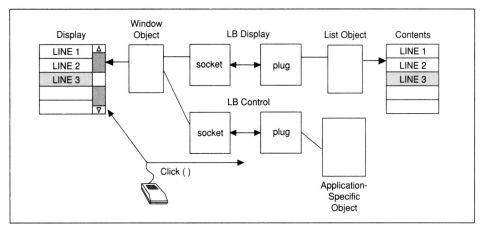

Figure 4-5. List box control connection

chapter, but the connection definitions and an array of string pointers implementation of *LBDisplay::plug* are examined here.

The connection classes presented in this section employ an internal/external protocol, as described in Chapter 3. The protocol is a simple one-to-one matching, which allows the external functions to be available on the side where they are used without using the connection directly. The display connection plug, *LBDisplay::plug*, is what the string array component will be based upon. It provides two internal functions, *GetCount* and *GetText*. These are used to obtain the size of the array and the contents. The external functions call the component to notify the other end of the connection of changes to the array. For example, if an array entry is changed, the *Update* function can be called to notify the list box control.

The connection definition is normally placed into a header file and a C++ source file; both are presented next. There are two reasons for this split. The first is to have the functions defined only once. The second is to allow circular references necessary for the internal/external function definitions because the plug needs to access the socket functions, and vice versa. Now that you have the basics, here is the code:

```
DECLARE_CONNECTION
  ( LBDisplay
  , LBDisplayPlug
  , LBDisplaySocket
  )

typedef int LBEntry ;

class LBDisplayPlug : public LBDisplay::plug
{
  protected:
    DECLARE_PLUG ()
    friend  LBDisplaySocket ;

    virtual LBEntry GetCount () = 0 ;
    virtual void    GetText ( LBEntry entry, char * buffer, int
size ) = 0 ;

  public:
    virtual void UpdateAll    () ;
    virtual void Update       ( LBEntry entry ) ;
    virtual void Add          ( LBEntry entry ) ;
    virtual void Delete       ( LBEntry entry ) ;
    virtual void EnableUpdate ( LBEntry bFlag ) ;
} ;


class LBDisplaySocket : public LBDisplay::socket
{
  public:
    virtual LBEntry GetCount () ;
    virtual void    GetText ( LBEntry entry, char * buffer, int
size ) ;

  protected:
    DECLARE_PLUG ()
    friend  LBDisplayPlug ;

    virtual void UpdateAll    () {}
    virtual void Update       ( LBEntry entry ) { UpdateAll () ; }
```

```
      virtual void Add          ( LBEntry entry ) { UpdateAll () ; }
      virtual void Delete       ( LBEntry entry ) { UpdateAll () ; }
      virtual void EnableUpdate ( BOOL  bFlag ) { if ( bFlag )
UpdateAll () ;}
  } ;



// ==== LBDisplay Function Definitions  ====
//
// Forwards external functions to internal functions
// at the other end.

void LBDisplayPlug::UpdateAll ()
{
  pOther -> UpdateAll () ;
}


void LBDisplayPlug::Update ( LBEntry entry )
{
  pOther -> Update ( entry ) ;
}


void LBDisplayPlug::Add ( LBEntry entry )
{
  pOther -> Add ( entry ) ;
}


void LBDisplayPlug::Delete ( LBEntry entry )
{
  pOther -> Delete ( entry ) ;
}


void LBDisplayPlug::EnableUpdate ( LBEntry bFlag )
{
  pOther -> EnableUpdate ( bFlag ) ;
}



LBEntry LBDisplaySocket::GetCount ()
{
```

```
    return pOther -> GetCount () ;
  }


  void LBDisplaySocket::GetText ( LBEntry entry, char * buffer, int
  size )
  {
    pOther -> GetText ( entry, buffer, size ) ;
  }
```

The *LBEntry* type definition lets you easily change the kind of index being used. Sixteen-bit integers are fine in most cases, but 32-bit integers come in handy sometimes. The internal function body definitions should appear in the source file while the class definitions appear in the header file. The plug definition is an abstract class that can be used for subclasses like the string array example defined next. The socket definition, on the other hand, is not an abstract class, although what it does implement is not very useful. The list box component implemented in the next chapter will redefine these functions to perform something useful. Even so, the definitions presented can be useful. The *UpdateAll* function normally gets the current size of the array and then displays the appropriate entries. This is usually the worst case scenario, but it is workable in all the kinds of internal functions that are supported. For example, deleting an entry can be handled via *UpdateAll*. Having a specific function for handling a delete operation could make the support operate more efficiently.

The *StrArrayLBDisplayPlug* implements an *LBDisplayPlug* subclass. A pointer to an array of string pointers is used to track the strings on the plug side. In this particular implementation, the size of the array and the array pointer are public. The *UpdateAll* function should be called if these are changed. An *Update* function is included to show how this might change. Now for the source code:

```
    class StrArrayLBDisplayPlug : public LBDisplayPlug
    {
      public:
        char ** pArray ;
        LBEntry nSize ;
```

```
StrArrayLBDisplayPlug ()
  : nSize  ( 0 )
  {}

StrArrayLBDisplayPlug
( const char ** pNewArray, LBEntry nNewSize )
  : pArray ( pNewArray )
  , nSize  ( nNewSize )
  {}

LBEntry GetCount () { return nSize ; }

void GetText ( LBEntry entry, char * buffer, int size )
{
  strncpy ( buffer, pArray [ entry ], size ) ;
}

void Update ( LBEntry entry, const char * pText )
{
  pArray [ entry ] = pText ;
  Update ( entry ) ;
}
} ;
```

Two constructor functions are provided. The first takes no parameters and starts with a list of zero elements. Changing the size or the pointer must be accompanied by a call to *UpdateAll* to let the other end of the connection know about the change. The *Update* function shows how this might be done using an external function—it changes the pointer and notifies the other end. Similar functions could be defined for adding and deleting and even changing the array pointer and its size.

One thing to note in this implementation is that the *pOther* pointer is used directly, without checking, if it is a null pointer, which is the case when the plug is not connected. This could be done in these functions but it obviously slows things down. The trade-off is where the checking should be done; for this implementation, the checking should be done before the plug is used.

The list box control connection provides the other side of the list box coin. It handles information from the list box, such as mouse clicks and character input. It also lets the other end set the cursor position and what item is at the top of the list area. The connection does not provide a fine-grain control available on most list box controls, such as those in Microsoft Windows. For example, it does not pass messages about the list box scroll bar positioning via the mouse or any of the dozens of other messages a list box can receive. Instead, this connection is designed to provide the basic support normally required by text-oriented list boxes. An alternative connection can be defined that includes these features or an additional connection could be included. The one GUI-specific aspect of this sample connection is the *GetParent* function, which returns a window object pointer for the Microsoft Foundation Class (MFC). This was included to allow the socket end of the connection to use the same parent window as the list box control for subsequent windows or message windows that might be presented when a selection was made or a particular key was pressed. An alternative to this is to provide the same functionality in a different connection. In any case, here is the control connection that will be used as the basis of a list box component in the next chapter:

```
DECLARE_CONNECTION
  ( LBControl
  , LBControlPlug
  , LBControlSocket
  )

class LBControlPlug : public LBControl::plug
{
  protected:
    DECLARE_PLUG ()
    friend  WCControlBase ;

    virtual LBEntry GetCurSel   ()                 { return -1 ; }
    virtual void    SetCurSel   ( LBEntry entry) {}
```

```
    virtual LBEntry GetTopIndex ()              { return -1 ; }
    virtual void    SetTopIndex ( LBEntry )     {}
    virtual CWnd *  GetParent   ()              { return 0 ; }

  public:
    virtual void OnChar      ( UINT nChar, UINT nRepCnt, UINT
nFlags ) ;
    virtual void Click       ( LBEntry entry ) ;
    virtual void DoubleClick ( LBEntry entry ) ;
} ;



class LBControlSocket : public LBControl::socket
{
  protected:
    DECLARE_PLUG ()
    friend  LBControlPlug ;

    virtual void OnChar      ( UINT nChar, UINT nRepCnt, UINT
nFlags ) {}
    virtual void Click       ( LBEntry entry ) {}
    virtual void DoubleClick ( LBEntry entry ) { Click ( entry ) ;
}

  public:
    virtual LBEntry GetCurSel   () ;
    virtual void    SetCurSel   ( LBEntry entry) ;
    virtual LBEntry GetTopIndex () ;
    virtual void    SetTopIndex ( LBEntry ) ;
    virtual CWnd *  GetParent   () ;
} ;

// ==== LBControl Function Definitions  ====
//
// Forwards external functions to internal functions
// at the other end.

void LBControlPlug::OnChar ( UINT nChar, UINT nRepCnt, UINT nFlags
)
{
```

```
  pOther -> OnChar ( nChar, nRepCnt, nFlags ) ;
}

void LBControlPlug::Click ( LBEntry entry )
{
  pOther -> Click ( entry ) ;
}

void LBControlPlug::DoubleClick ( LBEntry entry )
{
  pOther -> DoubleClick ( entry ) ;
}



LBEntry LBControlSocket::GetCurSel ()
{
  return pOther -> GetCurSel () ;
}

void LBControlSocket::SetCurSel ( LBEntry entry)
{
  pOther -> SetCurSel ( entry ) ;
}

LBEntry LBControlSocket::GetTopIndex ()
{
  return pOther -> GetTopIndex () ;
}

void LBControlSocket::SetTopIndex ( LBEntry entry )
{
  pOther -> SetTopIndex ( entry ) ;
}

CWnd *  LBControlSocket::GetParent ()
{
  return pOther -> GetParent () ;
}
```

The layout of this connection is very similar to the *LBDisplay* connection. The main difference is that the *LBControl* connection has a plug and socket that are not abstract classes. However, the default class definitions simply do nothing when an internal function is called.

Plugs for these two connections, *LBDisplay* and *LBControl*, are normally part of a single component. In fact, they tend to be part of a compound plug. Compound plugs are discussed in more detail in Chapter 7, but a simple form is used here. Figure 4-6 shows how a basic compound works, while Figure 4-7

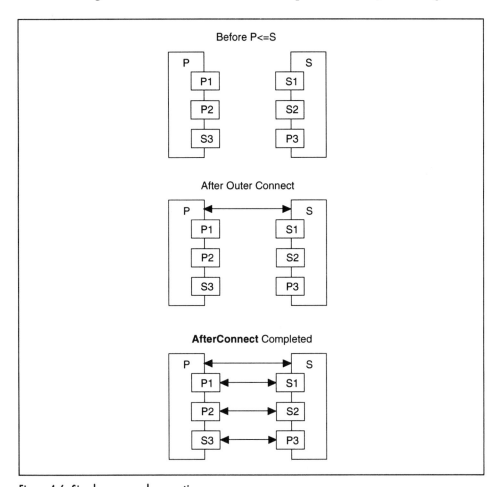

Figure 4-6. Simple compound connection

shows how this particular implementation, *LBConnect*, works. The *LBConnect* plugs contain functions that return references to a set of display and control plugs. The purpose is to relate the two as well as to provide a single connection for general use without requiring that two individual connections be made. The *LBConnect* plugs only provide connection support for the two

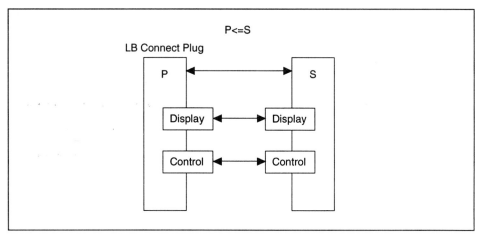

Figure 4-7. List box compound connection

internal plugs. As you will see in the source code, the internal plugs are actually obtained from public functions.

```
DECLARE_CONNECTION
  ( LBConnect
  , LBConnectPlug
  , LBConnectSocket
  )

class LBConnectPlug : public LBConnect::plug
{
  public:
    DECLARE_PLUG ()

    LBDisplay::plug & DisplayPlug () = 0 ;
    LBControl::plug & ControlPlug () = 0 ;
```

```
} ;

class LBSocketPlug : public LBSocket::plug
{
  protected:
    void afterConnect ( otherPlug & pPlug )
    {
      DisplaySocket () <= pPlug -> DisplayPlug () ;
      ControlSocket () <= pPlug -> ControlPlug () ;
    }

    void beforeDisconnect ( otherPlug & pPlug )
    {
      - DisplaySocket () ;
      - ControlSocket () ;
    }

  public:
    DECLARE_PLUG ()

    LBDisplay::socket & DisplaySocket () = 0 ;
    LBControl::socket & ControlSocket() = 0 ;
} ;
```

There are four notable items in this source code: it uses abstract classes; it contains the compound plug mechanisms of *afterConnect* and *beforeDisconnect*; the plug reference functions are public, and the reference functions return references to ends, not plugs. The abstract nature of the plugs means that you cannot look at an example of a connection statement, but if you assume that there is an *LBConnect* plug and socket pair available, the connection operation would look like this:

```
LBConnectPlug1   Plug ;
LBConnectSocket1 Socket ;

Plug <= Socket ;
```

It's not very exciting, but this is all that is required to make a compound connection. The plug's *afterConnect* function makes the internal connections. The *beforeDisconnect* does the reverse operation when the *Plug* or *Socket* is disconnected or reconnected to another plug.

The plug reference functions are public to allow internal connections to be made if you just happen to have the simpler component available. This is similar to how a stereo connection between an amplifier and a tuner work. There are two sets of wires, one set for each channel. They plug in as one logical group, and often the cables are made this way, but there are two distinct plugs at each end of the connection. It is possible to get a cable with only one plug at each end and to connect only one channel between the amplifier and tuner. Of course, all you get is mono sound, but that may be what you want.

The use of the connection *::plug* and *::socket* references means that an end is specified as the reference type. An end type in a connection is either a plug or a redirector. This would not be the case if the return type is an *LBDisplayPlug* reference, because a *::plugRedirector* could not be used in its place.

Text Control

The text control is simpler than the list box control. You will combine it with the list box control in the next section to create the combo box control. Some GUI text controls, like the one in Microsoft Windows, can be used in a variety of modes, from a single line of text to multiple lines of text and with a variety of options. The text control presented here is the simplest kind: one

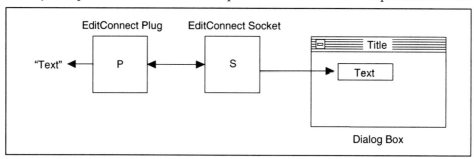

Figure 4-8. Text control connection

line of text of arbitrary length. Access to the text is provided but not to any of the functions that might be available, such as cutting and pasting operations, scrolling, or selection. This can be provided using plugs, but it would make the example overly complex.

Figure 4-8 shows the basic text control connection. The text control provides a way to get text in either direction, and the *Update* function is used to notify the text control that the text needs to be changed. It is up to the text control to ask for the new text via the external *GetText* function.

```
DECLARE_CONNECTION
  ( EditConnect
  , EditConnectPlug
  , EditConnectSocket
  )


class EditConnectPlug : public EditConnect::plug
{
  protected:
    friend EditConnectSocket ;

    virtual void GetMyText ( char * buffer, int nSize ) ;

  public:
    DECLARE_PLUG ()

    virtual void GetText ( char * buffer, int nSize ) ;
    virtual void Update () ;
} ;


class EditConnectSocket : public EditConnect::socket
{
  protected:
    friend EditConnectPlug ;

    virtual void GetMyText ( char * buffer, int nSize ) ;
```

```
      virtual void Update () {}

      void afterConnect ( otherPlug * pPlug )
      {
        Update () ;
      }

   public:
     DECLARE_PLUG ()

      virtual void GetText ( char * buffer, int nSize ) ;
} ;

// ==== EditConnect Function Definitions  ====
//
// Forwards external functions to internal functions at the other
end.


void EditConnectPlug::GetMyText ( char * buffer, int nSize )
{
  buffer [ 0 ] = 0 ;
}


void EditConnectPlug::GetText ( char * buffer, int nSize )
{
  pOther -> GetMyText ( buffer, nSize ) ;
}


void Update ()
{
  pOther -> Update () ;
}


void EditConnectSocket::GetMyText ( char * buffer, int nSize )
{
```

```
    buffer [ 0 ] = 0 ;
}


void EditConnectSocket::GetText ( char * buffer, int nSize )
{
    pOther -> GetMyText ( buffer, nSize ) ;
}
```

The next example is based on the *EditConnectPlug*. It implements a source of text for a text control via a pointer to a buffer and a maximum buffer size. In addition, it assumes that a new value should be obtained from the text control before the connection is broken. This is done by redefining the *beforeDisconnect* function, as shown in the following code.

```
class StrEditConnectPlug : public EditConnectPlug
{
  protected:
    void GetMyText ( char * buffer, int nSize )
    {
      strncpy ( buffer, pBuffer, nSize ) ;
    }

    void beforeDisconnect ( otherPlug * pSocket )
    {
      GetText ( pBuffer, nSize ) ;
    }

  public:
    char * pBuffer ;
    int    nSize ;

    StrEditConnectPlug
      ( char * pNewBuffer
      , int    nNewSize
      )
      : pBuffer ( pNewBuffer )
      , nSize   ( nNewSize )
      {}
} ;
```

There are a number of different ways to implement a text control connection and its components. This is just one, albeit limited, way. Let's move on to the combo box control.

Combo Box Control

A combo box is a combination of a list box and text control. The connection classes are based on this simple premise and show how components can be combined to form more complex components. Figure 4-9 shows what a combo box connection looks like from a logical standpoint. Figure 4-10 shows the internals of the combo box's compound connection, which also contains a compound connection, *LBConnect*. The combo box connection, *CBConnect*, is almost identical to the list box connection, *LBConnect*. Only the names

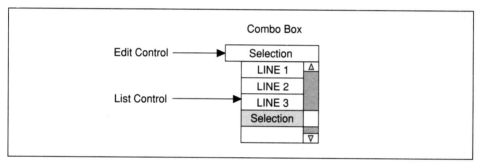

Figure 4-9. Combo box control connection

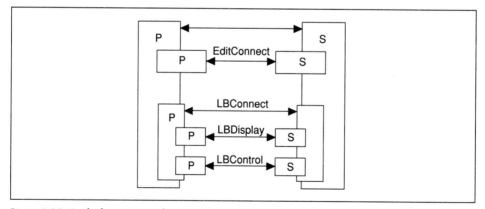

Figure 4-10. Combo box compound connection

have been changed to protect the differences. The *LBConnect* compound connection is used within the combo box connection and, like the list box connection, the reference functions are public. The source code looks like this:

```
DECLARE_CONNECTION
  ( CBConnect
  , CBConnectPlug
  , CBConnectSocket
  )

class CBConnectPlug : public CBConnect::plug
{
  public:
    DECLARE_PLUG ()

    LBConnect::plug   & ListPlug () = 0 ;
    EditConnect::plug & EditPlug () = 0 ;
} ;

class CBSocketPlug : public CBSocket::plug
{
  protected:
    void afterConnect ( otherPlug & pPlug )
    {
      ListSocket () <= pPlug -> ListPlug () ;
      EditSocket () <= pPlug -> EditPlug () ;
    }

    void beforeDisconnect ( otherPlug & pPlug )
    {
      - ListSocket () ;
      - EditSocket () ;
    }

  public:
    DECLARE_PLUG ()

    LBConnect::socket   & ListSocket () = 0 ;
    EditConnect::socket & EditSocket () = 0 ;
```

```
} ;
```

Although it wasn't done for the list box example, a pair of plugs will be defined for this connection based upon public redirectors. These components can be used to define new components or used to link existing components together, by first attaching the redirectors to the appropriate plugs and then using the redirector components to make the final connections. The code for the two redirector-based components is as follows:

```
class CBConnectRedirectorPlug : public CBConnectPlugocket () {
return Socket ; }
} ;
```

General Controls

The connections presented in this chapter are suitable for building general controls as well as the specific controls in which they will be used in the next chapter. Controls and connections should not be considered as unique to the GUI domain. They are just as applicable when used inside a program or as an interface to a component. For example, the list box display interface, *LBDisplay*, can be used to present information; while the control interface, *LBControl*, can be used along similar lines but to control a selectable list.

5 Basic Windows and Plugs

Windows and plugs work well together. Windowing systems come in a variety of forms, but by far the most popular environment is Microsoft Windows. In this chapter you'll see how to implement Windows elements using plugs.

A number of object-oriented libraries are available for Windows, including the Microsoft Foundation Class (MFC) and Borland's Object Windows Library (OWL). These libraries tend to be large and all-encompassing, making coverage of a complete integration with plugs beyond the scope of this book. Instead, a limited but useful subset using MFC will be examined, because it is the simpler of the two libraries.

I assume for this chapter that you have at least a passing familiarity with how Microsoft Windows works at the API level, including event-driven programming, windows, and controls. You can still figure out how the samples work even if you have not worked with Windows, but it helps if you have.

The class definitions presented in this chapter often include the definitions of the functions within the class definition. This is not really the best way to implement a header file, where the class definitions are normally found. It makes the header file larger, thereby slowing down compilation and adding to the overhead in the object file for each source file that includes a header file. However, for our purposes, it simplifies the example significantly.

One approach to using plugs with objects from MFC is to use the MFC objects as the base classes for a plug. MFC window objects include classes such as *CButton, CListBox, CComboBox, or CEdit*. (Yes, all MFC class names start with a capital C.) Figure 5-1 shows the MFC class structure. The window classes are all based on the *CWnd* class. Some of the list classes are also used in the examples. You could build a plug from a basic window object, but plugs are more suitable for sophisticated controls or dialog boxes.

This chapter presents three connection implementations based on the connections defined in the previous chapter and a matching MFC window class. They include a text control, a list box control, and a combo box control. The text control, shown in Figure 5-2, is implemented using a *CEdit* object. The list box control, shown in Figure 5-3, is implemented using a *CListBox* object. The combo box control, shown in Figure 5-4, uses the same connection classes as the text and list box controls but interfaces them with a *CComboBox* object. Microsoft Windows implements the combo box using a Windows text control window and a list box window, but it presents this as a single window

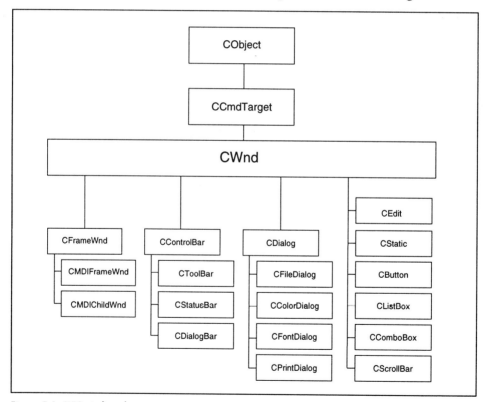

Figure 5-1. MFC window classes

object. This is why the combo box is a subclass of *CWnd* instead of a combination of *CListBox* and *CEdit*. The dual nature of the combo box is more apparent with our plug-based presentation.

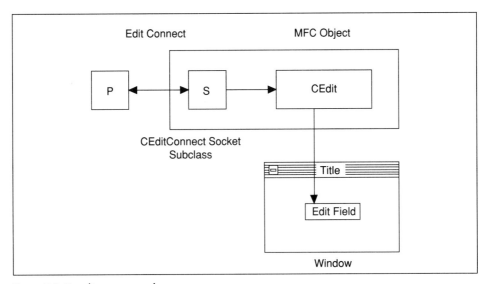

Figure 5-2. Text/integer control

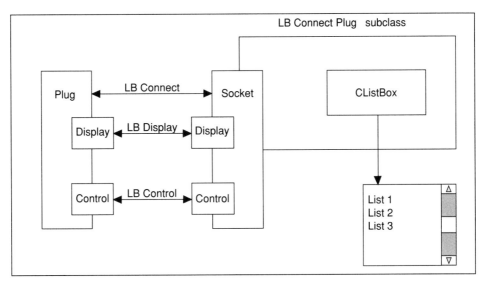

Figure 5-3. List box control

The components presented in this chapter are just one way to implement part of a connection. There are a variety of other ways to implement them; some more desirable than others. For example, the list box and the list portion of the combo box are implemented using the corresponding conventional MFC classes. The objects normally keep a copy of the strings and handle the screen update. Although this method is used, you could implement a version that does not keep a copy of the strings. The objects would then have to use the connection to obtain the text for an entry any time the entry needed to be updated. This becomes more desirable as the number of entries becomes large (more than 100), because it takes time and space to add these

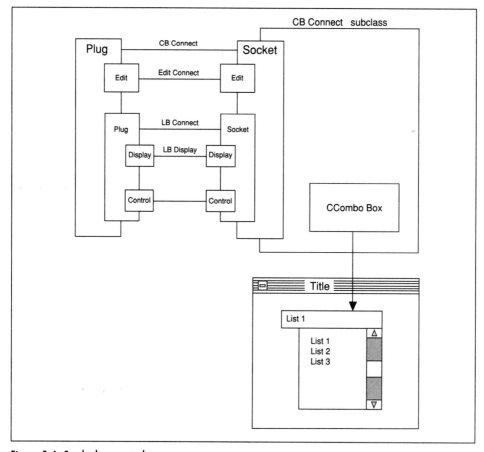

Figure 5-4. Combo box control

strings to the list box. Normally, few of the strings are ever displayed and only a few, usually under 20, are displayed at any one time. The advantage of our connections and plugs becomes clear when you consider the amount of work that must be done to replace one type of component with another. The connection provides the standard and the components provide the choice of implementation.

MFC also provides general classes unrelated to the Windows interface. Two of these, *CStringList* and *CStringArray,* are used to implement an alternative to the string array list box plug class presented in the previous chapter. These two implementations will provide not only an *LBDisplay* connection but a full *LBConnect* connection, which also include the *LBControl* connection.

A simple Windows application using these new classes is presented at the end of the chapter. One thing to keep in mind while you look at these plug class definitions is that the objects of these are connected using a very simple operation even though the class definition is rather complex. Some operations for various parts, like the window object or string array, will also be used at the same logical level as the connection operation, but most operations will be hidden. For example, you would position a window object and add items to a string array.

List Box Control Plugs

The two control plug classes are called *CStringListLBPlug* and *CStringArrayLBPlug.* Both employ the MFC *CString* class, which is a dynamically allocated string object. Without going into the *CString* class too deeply, essentially, it provides a Basic-style string that keeps track of its own storage. The string itself is a C string with a zero terminator. A set of operations are defined for the class, including assignment, conversions, and merge operations such as appending to the end of the string. The *CString* class also defines conversion functions, so that a *const char* * type pointer can be obtained by simply using an object's name, as in a normal C string pointer or array name. You don't need to concern yourself with the other functions or features of the *CString* class, and any specific functions used in the examples will be explained when the example is presented. Most class libraries like MFC and OWL provide classes of this sort, and plug classes can be defined using the basic classes provided.

The two classes, *CStringList* and *CStringArray,* are functionally the same but they are implemented differently. The first employs a doubly linked list while the other employs an array. Both classes can add and delete entries at any point. The linked list version does this in the normal fashion by adding and deleting new elements that are dynamically allocated. The array version works by shifting entries and reallocating a new array if the current one is too small for an operation to be performed. They will look the same across a connection.

In addition to providing access to the strings in these objects, our implementations will track the addition and deletion of strings in a list box when the plug is connected. Multiple inheritance is used to implement the three plug classes because this approach is syntactically simpler. It is also functionally equivalent to implementing individual classes that have a reference to a related object using single inheritance.

First, let's look at *CStringListLBPlug,* which utilizes the doubly linked list. Microsoft's C++ compiler does not support C++ templates so it implements lists using void pointers. The type POSITION is a *void* pointer. The *CStringList* class implements a *FindIndex* function that returns a POSITION. The function allows the list to be indexed as a base *0* array, which is just what we want. The *GetAt, SetAt,* and *RemoveAt* functions take a POSITION parameter. The functions are used to implement a complementary set of *LBControl* plug functions. In particular, there are *Update, Add,* and *Delete* functions that operate on both the string list and the control if a connection is made. The source code for this class is as follows:

```
class CStringListLBPlug
  : public LBConnect
  , public LBControl
  , public LBDisplay
{
```

```
public:
  CStringList StringList ;

  LBDisplay::plug & DisplayPlug () { return * this ; }
  LBControl::plug & ControlPlug () { return * this ; }

protected:
  LBEntry GetCount () { return StringList.GetCount () ; }

  void GetText ( LBEntry entry, char * buffer, int size )
  {
    strncpy (buffer, StringList.GetAt(StringList.FindIndex(entry)),
      size) ;
  }

  virtual void Update ( LBEntry entry, const char * pString )
  {
    StringList.SetAt ( StringList.FindIndex ( entry ), pString ) ;
    if ( connected ())
      pOther -> Update ( entry ) ;
  }

  virtual void Add ( LBEntry entry, const char * pString )
  {
    StringList.AddBefore ( StringList.FindIndex ( entry ),
      pString ) ;
    if ( connected ())
      pOther -> Add ( entry ) ;
  }

  virtual void Delete ( LBEntry entry )
  {
    StringList.RemoveAt ( StringList.FindIndex ( entry )) ;
    if ( connected ())
      pOther -> Delete ( entry ) ;
  }
} ;
```

The *DisplayPlug* and *ControlPlug* functions return the proper pointer because C++ knows which one to use by the return type of the function. The C++ multiple inheritance support creates distinct objects that can reference each other as well as the main object of the main class, which contains the other objects. The returned pointers reference the internal objects, not the main object.

The *CStringArrayLBPlug* source, shown next, looks a lot like the previous example.

```
class CStringArrayLBPlug
  : public LBConnect
  , public LBControl
  , public LBDisplay
{
  public:
    CStringArray StringArray ;

    LBDisplay::plug & DisplayPlug () { return * this ; }
    LBControl::plug & ControlPlug () { return * this ; }

  protected:
    LBEntry GetCount () { return StringArray.GetSize () ; }

    void GetText ( LBEntry entry, char * buffer, int size )
    {
      strncpy ( buffer, StringArray.GetAt ( entry ), size ) ;
    }

    virtual void Update ( LBEntry entry, const char * pString )
    {
      StringArray.SetAt ( entry, pString ) ;
      if ( connected ())
        pOther -> Update ( entry ) ;
    }

    virtual void Add ( LBEntry entry, const char * pString )
    {
      StringArray.InsertAt ( entry, pString ) ;
```

```
        if ( connected ())
          pOther -> Add ( entry ) ;
      }

      virtual void Delete ( LBEntry entry )
      {
        StringArray.RemoveAt ( entry ) ;
        if ( connected ())
          pOther -> Delete ( entry ) ;
      }
  } ;
```

Not many changes—*GetSize* replaces *GetCount,* and the *FindIndex* function is not required because the array functions require an index and not a *POSITION.*

Next take a look at the other end of the connection.

List Box Control Socket

The list box control socket is a bit more complicated than the plug side. The plug definition essentially ignored the control side, leaving any redefinition of those functions to a subclass. The socket, on the other hand, must define both the display and control sockets. There are also some support functions added to the class definition in addition to the superclass functions, which are redefined. These are used to assist in a clean update, because the *CListBox* does not come with all the functions needed for implementing the socket functions.

The source code for the class definition is given first, followed by the function definitions for the three different sections. Finally, a window class definition that uses one of the *CListBoxLBConnectSocket* objects is presented. Here is the source code:

```
class CListBoxLBConnectSocket
  : public LBConnectSocket
  , public LBDisplaySocket
  , public LBControlSocket
{
    // Note: this will not work with a sorted list box
```

```
public:
  CListBox & ListBox ;
  int        nEnableUpdate ;

  LBConnect::socket & ListSocket    () { return * this ; }
  LBDisplay::socket & DisplaySocket () { return * this ; }
  LBControl::socket & ControlSocket () { return * this ; }

  CListBoxLBDisplaySocket ( CListBox & NewListBox )
    : ListBox        ( NewListBox )
    , nEnableUpdate ( 1 )   // list box is enabled by default
    {}

protected:
  // — LBDisplaySocket functions —

  void afterConnect     ( otherPlug * pPlug ) ;
  void beforeDisconnect ( otherPlug * pPlug ) ;

  void UpdateAll    () ;
  void Update       ( LBEntry entry ) ;
  void Add          ( LBEntry entry ) ;
  void Delete       ( LBEntry entry ) ;
  void EnableUpdate ( BOOL bFlag ) ;

  // — LBControl functions —

  LBEntry GetCurSel   () ;
  void    SetCurSel   ( LBEntry entry) ;
  LBEntry GetTopIndex () ;
  void    SetTopIndex ( LBEntry ) ;
  CWnd *  GetParent   () ;

public:
  void OnChar       ( UINT nChar, UINT nRepCnt, UINT nFlags ) ;
  void Click        () ;
  void DoubleClick () ;

protected:
```

```
// — Support functions —

virtual void BeginUpdate () ;
virtual void EndUpdate () ;
} ;
```

The public portion of the class includes the two internal objects: the list box reference, *ListBox,* and the update enable flag, *bUpdateEnable.* This is done more as a convenience, in case they need to be manipulated directly by whatever code is used to define the object. They cannot be accessed through any of the three connections that can be made. Multiple inheritance is used so this one class definition can be used to redefine the appropriate class functions. The class definition is divided into four sections, three along the lines of the superclass definitions, the fourth for internal functions.

The constructor definition initializes the list box reference and the update flag. By default, a window starts out with updates enabled, so it is assumed that the window the object will reference is in this same condition. You could poll the object and determine its setting instead. The enable update flag is implemented as a counter, allowing updates to be disabled from the other end of the connection, as well as allowing the internal functions to disable the list box updates within its internal functions.

Since they are so simple, the *LBConnect* function bodies are defined in the class definition. They return references to the internal sockets, which are obtained by the ability of C++ to reference the appropriate component created via inheritance.

The description of the other functions comes next, with the same grouping.

The following function definitions cover the *LBDisplay* functions. These handle changes from the plug side and reflect these changes in what the list box displays. They utilize the internal *BeginUpdate* and *EndUpdate* functions.

```
// ====  Function definitions  ====
//
// —  LBDisplay functions  —

void CListBoxLBConnectSocket::afterConnect
  ( LBDisplaySocket::otherPlug * pPlug )
{
  LBDisplaySocket::afterConnect ( pPlug ) ;
  UpdateAll () ;
}


void CListBoxLBConnectSocket::beforeDisconnect
  ( LBDisplaySocket::otherPlug * pPlug )
{
  ListBox.ResetContent () ;
}


void CListBoxLBConnectSocket::UpdateAll ()
{
  // —  Disable update when updating  —

  BeginUpdate () ;

  // —  Clear out the list box and add from the list  —

  ListBox.ResetContent () ;
  int nSize = GetCount () ;

  for ( LBEntry i = 0 ; i < nSize ; ++ i )
  {
    char buffer [ 256 ] ;
    GetText ( buffer, i, sizeof ( buffer )) ;

    ListBox.AddString ( buffer ) ;
  }

  // —  Turn update back on if enabled  —

  EndUpdate () ;
}
```

```
void CListBoxLBConnectSocket::Update ( LBEntry entry )
{
  // —  Update an entry   —
  // CListBox has no update/set function.
  // This achieves the same effect: delete the entry
  // and then add the new value. Disable update to
  // prevent the delete/add operations from being shown.

  BeginUpdate () ;
  CListBox::DeleteString ( entry ) ;
  Add ( entry ) ;
  EndUpdate () ;
}

void CListBoxLBConnectSocket::Add ( LBEntry entry )
{
  char buffer [ 256 ] ;
  GetText ( buffer, i, sizeof ( buffer )) ;

  CListBox::InsertString ( entry, buffer ) ;
}

void CListBoxLBConnectSocket::Delete ( LBEntry entry )
{
  CListBox::DeleteString ( entry ) ;
}

void CListBoxLBConnectSocket::EnableUpdate ( BOOL bFlag )
{
  // —  Allows multiple calls to be made  —

  if ( bFlag )
  {
    ++ nEnableUpdate ;
    if ( nEnableUpdate == 1 )
    {
      ListBox.SetRedraw ( TRUE ) ;
    }
  }
```

```
    else
    {
      -- nEnableUpdate ;
      if ( nEnableUpdate == 0 )
      {
        ListBox.SetRedraw ( FALSE ) ;
      }
    }
  }
```

The *afterConnect* function is included in this group because it calls the *UpdateAll* function. It seems reasonable to initialize the list box using the connection once the connection is made. Note the parameter definition for *pPlug*. C++ function overloading allows you to differentiate which function you are redefining because the parameter types are different. This function will be called by the *LBDisplay* portion of the object when an *LBDisplay* connection is made. The *beforeDisconnect* function does a similar operation and prevents the old contents of the list box from being shown after the connection is broken.

UpdateAll brackets its operations with the *BeginUpdate* and *EndUpdate* functions. This allows the changes to be made to the list box without having all the changes seen on the screen as they occur. The contents of the list box are cleared and each entry is obtained from the plug and added to the list. The Update function uses a delete and add operation because the *CListBox* object does not support an update function directly. The *Delete* and *Add* functions use the *CListBox* functions because they do the same operation. You could leave the redefinitions of the *Update, Add,* and *Delete* functions out of this class definition and obtain the same display results, but at a much lower performance. The difference is that default definitions call *UpdateAll*, which needs to turn off updates, delete all entries from the list box, and restore them—a lot of work to change just one line in a list box, but it works. The *EnableUpdate* function implements the control portion of the update flag. It forces the list box to redraw itself if the flag is enabled after being disabled. Not that the *UpdateWindow* is different from the *UpdateAll*. The latter updates the contents of the list box while the former updates the screen.

The *LBControl* functions are divided into two groups: internal and external. The internal functions are used by the other end of the connection. The external functions are called from this end of the connection. The internal functions do not check for a connection but the external ones do. The external functions do nothing if there is no connection. This prevents errors if there is no connection and the list box is being displayed. The *LBControl* functions are rather simple. They call the appropriate list box of the *LBControl* function. These are specified using class prefixes to highlight the operation and to allow the use of the proper function. Otherwise the *CListBoxLBConnect-Socket* function would be called, resulting in a function calling itself until the program encountered a stack underflow.

```
// — LBControl functions —

LBEntry CListBoxLBConnectSocket::GetCurSel ()
{
  return ListBox.GetCurSel () ;
}


void CListBoxLBConnectSocket::SetCurSel ( LBEntry entry )
{
  ListBox.SetCurSel ( entry ) ;
}


LBEntry CListBoxLBConnectSocket::GetTopIndex ()
{
  return ListBox.GetTopIndex () ;
}


void CListBoxLBConnectSocket::SetTopIndex ( LBEntry entry )
{
  ListBox.SetTopIndex ( entry ) ;
}


CWnd * CListBoxLBConnectSocket::GetParent ()
{
  return ListBox.GetParent () ;
}
```

```
void CListBoxLBConnectSocket::OnChar ( UINT nChar, UINT nRepCnt,
UINT nFlags )
{
  if ( LBControl::connected () )
  {
    LBControl::OnChar ( nChar, nRepCnt, nFlags ) ;
  }
}


void CListBoxLBConnectSocket::Click ()
{
  if ( LBControl::connected () )
  {
    LBControl::Click ( ListBox.GetCurSel () ) ;
  }
}


void CListBoxLBConnectSocket::DoubleClick ()
{
  if ( LBControl::connected () )
  {
    LBControl::DoubleClick ( ListBox.GetCurSel () ) ;
  }
}
```

The support functions handle screen updates based on the *nEnableUpdate* value. The *SetRedraw* function sets the redraw flag for the list box that, unlike the *nEnableUpdate* flag, is just a boolean flag. The *UpdateWindow* call causes the list box to be redrawn on the screen.

```
// — Support function definitions —

void CListBoxLBConnectSocket::BeginUpdate ()
{
  if ( nEnableUpdate )
  {
    ListBox.SetRedraw ( FALSE ) ;
  }
```

```
    }


void CListBoxLBConnectSocket::EndUpdate ()
{
  if ( nEnableUpdate )
  {
    ListBox.SetRedraw ( TRUE ) ;
    ListBox.UpdateWindow () ;
  }
}
```

The List Box Sample

Now let's look at the sample based on the list box. It fills in the support for the *LBControl* connection. This approach is taken because it follows the MFC convention for control support, which has the parent window of a control receiving the messages for the control. The idea was to keep the control support in one place—the parent window class. The use of plugs changes this because the connections distribute the control.

The sample window definition, *CListBoxAndSocket,* uses a single list box, which it sizes to the specified size for the sample window. The window can be used as a general component to construct other windows with socketed list boxes. The #*define* in the example is used to define a constant required by MFC to identify a child window. The MFC message map facility is also used to handle messages to the main window. The messages that are handled are those from the list box and also to the main window.

Before you get too confused, the word *message* is used in this book to mean class functions that can be called with respect to an object. In this case, *messages* refer to a data structure that is used in the Microsoft windowing system. MFC window objects are part of a layer that sits on top of Windows, which has its own internal window objects. An MFC window object maps to one of the MFC window objects via a handle (integer), which is hidden in the MFC window object structure. The windowing system generates the message structures when an action occurs and places them into a queue, where they are then read and dispatched to a handling function associated with the related window object. This function is part of the MFC class definition if the windowing object is related to an MFC object. The default handling is to search a list of message types, the message map, to find a matching entry that also contains a pointer to a function. This function is called when the corresponding message is received. This is how the functions defined in our class definition are finally called.

There is actually much more to the message passing system, and I am not going to go into any more detail here. All you really need to know about the system is that an action, like clicking the mouse while the mouse pointer on the screen is over the list box, will wind up causing the function to be called. The message map shows the relationship between the MFC windows definition and the function. The definitions are included to make the example complete.

The definition portion of the sample window class is as follows:

```
#define ID_LIST_BOX     100

class CListBoxAndSocket : public CWnd
{
  public:
    CListBox                ListBox ;
    CListBoxLBConnectSocket Socket ;


    CListBoxAndSocket ()
      : Socket ( ListBox )
      {}

    afx_msg void OnSize        ( UINT nType, int cx, int cy ) ;
    afx_msg void OnShowWindow  ( BOOL bShow, UINT nStatus ) ;
    afx_msg void OnCreate      ( LPCREATESTRUCT lpCreateStruc ) ;
    afx_msg void OnChar        ( UINT nChar, UINT nRepCnt, UINT
nFlags ) ;

    afx_msg void ListBoxClick  () ;
```

```
    afx_msg void ListBoxDoubleClick () ;

    DECLARE_MESSAGE_MAP ()
} ;
```

The On functions, except *OnChar,* are used to forward any messages from the main window to the list box window. This allows the window to be moved and sized after it is created. The other functions are called when an action occurs after the list box control is displayed. The windowing system handles messages regarding displaying, input, and mouse control automatically.

Now take a look at the definitions required to implement this class. The message map is defined first, using MFC macros. This creates a global array and initializes it with pointers to the functions. The map can only be used with objects derived from *CListBoxAndSocket.* The *BEGIN_MESSAGE_MAP* macro requires the name of the class and its superclass. The macros that do not include parameters refer to functions with default names. They roughly correspond to the last part of the macro name plus the prefix On. The function operation will be covered after you have had a chance to look at the following source code:

```
// ====  Message map definition  ====

BEGIN_MESSAGE_MAP  ( CListBoxAndSocket, CWnd )
  ON_LB_SELCHAANGE ( ID_LIST_BOX, ListBoxClick )
  ON_LB_DBLCLK     ( ID_LIST_BOX, ListBoxDoubleClick )
  ON_WM_SIZE       ()
  ON_WM_SHOWWINDOW ()
  ON_WM_CHAR       ()
  ON_WM_CREATE     ()
END_MESSAGE_MAP ()


// ====  Function definitions  ====

afx_msg void CListBoxAndSocket::OnSize ( UINT nType, int cx, int cy
)
{
```

```
      ListBox.SetWindowPosition ( 0, 0, 0, cx, cy, SWP_SHOWWINDOW ) ;
   }


   afx_msg void CListBoxAndSocket::OnShowWindow ( BOOL bShow, UINT
   nStatus )
   {
     if ( bShow )
     {
       ListBox.ShowWindow ( SW_SHOWNORMAL ) ;
       ListBox.UpdateWindow () ;
     }
   }


   afx_msg void CListBoxAndSocket::OnCreate ( LPCREATESTRUCT lpCreate-
   eStruc )
   {
     RECT rect ;

     rect.top    = 0 ;
     rect.left   = 0 ;
     rect.bottom = lpCreateStruc -> cy ;
     rect.right  = lpCreateStruc -> cx ;

     ListBox.Create ( WS_CHILD | WS_VSCROLL | LBS_NOINTEGRALHEIGHT
                    , rect
                    , this
                    ) ;
   }


   afx_msg void CListBoxAndSocket::OnChar
     ( UINT nChar
     , UINT nRepCnt
     , UINT nFlags
     )
   {
     Socket.OnChar ( nChar, nRepCnt, nFlags ) ;
   }


   afx_msg void CListBoxAndSocket::ListBoxClick  ()
   {
```

```
      Socket.Click () ;
   }


   afx_msg void CListBoxAndSocket::ListBoxDoubleClick ()
   {
      Socket.DoubleClick () ;
   }
```

The *OnSize* function is called when the parent window is resized. It's not a frame window, so this will not be done using the mouse; but the window that contains the window you've created can do it via MFC functions defined with the *CWnd* class. The function makes the list window will the main window. The *OnShowWindow* function just passes on the ability to show the list box. You don't have to handle hiding the window because all child windows are automatically hidden if the parent is hidden.

The *OnCreate* function is called after the main window is created. *CWnd* defines a *Create* function. The window is already created at this point, and you can create the Microsoft Windows list box control window. The *CListBox* object does not create the Microsoft Windows window object when it is created; it must be done explicitly with another *Create* function call, as done here. The *OnCreate* function creates a list box window that fills the main window. The *OnSize* function handles any subsequent changes.

The remaining functions handle character input and mouse operations. The change of selection is translated into a *Click* function call. This can actually be generated using the keyboard, but this transparency is actually desirable.

In theory, it is possible to define a list box control using a single window, but this version is useful both as an example and because it can be used within a program. The next two controls will be implemented in a similar fashion and then used in a sample program. Although these controls are a bit complex compared to previous examples in other chapters, they are simple compared to some implementations in MFC-based applications. They are definition simpler than the definition of *CWnd,* which has hundreds of functions.

Edit Control

The edit control defined in this section is simpler than the list box presented in the previous section for two reasons. First, the base class, *EditConnectSocket,* is significantly simpler than any of the three connection sockets used in the list box example. Second, all of the support fits into a single *CEdit* window instead of having an additional window to contain it. This can be done because there are no additional messages to be handled, as in the list box. Note that this is done out of choice, to keep the interface and examples simple.

The edit control is based only upon *EditConnectSocket.* It contains a reference to a *CEdit* control that must be available before the socket is initialized. The constructor handles initialization of the edit control window reference, *Edit.* The two functions defined by the class include *GetMyText* and *Update.* Both use the *Edit* reference to access the edit control functions to get and set the window text displayed on the screen. The source code for this little socket follows.

```
class CEditEditConnectSocket : public EditConnectSocket
{
  public:
    CEdit & Edit ;

    CEditEditConnectSocket ( CEdit & NewEdit )
      : Edit ( NewEdit )
      {}

    void GetMyText ( char * buffer, int nSize )
    {
      Edit.GetWindowText ( buffer, nSize ) ;
    }

    void Update ()
    {
      char buffer [ 256 ] ;

      GetText ( buffer, sizeof ( buffer )) ;

      Edit.SetWindowText ( buffer ) ;
```

```
        }
    } ;
```

The *CEditEditConnectSocket* is a straightforward implementation of a plug based on an existing connection class, *EditConnect*, and an existing object, *CEdit*.

To fill out the connection, a matching plug implementation based upon a *CString* is presented. Like the edit control, this component is very simple. It utilizes the *GetBuffer* and *ReleaseBuffer CString* functions. The *GetBuffer* function allocates the specified amount of space while the *ReleaseBuffer* reduces the size to the length of the string. The functions are used in the *beforeDisconnect* function to retrieve a copy of the text in the edit control. This allows the control to be used for data entry. The *beforeDisconnect* function can be redefined so this is not done if the text is not to be retrieved. The assignment and append operators are also redefined so the edit control is automatically changed if a new value is assigned to the string. Finally, the *Update* function is redefined so the superclass version is only called if a connection is made, otherwise a null pointer would be used.

Here is the source code for the string component:

```
class CStringEditConnectPlug
  : public EditConnectPlug
  , public CString
{
  public:
    void beforeDisconnect ( otherPlug * pSocket )
    {
      EditConnectPlug::beforeDisconnect ( pSocket ) ;

      GetText ( GetBuffer ( 256 ), 256 ) ;
      ReleaseBuffer () ;
    }

    const CString & operator = ( const CString & rString )
    {
      operator = ( rString ) ;
```

```
        Update () ;
        return * this ;
      }


    const CString & operator = ( const char * pString )
      {
        operator = ( pString ) ;
        Update () ;
        return * this ;
      }


    const CString & operator = ( char cChar )
      {
        operator = ( cChar ) ;
        Update () ;
        return * this ;
      }


    void CString & operator += ( const CString & rString )
      {
        operator += ( rString ) ;
        Update () ;
      }


    void operator += ( const char * pString )
      {
        operator += ( pString ) ;
        Update () ;
      }


    void operator += ( char cChar )
      {
        operator += ( cChar ) ;
        Update () ;
      }

  protected:
    void GetMyText ( char * buffer, int nSize )
      {
        if ( IsEmpty ())
```

```
          buffer [ 0 ] = 0 ;
        else
          strncpy ( buffer, (const char *) * this, nSize ) ;
      }

    void Update ()
    {
      if ( connected ())
        EditConnectPlug::Update () ;
    }
} ;
```

Objects of this class can be used in the same way as normal *CString* objects. If multiple inheritance is not to your liking, you can define a pair of classes, one based on *CString* and another based on *EditConnectPlug,* which have references to each other. The effect is the same, as is the overhead, but the multiple inheritance version is easier to build and maintain.

The next control is a combo box. It uses the same connections used in the edit and list box components but implements them using a combo box.

Combo Box Control

A combo box is an edit field with a list box underneath it. Combo boxes come in a variety of styles, including those that do not allow editing of the edit field and those with list boxes that pop down upon request. They can all be used with the combo box component defined in this section, but there are no functions added to the edit and list box interfaces that are provided to handle the combo box features. Functions could be added later using subclasses or by other means. In any case, the edit and list box connections appear independently, even though they are implemented using a common base, the *CComboBox* class.

The combo box control consists of an *EditConnect::socket* and a list box *LBConnect::socket.* The latter contains an *LBDisplay::socket* and an *LBControl::socket.* For the most part, the definition of this class looks like a merger of the two other window components already presented in this chapter.

Coverage of the combo box will be brief—all of the comments presented in the previous sections are applicable here. The only difference is that the two components are combined, and a single combo box supplies the support for both the list box and edit control connections. All the sockets are available through function calls. As with the list box, there is a window class defined at the end of this section to contain the entire combo box and to provide support for the Windows input messages. One notable item is the use of *GetText*. This is used by both the edit and list box display connections. There will be no conflicts because the list box version includes an additional *LBEntry* parameter. Function overloading is allowed and handles the respective functions properly.

The definition for the main combo box class is as follows:

```
class CComboBoxLBConnectSocket
  : public LBConnectSocket
  , public LBDisplaySocket
  , public LBControlSocket
  , public EditConnectSocket
{
  // Note: this will not work with a sorted list box

  public:
    CComboBox & ComboBox ;
    int        nEnableUpdate ;

    EditConnect::socket & EditSocket    () { return * this ; }
    LBConnect::socket    & ListSocket   () { return * this ; }
    LBDisplay::socket    & DisplaySocket () { return * this ; }
    LBControl::socket    & ControlSocket () { return * this ; }

    CComboBoxLBDisplaySocket ( CComboBox & NewComboBox )
      : ComboBox        ( NewComboBox )
      , nEnableUpdate ( 1 )   // list box is enabled by default
      {}

  protected:
    // — EditConnect functions —
```

```
    void GetMyText ( char * buffer, int nSize ) ;
    void Update () ;


    // — LBDisplaySocket functions —

    void afterConnect     ( otherPlug * pPlug ) ;
    void beforeDisconnect ( otherPlug * pPlug ) ;

    void UpdateAll    () ;
    void Update       ( LBEntry entry ) ;
    void Add          ( LBEntry entry ) ;
    void Delete       ( LBEntry entry ) ;
    void EnableUpdate ( BOOL bFlag ) ;

    // — LBControl functions —

    LBEntry GetCurSel   () ;
    void    SetCurSel   ( LBEntry entry) ;
    LBEntry GetTopIndex () ;
    void    SetTopIndex ( LBEntry ) ;
    CWnd *  GetParent   () ;
public:
    void OnChar       ( UINT nChar, UINT nRepCnt, UINT nFlags ) ;
    void Click        () ;
    void DoubleClick () ;

protected:
    // — Support functions —

    virtual void BeginUpdate () ;
    virtual void EndUpdate () ;
} ;
```

The definition for the functions comes next. It is in the same order as the edit and list box controls, but without the intervening commentary. The only changes you will see are those related to the change from an edit and list box control to the combo box; the functionality is identical. Luckily the functions provided by the *CListBox* object use the same names and semantics as the *CComboBox*.

```
// ====  Function definitions  ====
//
// —  EditConnect functions  —

void CComboBoxLBConnectSocket::GetMyText ( char * buffer, int nSize
)
{
  ComboBox.GetWindowText ( buffer, nSize ) ;
}

CComboBoxLBConnectSocket::void CComboBoxLBConnectSocket::Update ()
{
  char buffer [ 256 ] ;

  GetText ( buffer, sizeof ( buffer )) ;

  ComboBox.SetWindowText ( buffer ) ;
}


// —  LBDisplay functions  —

void CComboBoxLBConnectSocket::afterConnect
  ( LBDisplaySocket::otherPlug * pPlug )
{
  LBDisplaySocket::afterConnect ( pPlug ) ;
  UpdateAll () ;
}

void CComboBoxLBConnectSocket::beforeDisconnect
  ( LBDisplaySocket::otherPlug * pPlug )
{
  ComboBox.ResetContent () ;
}

void CComboBoxLBConnectSocket::UpdateAll ()
```

```
{
  // —  Disable update when updating  —

  BeginUpdate () ;

  // —  Clear out the list box and add from the list  —

  ComboBox.ResetContent () ;
  int nSize = GetCount () ;

  for ( LBEntry i = 0 ; i < nSize ; ++ i )
  {
    char buffer [ 256 ] ;
    GetText ( buffer, i, sizeof ( buffer )) ;

    ComboBox.AddString ( buffer ) ;
  }

  // —  Turn update back on if enabled  —

  EndUpdate () ;
}

void CComboBoxLBConnectSocket::Update ( LBEntry entry )
{
  // —  Update an entry   —
  // CComboBox has no update/set function.
  // This achieves the same effect: delete the entry
  // and then add the new value. Disable update to
  // prevent the delete/add operations from being shown.

  BeginUpdate () ;
  CComboBox::DeleteString ( entry ) ;
  Add ( entry ) ;
  EndUpdate () ;
}

void CComboBoxLBConnectSocket::Add ( LBEntry entry )
{
  char buffer [ 256 ] ;
```

```
    GetText ( buffer, i, sizeof ( buffer )) ;

    CComboBox::InsertString ( entry, buffer ) ;
  }


void CComboBoxLBConnectSocket::Delete ( LBEntry entry )
{
    CComboBox::DeleteString ( entry ) ;
}


void CComboBoxLBConnectSocket::EnableUpdate ( BOOL bFlag )
{
    // —  Allows multiple calls to be made  —

    if ( bFlag )
    {
      ++ nEnableUpdate ;
      if ( nEnableUpdate == 1 )
      {
        ComboBox.SetRedraw ( TRUE ) ;
      }
    }
    else
    {
      — nEnableUpdate ;
      if ( nEnableUpdate == 0 )
      {
        ComboBox.SetRedraw ( FALSE ) ;
      }
    }
}



  // —  LBControl functions  —

LBEntry CComboBoxLBConnectSocket::GetCurSel ()
{
    return ComboBox.GetCurSel () ;
}
```

```
void CComboBoxLBConnectSocket::SetCurSel ( LBEntry entry )
{
  ComboBox.SetCurSel ( entry ) ;
}


LBEntry CComboBoxLBConnectSocket::GetTopIndex ()
{
  return ComboBox.GetTopIndex () ;
}


void CComboBoxLBConnectSocket::SetTopIndex ( LBEntry entry )
{
  ComboBox.SetTopIndex ( entry ) ;
}


CWnd * CComboBoxLBConnectSocket::GetParent ()
{
  return ComboBox.GetParent () ;
}


void CComboBoxLBConnectSocket::OnChar (UINT nChar,UINT nRepCnt,UINT
nFlags)
{
  if ( LBControl::connected ())
  {
    LBControl::OnChar ( nChar, nRepCnt, nFlags ) ;
  }
}


void CComboBoxLBConnectSocket::Click ()
{
  if ( LBControl::connected ())
  {
    LBControl::Click ( ComboBox.GetCurSel ()) ;
  }
}


void CComboBoxLBConnectSocket::DoubleClick ()
{
  if ( LBControl::connected ())
```

```
        {
          LBControl::DoubleClick ( ComboBox.GetCurSel ()) ;
        }
    }



    // — Support function definitions —

    void CComboBoxLBConnectSocket::BeginUpdate ()
    {
      if ( nEnableUpdate )
      {
        ComboBox.SetRedraw ( FALSE ) ;
      }
    }



    void CComboBoxLBConnectSocket::EndUpdate ()
    {
      if ( nEnableUpdate )
      {
        ComboBox.SetRedraw ( TRUE ) ;
        ComboBox.UpdateWindow () ;
      }
    }
```

The sample window definition for the combo box is identical to the list box
example. The comments regarding the list box version apply here. Refer to
the list box section for additional details.

Here is the definition portion of the sample window class:

```
    #define ID_COMBO_BOX    100

    class CComboBoxAndSocket : public CWnd
    {
      public:
        CComboBox                CposmboBox ;
        CComboBoxLBConnectSocket Socket ;
```

```
    CComboBoxAndSocket ()
      : Socket ( ComboBox )
      {}

    afx_msg void OnSize        ( UINT nType, int cx, int cy ) ;
    afx_msg void OnShowWindow  ( BOOL bShow, UINT nStatus ) ;
    afx_msg void OnCreate      ( LPCREATESTRUCT lpCreateStruc ) ;
    afx_msg void OnChar        ( UINT nChar, UINT nRepCnt, UINT
nFlags ) ;

    afx_msg void ComboBoxClick  () ;
    afx_msg void ComboBoxDoubleClick () ;

    DECLARE_MESSAGE_MAP ()
} ;
```

Just to fill out the definition, here is the rest of the code for the combo box example:

```
// ====  Message map definition  ====

BEGIN_MESSAGE_MAP ( CComboBoxAndSocket, CWnd )
  ON_LB_SELCHAANGE ( ID_COMBO_BOX, ComboBoxClick )
  ON_LB_DBLCLK     ( ID_COMBO_BOX, ComboBoxDoubleClick )
  ON_WM_SIZE       ()
  ON_WM_SHOWWINDOW ()
  ON_WM_CHAR       ()
  ON_WM_CREATE     ()
END_MESSAGE_MAP ()


// ====  Function definitions  ====

afx_msg void CComboBoxAndSocket::OnSize ( UINT nType, int cx, int
cy )
```

```
  {
    ComboBox.SetWindowPosition ( 0, 0, 0, cx, cy, SWP_SHOWWINDOW ) ;
  }


afx_msg void CComboBoxAndSocket::OnShowWindow ( BOOL bShow, UINT
nStatus )
  {
    if ( bShow )
    {
      ComboBox.ShowWindow ( SW_SHOWNORMAL ) ;
      ComboBox.UpdateWindow () ;
    }
  }


afx_msg void CComboBoxAndSocket::OnCreate ( LPCREATESTRUCT lpCreat-
eStruc )
  {
    RECT rect ;

    rect.top    = 0 ;
    rect.left   = 0 ;
    rect.bottom = lpCreateStruc -> cy ;
    rect.right  = lpCreateStruc -> cx ;

    ComboBox.Create ( WS_CHILD | WS_VSCROLL | CBS_NOINTEGRALHEIGHT
                  , rect
                  , this
                  ) ;
  }


afx_msg void CComboBoxAndSocket::OnChar
  ( UINT nChar
  , UINT nRepCnt
  , UINT nFlags
  )
  {
    Socket.OnChar ( nChar, nRepCnt, nFlags ) ;
  }


afx_msg void CComboBoxAndSocket::ComboBoxClick  ()
```

```
{
  Socket.Click () ;
}


afx_msg void CComboBoxAndSocket::ComboBoxDoubleClick ()
{
  Socket.DoubleClick () ;
}
```

Now that all the parts are defined, the next section looks at a simple program.

A Simple Windows Application

The windows application contains one frame window in which an edit control, a list box, and a combo box are placed. The placement uses fixed values. (Normally, fixed values are not used for window placement because the size of text is different on different displays. An application usually sizes the windows based upon some system-specific value obtained from the environment, such as the size of the text being used.)

Two more classes are introduced, *CWinApp* and *CFrameWnd*. An MFC program usually has one global object from a subclass of *CWinApp*. The default startup code for the program calls various functions of the object and this gets the program going. In particular, the *InitInstance* function is called once when the program is started. The *CFrameWnd* class is used to create a window with a border and title bar on top. The windows you create will be placed in this window. The frame window will be created in the application's *InitInstance* function.

The frame window contains the sockets for the various controls, which are created and placed when the frame window is created. No connections are made when the frame window is created. The matching plugs are contained in the application object, which also contains the frame window object. The connections between the plugs and sockets are made after the Windows frame window has been created using the *Create* function.

The frame window includes a message map like the ones defined in the window classes that support the list box and combo box. The *OnDestroy* message is the only one handled in this application. The function is called just before the Windows frame window is destroyed, which is done by selecting the *Close* option on the system menu. The function calls *PostQuitMessage*, which shuts down the application.

When the application is started, it creates a frame window, puts up some control windows that you can see, and cleans up when you select the *Close* option from the system menu. It's not very exciting, but it does show how the connections are made and components initialized.

Here are the class definitions:

```
class MyFrameWnd : public CFrameWnd
{
  public:
    CListBoxAndSocket   ListBox ;
    CComboBoxAndSocket City ;
    CEdit              Edit ;
    CEditEditConnectSocket EditSocket ;

    MyFrameWnd ()
      : EditSocket ( Edit )
      {}

    BOOL Create () ;

    afx_msg void OnDestroy () ;

    DECLARE_MESSAGE_MAP ()
} ;


class MyApp : public CWinApp
{
  public:
```

```
        MyFrameWnd FrameWnd ;

        CStringListLBPlug StringList1 ;
        CStringListLBPlug StringList2 ;

        CStringEditConnectPlug String1 ;
        CStringEditConnectPlug String2 ;

        BOOL InitInstance () ;
    } ;
```

Unlike the other components, these classes have a limited number of functions and a number of objects. The objects are used in the rest of the function definitions that follow.

```
    // — Global application object definition —

    MyApp TheApp ;


    // ====  MyFrameWnd Function Definitions  ====

    BOOL MyFrameWnd::Create ()
    {
      RECT rectMain     ( 10,   10, 310, 410 ) ;
      RECT rectEdit     (  0,    0, 310,  10 ) ;
      RECT rectListBox  (  0,   10, 310, 210 ) ;
      RECT rectComboBox (  0,  210, 310, 410 ) ;

      return    Create            ( 0 // use default class name
                                  , "Sample Window Title"
                                  , WS_VISIBLE | WS_OVERLAPPED |
    DS_MODALFRAME
                                  , rectMain
                                  , 0 // parent is desktop
                                  , 0 // no menu
                                  )
```

```
          && Edit.Create      ( WS_VISIBLE | ES_LEFT
                              , rectEdit
                              , this // parent
                              , 1    // ID, not used
                              )
          && ListBox.Create   ( 0  // use default class name
                              , "" // no title
                              , WS_VISIBLE
                              , rectListBox
                              , this // parent
                              , 2    // ID, not used
                              )
          && ComboBox.Create  ( 0  // use default class name
                              , "" // no title
                              , WS_VISIBLE
                              , rectComboBox
                              , this // parent
                              , 3    // ID, not used
                              )
          ;
  }


// ====  MyApp Function Definitions   ====

BEGIN_MESSAGE_MAP ( MyApp, CWinApp )
  WM_DESTROY ()
END_MESSAGE_MAP ()


BOOL MyApp::InitInstance ()
{
  if ( FrameWnd.Create ())
  {
    // —  Initialize the plugs  —

    String1 = "String 1" ;
    String2 = "String 2" ;

    StringList1.AddString ( Line 1" ) ;
```

```
            StringList1.AddString ( "Line 2" ) ;
            StringList1.AddString ( "Line 3" ) ;
            StringList1.AddString ( "Line 4" ) ;
            StringList1.AddString ( "Line 5" ) ;

            StringList2.AddString ( "Line A" ) ;
            StringList2.AddString ( "Line B" ) ;
            StringList2.AddString ( "Line C" ) ;
            StringList2.AddString ( "Line D" ) ;
            StringList2.AddString ( "Line E" ) ;

            // — Connect to the sockets —

            StringList1 <= FrameWnd.ListBox.Socket () ;
            StringList2 <= FrameWnd.ComboBox.Socket () ;

            String1 <= FrameWnd.EditSocket ;
            String2 <= FrameWnd.ComboBox.EditSocket () ;

            // — Show our windows —

            FrameWnd.ShowWindow ( SWP_SHOWNORMAL ) ;
            FrameWnd.UpdateWindow () ;
            return TRUE ;
        }

    return FALSE ;
}

void MyApp::OnDestroy ()
{
  ::PostQuitMessage ( 0 ) ;
}
```

The single global variable, *TheApp*, contains all the objects in the program. This definition is followed by the *Create* function for the frame window, where the constants reside. The *RECT* structure contains the left, top, right, and bottom positions for the windows. The main window position is with respect to the desktop while the others are with respect to the main window; hence the *0,0* top left position for the edit control. The function returns *TRUE* if all the windows are created. Any functions that have been created will be deleted automatically if any one function fails to be created. The parameters for the *Create* functions are different for each class, but the values should make their use apparent. It is unnecessary to know what the parameters are to understand the example, unless you want to learn more about MFC. Essentially the *Create* parameters include attributes such as *WS_VISIBLE,* a position rectangle, and a parent window. The parent window for the frame window is the desktop indicated by a 0 value. The frame window is the parent for the other windows. The *this* variable points to the frame window object, which is the parent.

The *InitInstance* application object function is where the rest of the work is done. It first creates the frame window and, if successful, fills up the strings and string lists with data to be displayed. These plugs are then connected to the sockets associated with the windows. Finally the MFC window functions are called, to display the windows with their contents. The windows remain on the screen when the *InitInstance* function returns.

The frame window and its children remain on the screen until the *Close* option is selected from the system menu. This causes the *OnDestroy* function to be called, which finally adds a *WM_Quit* message to the message queue. The standard functions for the *CWinApp* class finish cleaning up and the application terminates. I have left out quite a few details, but this explanation should be sufficient to see how the plugs work.

The connections remain while the window is on the screen. The value of the edit field is copied back into the strings when the window is closed. About the only change that can occur in this data is a change made to the edit field or a selection of an entry from the combo box. In the latter case, the edit field associated with the combo box will be changed to the selection.

The plugs and components used in this chapter are more complex than those in previous chapters, with the possible exception of the use of compound plug connections in the list and combo boxes. Now that you've seen how to develop some more complex objects using plugs, it's a good time to take up a topic that necessarily comes up whenever you are developing complex bodies of code: *debugging*. The next chapter covers how to debug plugs.

6 Debugging with Plugs

By debugging with plugs, I mean debugging a program that is constructed with plugs. There are two ways to do this: The first is to include a control/status plug as part of a component. A connection is made to the plug when debugging the component. This is similar to including extra debugging functions in a class definition. This approach also requires additional design work when the connection is implemented. The second way does not require additional functions or plugs within a component; it uses a filter component with a matching plug and socket pair. The filter can be placed between a matching socket and plug connection, as shown in Figure 6-1. A debugging filter passes information in either direction without modification and records connections, function calls, and associated parameters. It may also be capable of invoking an external debugger via breakpoints.

This chapter addresses only the second approach to debugging. The first approach is component specific, and it is along the lines of conventional debugging techniques. The second approach is specific to plugs and connections

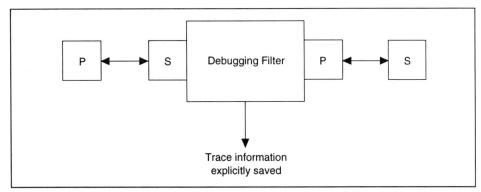

Figure 6-1. Debugging filter

and is one of the reasons plugs were designed the way they are. For example, including a filter between a matching plug and socket is a straightforward process. Instead of using

```
A <= B
the following is used:
A <= DebugFilter.B () ;
B <= DebugFilter.A () ;
```

This assumes *A* and *B* are the matching plug and socket and the *DebugFilter* component has two functions that return references to the same kind of plug and socket. *A* is now connected to *B* through the *DebugFilter* component. The example is appropriate if you have access to the source code that performs the connection, but there are other ways of getting the filter between *A* and *B* that are unique to plugs.

Each plug class definition includes the *addBefore* and *addAfter* function. These functions are essentially identical. The difference is related to the use of redirectors, which is described later in this chapter. The previous example can be replaced with the following:

```
A.addBefore ( & DebugFilter.B (), & DebugFilter.A ()) ;
```

The parameters to *addBefore* and *addAfter* are pointers to a socket and plug. The assumption is that *A* is already connected to *B*. The *addBefore* function temporarily disconnects *A* and *B* and reconnects them to the DebugFilter plugs. The interesting thing to note about the last example is that there is no mention of the plug *B*. You will see how *addBefore* and *addAfter* work and their relationship to debugging in this chapter.

The first section of the chapter introduces basic debugging filters similar to those just discussed and describes *addBefore* and *addAfter* in more detail. Then *tee filters*, an extension of a basic filter, are introduced. A *tee filter* is a component with three plugs, as shown in Figure 6-2. The tee filter adds one plug to the basic filter component. The extra plug provides a standard way of getting information from a debugging filter. Tee connections to windows and files are also discussed.

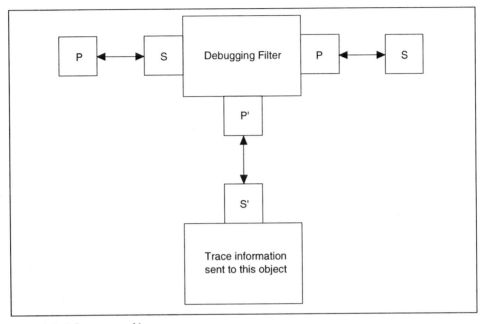

Figure 6-2. Debugging tee filter

The next section addresses redirectors and completes the discussion of *addBefore* and *addAfter*. It also addresses how debugging redirectors are constructed. A section on debugging with dynamic plugs is included, even though the next chapter covers dynamic plugs. The section here covers the reasons why dynamic components are needed in debugging situations. The last section in the chapter diverges from the rest. It discusses the *plugCheck* macro, which can be used to assist in tracking down the use of plugs that are not connected but need to be.

Basic Debugging with Plugs Using Filters

The basic idea of debugging with plugs is to monitor the functions being called across a connection. This can be done by replacing a single connection between a pair of plugs with two connections that include the original pair plus two more plugs of the same type. The two additional plugs, actually a plug and matching socket, are normally part of the same component. The simplest case is a component that only contains the two plugs. This component is called a *filter*.

This section presents a number of simple filters and discusses the restrictions that are placed on the definition of a connection. In particular, the plug class definitions may only contain virtual or static function definitions and type definitions. There may not be non-virtual function definitions other than static function definitions. Variable definitions are also not allowed. The reason for these restrictions is to allow filters to be used transparently, which in turn allows them to be used in any situation where a connection is defined using these restrictions. In essence, these restrictions describe a polymorphic base class definition from which each subclass is interchangeable, plus you can define a filter that can readily forward any function call. The most general case extends these restrictions so that the virtual function definitions are also pure. Comments or documentation are needed to describe the semantics of this type of function since there is no associated source code for the function. A class with a *pure virtual* function definition is called an *abstract class*. Abstract classes have the advantage of requiring a subclass definition that implements the pure functions before an object can be defined. Abstract plug classes are not required to build a filter but virtual functions are.

I will assume that the plug connections being debugged use plugs implemented with abstract class definitions. This is what I recommend, and it makes it possible for you to trace the various function calls. For example:

```
DECLARE_CONNECTION
  ( FooBar
  , FooBarPlug
  , FooBarSocket
  )

class FooBarPlug : public FooBar::plug
{
  public:
    DECLARE_PLUG ()
```

```
      virtual int foo () = 0 ;
      virtual int bar () = 0 ;
} ;

class FooBarSocket : public FooBar::socket
{
  public:
    DECLARE_PLUG ()

    virtual int poof () = 0 ;
    virtual int boom () = 0 ;
} ;
```

This connection is suitable for debugging with another pair of plugs because all of the methods in both base classes are virtual. They are also pure virtual functions, which means there should be some associated documentation for them; but it is not provided here since it is not needed to complete our example. Note that there is no requirement to limit the number of parameters even though all the functions in this example use the same function prototype. This makes it possible to define a class like the following:

```
class FooBarTraceClass1
  : public FooBarPlug
  , public FooBarSocket
{
  public:
    virtual void Show ( char * traceText ) = 0 ;

    FooBarPlug   & Plug ()   { return * this ; }
    FooBarSocket & Socket () { return * this ; }

    virtual int foo ()
    {
      Show ( "Calling foo" ) ;
      int result = FooBarSocket::pOther -> foo () ;
      char resultText [ 80 ] ;
```

```
        sprintf ( resultText, "foo returned %d", result ) ;
        Show ( resultText ) ;
        return result ;
    }
    virtual int bar ()
    {
        Show ( "Calling bar" ) ;
        int result = FooBarSocket::pOther -> bar () ;
        char resultText [ 80 ] ;
        sprintf ( resultText, "bar returned %d", result ) ;
        Show ( resultText ) ;
        return result ;
    }
    virtual int poof ()
    {
        Show ( "Calling poof" ) ;
        int result = FooBarPlug::pOther -> poof () ;
        char resultText [ 80 ] ;
        sprintf ( resultText, "poof returned %d", result ) ;
        Show ( resultText ) ;
        return result ;
    }
    virtual int boom ()
    {
        Show ( "Calling boom" ) ;
        int result = FooBarPlug::pOther -> boom () ;
        char resultText [ 80 ] ;
        sprintf ( resultText, "boom returned %d", result ) ;
        Show ( resultText ) ;
        return result ;
    }
} ;
```

This new class can be used as a basis for a class that can really be used to display the operations associated with the two plug classes. The *Show* function must be implemented to make this all work. Each function in both the plug and socket must be implemented. The simplest case would be to just call the appropriate function using the other plug. In this case you also call the *Show* function before and after this call. One thing the functions do not do is to check the validity of the appropriate *pOther*. This could be done in two ways. The first is what has been done here—ignore the error, but display an error message and let the system continue on its merry way. This may be appropriate if other debugging hooks are included. The second way is to add an additional function—let's call it *FatalError*—which would take control when something goes wrong. The implementation for the *Show* function is left to a subclass. It could be as simple as,

```
void Show ( const char * traceText )
{
  printf ( "%s", traceText ) ;
}
```

or it could employ any number of other recording or display techniques.

One issue that needs to be addressed is the use of multiple inheritance. In the prior example there is no name conflict between the plug and socket functions, which allows us to easily redefine the initial connection class functions. This will not be the case if both the plug and socket have a function with the same name. The best way around this problem is to define four classes instead of just one, as in:

```
class ShowClass
{
  public:
    virtual void Show ( const char * ) = 0 ;
} ;

class ForwardingFooBarPlug : public FooBarPlug
{
  protected:
    FooBarSocket & MySocket ;
    ShowClass     & MyShow ;

  public:
    ForwardingFooBarPlug
```

```
        ( FooBarSocket & MyNewSocket
        , ShowClass    & MyNewShow
        )
        : MySocket ( MyNewSocket )
        , MyShow   ( MyNewShow )
        { }


    virtual int foo ()
    {
      Show ( "Calling foo" ) ;
      int result = MySocket -> foo () ;
      char resultText [ 80 ] ;
      sprintf ( resultText, "foo returned %d", result ) ;
      Show ( resultText ) ;
      return result ;
    }
    virtual int bar ()
    {
      Show ( "Calling bar" ) ;
      int result = FooBarSocket::pOther -> bar () ;
      char resultText [ 80 ] ;
      sprintf ( resultText, "bar returned %d", result ) ;
      Show ( resultText ) ;
      return result ;
    }
} ;


class ForwardingFooBarSocket : public FooBarSocket
{
  protected:
    FooBarPlug & MyPlug ;

  public:
    ForwardingFooBarSocket
      ( FooBarPlug & MyNewPlug
      , ShowClass   & MyNewShow
      )
      : MyPlug ( MyNewPlug )
      , MyShow ( MyNewShow )
      { }
```

```
    virtual int poof ()
    {
      MyShow.Show ( "Calling poof" ) ;
      int result = MyPlug -> poof () ;
      char resultText [ 80 ] ;
      sprintf ( resultText, "poof returned %d", result ) ;
      MyShow.Show ( resultText ) ;
      return result ;
    }
    virtual int boom ()
    {
      MyShow.Show ( "Calling boom" ) ;
      int result = MyPlug -> boom () ;
      char resultText [ 80 ] ;
      sprintf ( resultText, "boom returned %d", result ) ;
      MyShow.Show ( resultText ) ;
      return result ;
    }
} ;

class FooBarFilter
{
  public:
    virtual FooBarPlug   & Plug () = 0 ;
    virtual FooBarSocket & Socket () = 0 ;
} ;

class FooBarTraceClass2 : public FooBarFilter
{
  protected:
    ForwardingFooBarSocket    MySocket ;
    ForwardingFooBarPlug      MyPlug ;

  public:
    FooBarTraceClass2 ( ShowClass & MyShow )
      , MySocket ( MyPlug,   MyShow )
      , MyPlug   ( MySocket, MyShow )
      {}
```

```
        FooBarPlug   & Plug ()   { return MyPlug ; }
        FooBarSocket & Socket () { return MySocket ; }
    } ;
```

The *ShowClass* lets the plug and socket classes utilize the *Show* function. The plug and socket objects access the complementary plug in the trace filter using an explicitly defined local reference variable that is initialized by the respective constructor. The *ShowClass* reference variable is also initialized at the same time. The *FooBarFilter* abstract filter class is introduced in this example as well. This class defines the interface for a simple filter. It allows additional filters to be defined using this base, not just the one class defined here. This class becomes important in the next section, when tee filters, which are based upon the filter class, are considered. The forwarding socket and plug classes are a standard to implement filters. These classes both forward the function calls as well as note them using the ShowClass.

Although *FooBarTraceClass2* has a more verbose definition than *FooBarTraceClass1*, they are effectively the same in both operation and implementation. The multiple inheritance used in *FooBarTraceClass1* essentially hides the use of references. The references still exist and can, in theory, be more efficiently implemented, but normally the two class definitions are the same in both internal form and function. The advantage of *FooBarTraceClass2* is the ability to readily redefine any plug function. This becomes more important when plug functions have the same name for both the plug and socket classes.

Defining and implementing a trace component can require a good deal of work. Luckily a generic implementation will be suitable for tracing function calls between any plug/socket implementation. Trace plugs should be supplied with the plugs they trace, making the use of plugs and trace plugs easy. This brings up the second part of the discussion regarding the use of trace plugs.

Obviously the goal is to transparently trace the operations being performed through a connection. The trace object must contain a plug and a socket because it is to be placed in the system between a plug and socket. This can be done when the connection is made. For example,

```
A <= B ;
```

is replaced by,

```
A <= TraceFilter ;
B <= TraceFilter ;
```

where *TraceFilter* is an object with a definition similar to *FooBarTraceClass1*. This syntax works because the *TraceFilter* is built from a plug and a socket, and C++ picks the appropriate portion to make a connection depending upon the type of *A* and *B*. Although it is possible to use this C++ feature, it is preferable to use virtual functions to obtain the references to the plugs, as in:

```
A <= TraceFilter.Socket () ;
B <= TraceFilter.Plug () ;
```

This is the approach given in the trace filter class example at the beginning of this section. Actually, the class can be used in both ways but the explicit use of a function to obtain the reference is preferred to the implicit method.

An alternative to adding a trace filter at the point of the initial connection is to insert the trace connection after the initial connection is made. This approach is used more often because a system of plug connection is normally built up by a function that you don't wish to make major changes to. In fact, the original construction can be done by a portion of the program for which you may not have any source code, and therefore could not make modifications even if you wanted to. With plugs, you can still make the modifications as long as you have access to at least one side of a connection. A component class definition like the following can provide the access to the internals of the component.

```
class Component123
{
   public: // -- debugging points --
      virtual FooBarPlug   & DebugPlug () = 0 ;
      virtual FooBarSocket & DebugSocket () = 0 ;
```

```
public:  // — other definitions go here —
   virtual FooBarPlug   & SamplePlug () = 0 ;
   virtual FooBarSocket & SampleSocket () = 0 ;
} ;
```

Additional comments or documentation should describe what the *DebugPlug* and *DebugSocket* do and when you can connect to them. Likewise, the other plugs and sockets that may be for general use are also subject to manipulation via the debug filters, or any other connections for that matter.

To insert a trace object within a connection, the *addBefore* or *addAfter* plug functions are used. An example might look like this:

```
A.addBefore ( TraceFilter.Socket(), TraceFilter.Plug ()) ;
```

The *addBefore* and *addAfter* functions take the same parameters and perform essentially the same function. They temporarily disconnect a plug connection and reconnect the disconnected ends to the parameters passed to the function. The end result is the same; the trace object now sits between the plug and socket to be traced.

The difference between the two functions is with respect to any associated redirectors. The *addBefore* function will change any redirector pointing to the plug to point to the new plug, which, in this case, would be one end of the trace plug.

A simple removal procedure of a trace plug object looks like this:

```
(* - plug::TraceFilter.Socket ())
   <= (* - socket::TraceFilter.Plug ()) ;
```

This idiom temporarily disconnects both the plug and socket portions of the trace plug object and connects the ends together, leaving the trace plug unconnected. Unfortunately, the disconnection procedure does not take redirectors into account. This is important if you use *addBefore*, which changes any redirector that points to the initial plug. Restoring redirectors to the initial state before the *addBefore* function is used may be rather involved if the trace filter also has redirectors associated with it, because only the original redirectors should be restored.

The *addBefore* and *addAfter* functions can be used for trace filters, but they can also be used when building more complex plug structures. These issues are discussed later in this book. I just wanted to let you know that *addBefore* and *addAfter* are not unique to trace filters.

The functions that are traced and the method of tracing the operations is not restricted to the simple examples presented in this section. You can just as readily trace the plug functions, such as *connected,* and even operators, such as <=. Tracing the *afterConnect* and *beforeDisconnect* functions lets you follow the connections made with a plug.

The amount of information displayed and the way it is displayed is based upon the requirements of the designer and debugger, who is often the same programmer. For example, you may be trying to find when and how a particular connection is broken but only after a certain function has been called. This test can be added to the trace filter forwarding function, *disconnected,* or possibly *beforeDisconnect.*

The next section addresses how the *ShowClass* might be implemented. Remember that the techniques presented in this chapter are just that, techniques. They are not the only method by which debugging can be implemented using plugs and filters.

Basic Debugging with Tee Filters

The previous section introduced filters and how to connect them within existing components. The definition of the *ShowClass* was deliberately left out until this section. A subclass that implements the *Show* function in a standard C environment could be as simple as:

```
class PrintfShowClass : public ShowClass
{
  public:
    virtual void Show ( const char * text )
      { printf ( "%s", text ) ; }
} ;
```

It could also be used to display or record the information using files (see Figure 6-3) or windows (see Figure 6-4). One way to implement these filters is to follow the same pattern as the previous example, as in:

```
class FileShowClass : public ShowClass
{
  public:
    FileShowClass ()
      : file ( 0 )
      {}

    FILE * file ;

    virtual void Show ( const char * text )
    {
      if ( file )
        fprintf ( file, "%s", text ) ;
    }
} ;
class MessageBoxShowClass : public ShowClass
{
  public:
    virtual void Show ( const char * text )
      { ::MessageBox ( 0, text, "ShowClass", MB_OK ) ; }
} ;
```

You now have three classes that can be used interchangeably with the *Foo-BarTraceClass2* objects. The problem with these designs is there is no standard way of hooking these filters into any other part of the program. The closest is the file version, which expects an open file before the *Show* function is used. The function does not cause an error if the file is not open. The

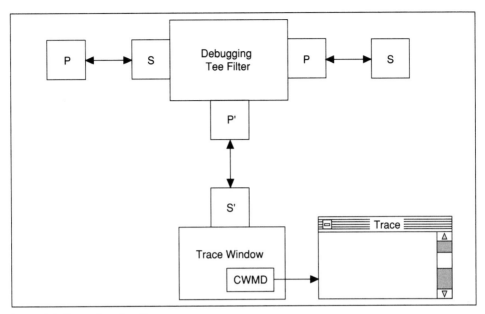

Figure 6-3. Tee and window diagram

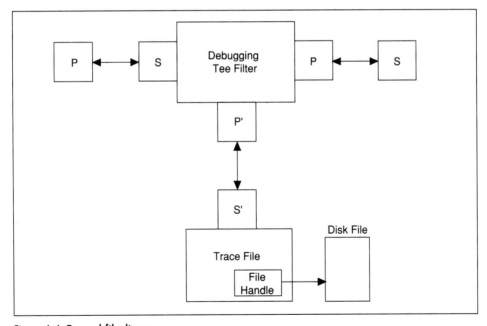

Figure 6-4. Tee and file diagram

215

file handle used by the class can be changed using standard C library functions, but this is the limit of the changes. So what is the alternative?

The answer is a tee filter. Most debugging filters are built as tee filters. A tee filter is a subclass of a filter with an extra plug (or socket) as part of the component. The extra plug does not have to be, and typically is not, of the same connection type as the other two plugs that are part of the filter. One possibility is to use the *StrStream1Plug* presented in Chapter 3 in a definition like this:

```
class StrStream1ShowClass : public ShowClass
{
  protected:
    StrStream1Plug MyPlug ;

  public:
    StrStream1Plug & Plug () { return MyPlug ; }

    virtual void Show ( const char * text )
      { MyPlug.Process ( text ) ; }
} ;
```

Then an object of this *ShowClass* subclass is integrated with the *FooBarTraceClass2* filter, and you get this:

```
class FooBarTraceClass3 : public FooBarTraceClass2
{
  protected:
    StrStream1ShowClass MyShow ;

  public:
    FooBarTraceClass3 ()
      : FooBarTraceClass2 ( MyShow )
      {}

    StrStream1Plug & TracePlug ()
    { return MyPlug.Plug() ; }
} ;
```

The *TracePlug* can now be used in a *StrStream1* connection with a matching socket. All the linkages created by the *FooBarTraceClass2* constructor are handled by the *FooBarTraceClass3* constructor, including the *ShowClass* object reference. Do you need to debug the *TracePlug* portion of the filter? Just grab a similar *StrStream1* filter, or build one.

Debugging filters and tee filters are only the starting point. Compound plug connections utilize many internal connections, and compound debugging filters may address only a few or even one of these internal connections. To see how this works, start with a simple compound connection that uses some of the previously defined connection classes, as in:

```
DECLARE_CONNECTION
    ( CompoundSample
    , CompoundSamplePlug
    , CompoundSampleSocket
    )

class CompoundSamplePlug : public CompoundSample::plug
{
  protected:
    friend CompoundSampleSocket ;
    virtual FooBar::plug & Plug1 () = 0 ;
    virtual FooBar::plug & Plug2 () = 0 ;
    virtual FooBar::plug & Plug3 () = 0 ;

  public:
    DECLARE_PLUG ()
} ;

class CompoundSampleSocket : public CompoundSample::socket
{
  protected:
    virtual FooBar::socket & Socket1 () = 0 ;
    virtual FooBar::socket & Socket2 () = 0 ;
    virtual FooBar::socket & Socket3 () = 0 ;

  public:
```

```
DECLARE_PLUG ()

void afterConnect ( CompoundSamplePlug * pPlug )
{
  CompoundSample::socket::afterConnect ( pPlug ) ;

  Socket1 () <= pOther -> Plug1 () ;
  Socket2 () <= pOther -> Plug2 () ;
  Socket3 () <= pOther -> Plug3 () ;
}

void beforeDisconnect ( CompoundSamplePlug * pPlug )
{
  CompoundSample::socket::beforeDisconnect ( pPlug ) ;

  - Socket1 () ;
  - Socket2 () ;
  - Socket3 () ;
}
} ;
```

This defines a simple compound connection with three internal connections that match the type for which a *StrStream1* debugging tee filter has been defined. The intention now is to make a debugging tee filter for this compound connection that inserts a debugging *FooBarTraceClass3* tee filter in between the second internal connection. The other two internal connections will not be affected. To do this you need forwarding classes for the compound plug and socket classes like those for the simple connections in the previous section. The main difference is that the forwarding classes also utilize a redirector reference for each internal connection. These redirectors are used to redirect a plug when the outer compound connection is made by the opposite end of the compound filter. The *afterConnect* function does this first and then attempts to make a connection using the normal means in the superclass.

You can follow the global steps of connecting the compound filter to see how all this works together. First, start with an unconnected compound filter and a compound plug and socket to which it will be connected. Then connect the plug to the socket of the compound filter. This causes the redirectors to be set to the compound plug's internal plugs. An attempt is then made to connect to the other end. The first and third internal connections will not be made because the matching redirector is redirecting nothing. The second connection is made to the internal tee filter. Connecting the compound socket to the plug of the compound filter causes the other set of redirectors to be set up, followed by a connection attempt. The middle connection is made to the internal tee filter, while the first and third connections are made through the redirectors, which were set up when the compound plug was first connected to the compound filter.

The neat thing about this entire process is that the resulting connections are between the first and third internal connections of the compound plug and compound socket, and only the middle connection is made through the compound filter's internal tee filter. The respective redirectors in the compound tee filter are adjusted whenever the compound connection on either end is broken.

The forwarding class objects are used in the compound tee filter objects along with a host of redirectors. A basic abstract filter class is added for good measure. This is what the compound trace tee filter class definitions look like:

```
class ForwardingCompoundSamplePlug : public CompoundSamplePlug
{
  protected:
    FooBar::socketRedirector & Redirector1 ;
    FooBar::socketRedirector & Redirector2 ;
    FooBar::socketRedirector & Redirector3 ;

    FooBar::plug & plug1 ;
    FooBar::plug & plug2 ;
    FooBar::plug & plug3 ;

    FooBar::plug & Plug1 () { return plug1 ; }
    FooBar::plug & Plug2 () { return plug2 ; }
    FooBar::plug & Plug3 () { return plug3 ; }
```

```
      public:
        ForwardingCompoundSamplePlug
          ( FooBar::socketRedirector & NewRedirector1
          , FooBar::socketRedirector & NewRedirector2
          , FooBar::socketRedirector & NewRedirector3
          , FooBar::plug & NewPlug1
          , FooBar::plug & NewPlug2
          , FooBar::plug & NewPlug3
          )
          : Redirector1 ( NewRedirector1 )
          , Redirector2 ( NewRedirector2 )
          , Redirector3 ( NewRedirector3 )
          , plug1 ( NewPlug1 )
          , plug2 ( NewPlug2 )
          , plug3 ( NewPlug3 )
          {}

      void afterConnect ( CompoundSampleSocket * pSocket )
      {
        OtherRedirector1.redirect ( pSocket -> Socket1 ()) ;
        OtherRedirector2.redirect ( pSocket -> Socket2 ()) ;
        OtherRedirector3.redirect ( pSocket -> Socket3 ()) ;

        CompoundSampleSocket::afterConnect ( pSocket ) ;
      }

      void beforeDisconnect ( CompoundSampleSocket * pSocket )
      {
        Redirector1.redirect ( 0 ) ;
        Redirector2.redirect ( 0 ) ;
        Redirector3.redirect ( 0 ) ;

        CompoundSampleSocket::beforeDisconnect ( pSocket ) ;
      }
} ;

class ForwardingCompoundSampleSocket
    : public CompoundSampleSocket
{
  protected:
```

```
    FooBar::plugRedirector & Redirector1 ;
    FooBar::plugRedirector & Redirector2 ;
    FooBar::plugRedirector & Redirector3 ;

    FooBar::socket & socket1 ;
    FooBar::socket & socket2 ;
    FooBar::socket & socket3 ;

    FooBarSocket * Socket1 () { return socket1 ; }
    FooBarSocket * Socket2 () { return socket2 ; }
    FooBarSocket * Socket3 () { return socket3 ; }

public:
  ForwardingCompoundSampleSocket
    ( FooBar::plugRedirector & NewRedirector1
    , FooBar::plugRedirector & NewRedirector2
    , FooBar::plugRedirector & NewRedirector3
    , FooBar::socket & NewSocket1
    , FooBar::socket & NewSocket2
    , FooBar::socket & NewSocket3
    )
    : Redirector1 ( NewRedirector1 )
    , Redirector2 ( NewRedirector2 )
    , Redirector3 ( NewRedirector3 )
    , socket1 ( NewSocket1 )
    , socket2 ( NewSocket2 )
    , socket3 ( NewSocket3 )
    {}

  void afterConnect ( CompoundSamplePlug * pPlug )
  {
    OtherRedirector1.redirect ( pPlug -> Plug1 ()) ;
    OtherRedirector2.redirect ( pPlug -> Plug2 ()) ;
    OtherRedirector3.redirect ( pPlug -> Plug3 ()) ;

    CompoundSamplePlug::afterConnect ( pPlug ) ;
  }

  void beforeDisconnect ( CompoundSamplePlug * pPlug )
  {
```

```
        Redirector1.redirect ( 0 ) ;
        Redirector2.redirect ( 0 ) ;
        Redirector3.redirect ( 0 ) ;

        CompoundSamplePlug::beforeDisconnect ( pPlug ) :
      }


      CompoundSample::socketRedirector Redirector1 ;
      CompoundSample::socketRedirector Redirector2 ;
      CompoundSample::socketRedirector Redirector3 ;
  } ;


class CompoundSampleFilter
{
  public:
    virtual CompoundSample::plug   & Plug () = 0 ;
    virtual CompoundSample::socket & Socket () = 0 ;
} ;


class CompoundSampleTeeTraceFilter
   : public CompoundSampleFilter
{
  protected:
    FooBarTraceClass3                  MyFilter ;
    ForwardingCompoundSamplePlug    MyPlug ;
    ForwardingCompoundSampleSocket MySocket ;

    FooBar::plugRedirector PlugRedirector1 ;
    FooBar::plugRedirector PlugRedirector2 ;
    FooBar::plugRedirector PlugRedirector3 ;

    FooBar::socketRedirector SocketRedirector1 ;
    FooBar::socketRedirector SocketRedirector2 ;
    FooBar::socketRedirector SocketRedirector3 ;

  public:
    CompoundSampleTeeTraceFilter ()
      : MyFilter ()
      , MyPlug    ( SocketRedirector1
                  , SocketRedirector2
```

```
                    , SocketRedirector3
                    , PlugRedirector1
                    , MyFilter.Plug ()
                    , PlugRedirector3
                    )
          , MySocket ( PlugRedirector1
                    , PlugRedirector2
                    , PlugRedirector3
                    , SocketRedirector1
                    , MyFilter.Socket ()
                    , SocketRedirector3
                    )
        { }

        StrStream1Plug & TracePlug () { return MyFilter.Plug() ; }
        CompoundSample::plug & Plug () { return MyPlug ; }
        CompoundSample::socket & Socket () { return MySocket ; }
    } ;
```

The *CompoundSampleTraceTeeFilter* constructor puts everything together. The forwarding compound plug and socket classes contain their respective redirectors. The constructor sets up the redirectors for the first and third internal connection to point to the redirectors in the other forwarding plug. Note that you still need the middle connection redirectors even though they are not used to make a connection. This is because the references are used to set up the initial redirection when a compound connection is initiated. The alternative is to use pointers instead and to check for null pointers before attempting to redirect. This causes a minimal increase in the amount of support code while eliminating a pair of redirectors. Either way works transparently with respect to the compound filter.

Debugging and Redirectors

The previous section showed how redirectors can be used as is in compound plugs to assist in debugging. In this section you will see how they interact with plugs and how they can be defined to assist in debugging.

A redirector can redirect any matching plug. For example, *FooBar::plugRedirector* can redirect *FooBar::plug*. It can also redirect another *FooBar::plugRedirector*. Redirectors are involved when connections are made and broken. They are not involved with internal protocol functions. If you are interested in debugging connections, then debugging redirectors may be the way to go. Otherwise, back up to the first section, on debugging filters, because these can be used to monitor the internal protocol functions.

When a redirector redirects a plug, as initiated by the redirect function of the redirector, it is added to the plug's redirector list. The redirector list is bidirectional and serves two purposes. First, the list allows redirectors to be used to make connections. The redirector uses the list in the direction toward the plug to obtain the plug reference and use it in the connection process. Then the plug uses the list in the other direction to pass information about what connection functions are being called. For example, the *afterConnect* function of each redirector in a list is called when the associated plug's *afterConnect* function is called. A similar thing is done for most other connection functions. Figure 6-5 shows how the connections would look with a set of redirectors and how the function calls progress for a particular function.

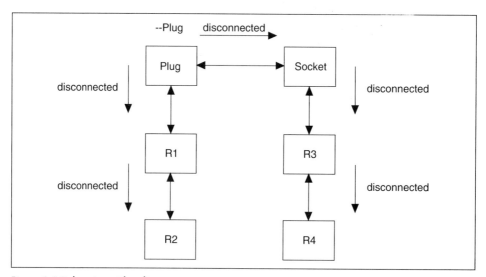

Figure 6-5 Debugging with redirectors

Normally the redirectors do nothing when the matching function is called, but they can use this information for debugging purposes. The information might be reported in a similar fashion to the debugging tee filters discussed earlier in this chapter.

The advantages of using the redirector over a filter are both simplicity and unobtrusiveness. A redirector is notified when a plug's connection functions are used, even if the redirector is not involved in initiating the connection. This means a debugging redirector could be added to a plug's redirector list simply to monitor the connections.

A simple redirector class definition for a prior sample class to track the *afterConnect* and *beforeDisconnect* functions looks like this:

```
class DebugFooBarPlugRedirector : public FooBar::plugRedirector
{
  protected:
    StrStream1Plug MyPlug ;

  public:
    StrStream1Plug & Plug () { return MyPlug ; }

    void afterConnect ( FooBarPlug * pPlug )
    {
      if ( MyPlug.connected ())
        MyPlug.Process ( "FooBar::plug::afterConnect" ) ;
      FooBar::plugRedirecor::afterConnect ( pPlug ) ;
    }

    void beforeDisconnect ( FooBarPlug * pPlug )
    {
      if ( MyPlug.connected ())
        MyPlug.Process ( "FooBar::plug::beforeDisconnect" ) ;
      FooBar::plugRedirecor::beforeDisconnect ( pPlug ) ;
    }
} ;
```

This redirector sends its notification out through the *StrStream1* plug if it is connected. The notification is simple and contains no specific information about which plug generated the information, but this information can be obtained and formatted if necessary. The point is that defining the class is a straightforward process. Using a redirector of this type is as simple as:

```
DebugFooBarPlugRedirector DebugRedirector ;

DebugRedirector.redirect ( AFooBarPlug ) ;
```

This assumes that *AFooBarPlug* is of type *FooBar::plug*. The debugging redirector can be removed from a plug's redirector list in the normal fashion, which is to let the redirector redirect a different plug or to call its redirect function with a *0* value.

In general, debugging redirectors are easier to create than a debugging filter and provide the same type of facility if only connections and connection functions need to be monitored. They are easy to install, and multiple redirectors can be associated with a single plug. If multiple plug connections need to be monitored at a single point, it is possible to create a forwarding redirector along the same lines as the forwarding plugs used earlier in this chapter. In this case the redirector simply forwards the calls to the appropriate object, which then checks the plug connections to be monitored.

Debugging with Dynamic Plugs

Dynamic plugs are covered in Chapter 8, but some aspects of dynamic plugs with respect to debugging need to be addressed here. Briefly, a dynamic plug or component is allocated out of free space and exists as long as there are a minimal number of references to it. For a plug, this normally means its connection. For a component, this may mean all its plugs or a specific subset, or even a subset and a specific set of conditions unrelated to the connections. In any case, the object frees itself when it is no longer needed.

Dynamic plugs can be both the object of a debugging session and a tool. The latter is of interest here since the former is essentially the same as debugging any plug or component as described in this chapter. Using dynamic plugs as a tool is important because of the way debugging connections are made and the fact that some of the things being debugged may include dynamic plugs and components.

Figure 6-6 highlights the need for dynamic debugging plugs and components. It shows how a debugging component is inserted into a system built from dynamic components. These components delete themselves when they are no longer needed and disconnect from the debugging component at that time.

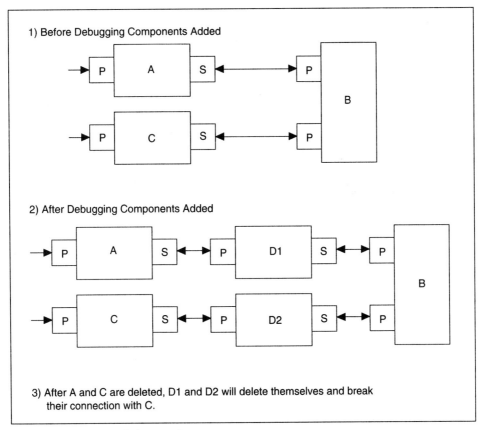

Figure 6-6 Debugging with dynamic plugs

Unfortunately the debugging component is still there after the things that it was watching are gone. Do this too many times and you run out of free space.

One solution is to make the debugging components dynamic too, so they will free themselves when they are no longer needed. The design of a dynamic debugging component is the same as for normal components and plugs. (Take a look at Chapter 8 to see how this is done.) The trick is to know what connections to check to determine when to free a component. This may include the connections of the component being debugged, or it may be the connections used to report the debug information. In any case, be sure to note the requirements and conditions in the documentation or comments.

In general, dynamic debugging components will be used in dynamic structures or where debugging components are dynamically placed. Non-dynamic debugging components are suitable if the debugging portion of the program is limited to a particular area and the number of dynamic debugging components is fixed or within the hierarchical design methodology described in Chapter 1.

Dynamic debugging components also become more interesting if they can be included as dynamic linked libraries, which are associated with a program at runtime. In this case the libraries can change depending upon whether debugging is to be performed actively, passively, or not at all. The level of complexity will be based on need and resources. At this point I have not needed to resort to anything quite so complex.

Debugging and the plugCheck Macro

The *plugCheck* macro is used in the default plug reference functions, * and ->. The default macro definition does nothing and generates no code. The macro definition is designed to be replaced by code that will check the value of the *pOther* pointer before it is returned by the respective function. In most cases, a *0* value will cause an error. If you are using a debugger, you will probably catch the error when the pointer is used. If you are not, the results can range from a general protection fault under a protected mode operating system like OS/2 or Windows, to eventually trashing the system in an unprotected environment like MS-DOS. In either case, you may want to include debugging support in your code for this type of error. This can be done by redefining the *plugCheck* macro.

Because it is a macro, *plugCheck* can be redefined any number of times. A particular definition takes effect only when the macro is expanded. Here, this is when the *DECLARE_CONNECTION* macro is used. This allows you to set the *plugCheck* macro definition to something useful, use the *DECLARE_CONNECTION* macro, and then change the *plugCheck* macro definition either back to its original null state or to something useful for the next use of the *DECLARE_CONNECTION* macro. For example:

```
#define plugCheck(c)\
  if(c==0)plugCheckError("Sample1Connection");


DECLARE_CONNECTION
   ( Sample1Connection
   , Sample1Plug
   , Sample1Socket
   )


#define plugCheck(c)\
  if(c==0)plugCheckError("Sample2Connection");


DECLARE_CONNECTION
   ( Sample2Connection
   , Sample2Plug
   , Sample2Socket
   )


#define plugCheck(c)
```

I have omitted the plug and socket class definitions. These can actually come later. The function *plugCheckError* is assumed to be a global function that takes a string parameter. It could put up a dialog box with the string when the error occurred and then terminate the program, thereby preventing a crash. A more sophisticated approach might be to determine the cause of the error and attempt some form of recovery. However, the latter is very dependent on the program and environment under which it is running and therefore beyond the scope of this book.

An *ASSERT* macro included in the Microsoft Foundation Class takes a single parameter that it checks for a non-zero value, which is ideal for this purpose. The macro generates the check and calls a function that puts up a dialog box with the line number and file name where the *ASSERT* macro was used. A *plugCheck* macro definition using this macro looks like this:

```
#define plugCheck(c) ASSERT(c)
```

I did not use the *ASSERT* macro inside the connection macro because you would not be able to selectively turn it on or off. The *plugCheck* macro approach allows this to be done. Take a look at Appendix A for more details on where the *plugCheck* macro is used.

Summary

A few possible enhancements for trace plugs come to mind. The first is a way to enable and disable, globally or selectively, the trace operations. A second enhancement is what gets displayed and how it is formatted. The list goes on and on, but these would seem like basic enhancements. Other purposes for debugging plugs might include the ability to set breakpoints on specific operations or combination of operations.

Debugging plugs can be very handy tools when developing a program. They can be used during development, or after a program has been developed when a bug needs to be fixed. The *addBefore* and *addAfter* functions make it practical to add hooks into the program structure, assuming the appropriate test points can be accessed. This is not always as easy as it sounds because connections may be dynamic. This brings us to the topic of the next chapter: dynamic plugs.

7 Components and Compound Plugs

The aim of this book is to show you how to build software from components, and this chapter shows you just what a component is. While examining components, you'll take a look at compound plugs, which will prove useful in component design.

Software components are not hard to understand. Like a hardware component, a software component is an object that can be hooked to other objects via standardized plug connections. Figure 7-1 shows just how close the two can be. The hardware connector and cable interface is described using the plug diagrams from this book. Now that a specific technical meaning has been given to the term software plug, this description is more than just an analogy with hardware. A software component is, technically, an object with one or more plugs associated with it. How the plugs are associated with an object and how a component is used and defined will be discussed in detail here.

When you consider what kinds of plugs are associated with the component, things get a little more interesting. The plugs associated with a component may be simple single-connection plugs or they may be compound plugs. A *compound plug* has more than one connection associated with it, and it has a plug protocol associated with these connections. So far in this book, the connection examples have all been simple connections; compound connections will be considered here.

There is a close relationship between components and compound plugs. A compound plug is actually a specialized component. The difference between components and compound plugs is in how they are built and used. Components are designed to show their plugs— at least the public ones—whereas a compound plug is designed to be viewed as a single (logical) plug. The internal plugs of a compound plug should not be used directly by the user of that compound plug; they should only be used internally.

This chapter covers a number of aspects in compound plug and component design and use. It begins with how a simple component is implemented. Then a simple compound plug design is introduced, followed by a detailed discussion of building components and compound plugs. A section on standard components presents some component designs that can be common to almost

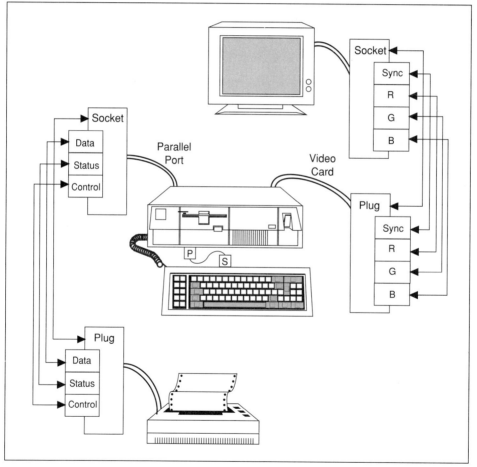

Figure 7-1. Computer example with compound plug correspondence

any connection definition, including filters and tee filters. Adapters and similar component designs are also discussed. The similarities and differences between compound plugs and components are covered in the last section. The distinction between the two gets a little blurry if you look too closely at the implementation, but there are reasons for having both and for using one instead of the other in particular circumstances.

Let's take a look at a simple component before getting into these discussions.

A Simple Component

A component is an object that contains public plug definitions, plug references, or pointers to plugs. A component may be allocated or passed to a function via a pointer. The definition for a component could look like this:

```
class PlugType1 ;
class PlugType2 ;
class SocketType3 ;

class Component1
{
  public:
    PlugType1 * plug1 ;
    PlugType2 * plug2 ;
    SocketType3 * socket3 ;

    int CommonVariable ;
};
```

There are several things to say about this code. The pointers contained in an object of class *Component1* can be used to make additional connections. The connection procedures and other related operations are defined by the designer of the class, who also decides on its purpose. Additional variables and functions can be defined within a component, with their use also defined by the designer. The reason for this approach is to make it possible to design and implement components in isolation from other parts of a program, which may also allow the components to be used in other programs.

Figure 7-2 shows a more complex component definition. There are two major differences between this and the previous example. The first is the use of an abstract class as a base. This allows additional component subclasses to be defined and used interchangeably. One component subclass is shown in Figure 7-2. Figure 7-3 shows how a component might be connected to other components. Unlike compound plugs, which are discussed in the next section, the component connections occur in arbitrary order and require explicit connection operations. Figure 7-3 also shows a compound plug, P3, being connected to another compound plug, C.

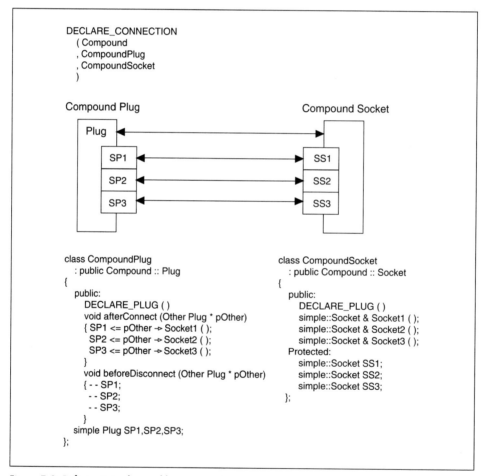

Figure 7-2. Defining interchangeable components

A Simple Compound Plug

Components are meant to be flexible in their purpose. Compound plugs are components with a fixed purpose and protocol. Compound plugs have a base class that contains plugs, references, or pointers to plugs. Does this sound just like a component? The difference is in the purpose. The purpose of a compound plug is to make connections with its base parts to plugs and sockets available from the other end of a connection.

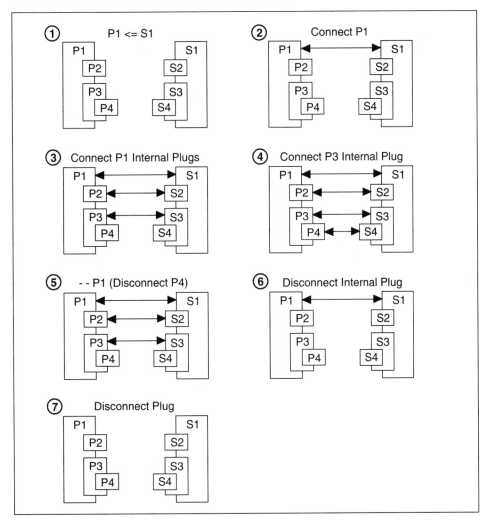

Figure 7-3. Connecting components

The protocol followed by compound plugs is the same as for normal plugs and, from a macro view, compound plugs are used and created just like simple plugs. The protocol for a compound plug is relatively simple. Connecting a compound plug causes it to make connections to its internal parts while disconnecting does the opposite.

Note that a component definition utilizes plugs, but it does not use any of the plug macros in this example. However, a component can itself be a plug, in which case the component class is usually a base class for one of the plug's macros.

Compound plugs imply compound connections. Defining compound connections is almost identical to defining simple connections. Both the plug and socket base classes must include function definitions for *afterConnect* and *beforeDisconnect*. For example, compare the following code for defining compound connections with the code in Chapter 1 for defining simple connections.

```
class PlugType1 ;
class SocketType1 ;

class PlugType2 ;
class SocketType2 ;

DECLARE_CONNECTION
    ( Compound1
    , CompoundPlug1
    , CompoundSocket1
    )

class CompoundPlug1 : public Compound1::plug
{
  public:
    DECLARE_PLUG ()

    PlugType1 p1a ;
    PlugType1 p1b ;
    SocketType2 s2 ;
} ;
```

```
class CompoundSocket1 : public Compound::socket
{
  public:
    DECLARE_PLUG ()

    SocketType1 s1a ;
    SocketType1 s1b ;
    PlugType2 p2 ;

    void afterConnect ( otherPlug * pb )
    {
      pb -> p1a <= s1a ;
      pb -> p1b <= s1b ;
      pb -> s2 <= p2 ;
    }

    void beforeDisconnect ( otherPlug * pb )
    {
      -- s1a ;
      -- s1b ;
      -- p2 ;
    }
} ;
```

Note that the socket base definitions make and break the internal connections. The choice is arbitrary, as is the order of the operations. In general, the users of a compound plug will not be concerned with the connection protocol since they are only using the connection functions for the compound plug itself. They do not access the lower level connections hidden in the objects and functions defined in the preceding code. However, designers can't ignore these things. If they are extending or enhancing compound plugs they must keep in mind the protocol and use of the connections involved. In particular, the parent class functions must be called from any redefined functions, such as *afterConnect* or *beforeDisconnect*, if the plugs are to operate properly.

Figure 7-4 shows another compound plug definition along with a diagram of what the plug looks like when connected to a matching socket. Note how a single connection operation invokes three subsequent connections. All four connections are maintained together, but they may be used independently. The outer connection can be used for additional functions, or it may simply be used to connect the internal plugs, as shown in the example.

Figure 7-5 shows the connect and disconnect operations for a different compound plug. This compound plug and matching socket also contain a compound plug, P3 and S3. Note that the connection progression is just the opposite of the disconnect progression. A compound connection may support any number of internal plug connections. These internal plugs may provide simple or compound connections.

Now let's take a look at components and compound plugs in more detail.

Building Components

Components contain public plugs or references to plugs. They may also contain public variables and functions. It is precisely in the public nature of a

```
class AbstractComponent
{
    public:
        virtual Simple::plug &Plug1 ( )= 0;
        virtual Simple::plug &Plug2 ( )= 0;
        virtual Compound::plug &Plug3 ( )= 0;
};
classComponent Class: public AbstractComponent
{
        protected:
            SimplePlug P1;
            SimplePlug P2;
            CompoundPlug P3;
        public:
            Simple::plug &Plug1 ( ) { Return P1; }
            Simple::plug &Plug2 ( ) { Return P2; }
            Compound::plug &Plug3 ( ) { Return P3; }
};
```

Figure 7-4. Defining a component

component where the difference between components and compound plugs shows itself. A compound plug may have public functions, but it should not have public plugs for general use. Also, a compound plug follows a protocol in which the non-public plugs are connected and disconnected in conjunction with the compound plug connection.

Several categories of components can be distinguished on the basis of their construction. The simplest case is the component that only has a few public plugs. (Public variables and functions can be part of any category.) The next case is a component which is itself a simple plug. The plug connection is used

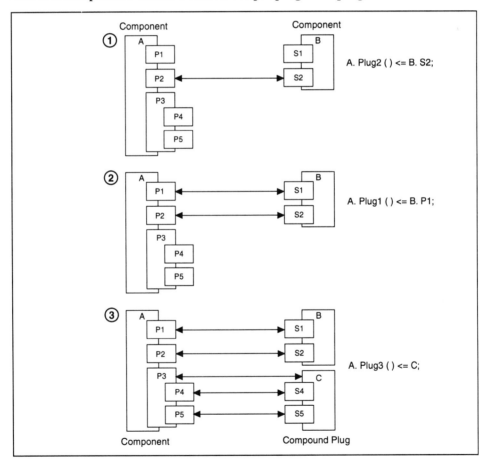

Figure 7-5. Connection process for a component

to gain access to the component's public plugs and members. Finally, the component may be a compound plug. Some examples will highlight the differences among these three categories.

The first example, the simplest case, is very similar to the one given at the beginning of the chapter. This example uses more member functions and elements.

```
class PlugType1 ;
class PlugType2 ;
class SocketType3 ;

class Component2
{
  public:
    PlugType1 * pPlug1 ;
    PlugType2 * pPlug2 ;
    SocketType3 * pSocket3 ;

    PlugType2 myPlug2 ;

    int CommonVariable ;

    void sample () ;

    Component2 ()
      : pPlug1 ( & plug1 )
      , pPlug2 ( & plug2 )
      , pSocket3 ( & socket3 )
      {}

  protected:
    void hidden () ;

    PlugType1 plug1 ;
    PlugType2 plug2 ;
    PlugType1 plug3 ;
    SocketType3 socket3 ;
} ;
```

This component class contains public and protected members. The public portion contains pointers to plugs and sockets as well as a public plug. The purpose of all public members should be described in comments or other documentation associated with the component. There is no particular protocol associated with a simple component and the access to it must be done using conventional programming techniques, including access via local or global variables or via pointers or references. The public portions of a component may be distinct or work in conjunction with one another.

The component can now be accessed via the plug connection. Making a component into a plug may be done simply to provide access to the plug instead of using a conventional pointer. However, adding the extra code to make it into a dynamic plug means that the component can be deallocated when it is no longer needed. Another reason to make a component into a simple plug is to hide the fact that there is a component at the other end of a connection. Functions are added to the other end of the connection to access the component instead of using it directly. The following is an example of this:

```
DECLARE_CONNECTION
  ( Component2B
  , Component2BPlug
  , Component2BSocket
  )

class Component2BPlug : public Component2::plug
{
  public:
    DECLARE_PLUG ()
} ;

class Component2BSocket : public Component2B::socket
{
  public:
    DECLARE_PLUG ()

    virtual void DoSomethingWithComponent2 ( PlugType3 * pPlug3 )=0;
    virtual void DoSomethingElseWithComponent2 ( int i ) = 0 ;
```

```
} ;

class Component2BSocket : public Component2BSocket!
{
  public
    void DoSomethingWithComponent2 ( PlugType3 * pPlug3 )
    {
      (* pPlug3) <= (* ( pOther -> pSocket3 )) ;
    }

    void DoSomethingElseWithComponent2 ( int i )
    {
      pOther -> CommonVariable = i ;
    }
} ;
```

Component2BPlug is implemented using multiple inheritance. The connection support is provided by the *Component2B::plug* class while the component support is provided by the *Component2 class*. The functions and variables contained in an object of type *Component2* will be part of the plug and can be accessed using the plug functions. The component portion can be hidden from general access by making it protected instead of public. In that case, the socket functions can be given access to the component by making the socket class a friend class.

Note that the functions implemented in *Component2BSocket* do not follow any particular protocol, and a description of the various member functions and any additional variables must be done either in comments or other documentation. *Component2BSocket* may also define plug-related methods to implement dynamic plug support or compound plug support. (This is covered in more detail in the next section.)

The points that should be made clear in any description of a component are what parts are related, what parts must be utilized, in what order, and what parts are utilized internally. In some cases the implementation may require the latter to be defined as public, so documentation is important.

Building Compound Plugs

Compound plugs are a very specific implementation of a component. In particular, they should look and be used just like simple plugs. The difference is what occurs when the plug is connected or disconnected and what members are used at that time.

Compound plugs are defined using the simple *DECLARE_CONNECTION* and *DECLARE_PLUG* macros in Appendix A. In general, a compound plug only redefines the *afterConnect* and *beforeDisconnect* functions. These functions are called after the basic connection has been made or just before it is broken. At this time the plug can use the connection to make or break additional connections using the basic connection. The additional connections are made using plugs/sockets available to the base class and matching sockets/plugs found at the other end.

The following example shows how to define a basic compound plug. The plugs involved in the compound connection are protected and cannot be used by any other part of the program except the plug at the other end of the connection. This access is provided by making the base class a *friend* of the other class, thereby granting access to *protected* variables.

```
// ====  Some Simple Plug Definitions  ====

DECLARE_CONNECTION
  ( SampleConnection1
  , Plug1
  , Socket1
  )

class Plug1 : public SampleConnection1::plug
{
  public:
    DECLARE_PLUG ()
} ;

class Socket1 : public SampleConnection1::socket
```

```
{
  public:
    DECLARE_PLUG ()
} ;


DECLARE_CONNECTION
  ( SampleConnection2
  , Plug2
  , Socket2
  )

class Plug2 : public SampleConnection2::plug
{
  public:
    DECLARE_PLUG ()
} ;

class Socket2 : public SampleConnection2::socket
{
  public:
    DECLARE_PLUG ()
} ;


// ====  Our Compound Plug Definition  ====

DECLARE_CONNECTION
  ( Compound1
  , CompoundPlug1
  , CompoundSocket1
  )

class CompoundSocket1 : Compound1::socket
{
  public:
    DECLARE_PLUG ()

    // public members go here
```

```
    protected:
      friend CompoundPlugBase1 ;
      Socket1 socket1 ;
      Socket2 socket2 ;
} ;


class CompoundPlug1 : public Compound1::plug
{
  public:
    DECLARE_PLUG ()

    // public members go here

  protected:
    Plug1 plug1 ;
    Plug2 plug2 ;

    void afterConnect ( CompoundSocketBase1 * pOther )
    {
      plug1 <= ( pOther -> socket1 ) ;
      plug2 <= ( pOther -> socket2 ) ;
    }

    void beforeDisconnect ( CompoundSocketBase1 * )
    {
    -- plug1 ;
    -- plug2 ;
    }
} ;
```

This example is a single-sided connection with fully accessible plugs. The single-sided nature comes from having one side of the compound plug performing both the connection and disconnection operations; the other side does nothing. This approach clearly shows what connections are to be made and which side makes them. However, this may not always be desirable. A number of other options are available including letting both sides unconditionally make and break connections, as well as conditionally performing these operations. Keep in mind that although all connections do not have to be made when the initial basic connection is made, all connections should be broken when the basic connection is broken.

This next example shows how internal connection maintenance can be split between the plugs. The example uses the basic plug definitions defined in the previous example.

```
DECLARE_CONNECTION
  ( Compound2
  , CompoundPlug2
  , CompoundSocket2
  )

class CompoundPlug2 : public Compound2::plug
{
  public:
    DECLARE_PLUG ()

    // public members go here

  protected:
    Plug1 plug1 ;
    Plug2 plug2 ;

    void afterConnect ( otherPlug * pOther ) ;
    void beforeDisconnect ( CompoundSocketBase2 * )
    {
    -- plug1 ;
    -- plug2 ;
    }
} ;

class CompoundSocket2 : public Compound2::socket
{
  public:
    DECLARE_PLUG ()
```

```
    // public members go here

protected:
  friend CompoundPlug2 ;
  Socket1 socket1 ;
  Socket2 socket2 ;

  void afterConnect ( otherPlug * ) ;
  void beforeDisconnect ( otherPlug * )
  {
    -- socket1 ;
    -- socket2 ;
  }
} ;


// ==== Function definitions normally found in a .CPP file  ====

void CompoundPlugBase2::afterConnect ( otherPlug * pOther )
{
  plug1 <= ( pOther -> socket1 ) ;
}

void CompoundSocketBase2::afterConnect ( otherPlug * pOther )
{
  socket2 <= ( pOther ->  plug2 ) ;
}
```

The differences between this example and the prior one are that here, both plugs do something in the *afterConnect* function and both sides disconnect their own plugs. The latter is redundant, but it will cause no problems because disconnecting a disconnected plug does nothing. One reason for splitting the connection operation to the corresponding sides is to implement a conditional connection procedure where it is easier to determine what connections are to be made based upon information available in a particular plug.

As mentioned, you can also implement a compound plug using the conventional plug definition macros. The base classes contain the plugs to be connected by the compound plug *afterConnect* function, but the actual work is done by classes that use the plug class as a superclass. This allows the actual connection work to be hidden, which is desirable, but it also leads to a problem. The plugs to be used by the compound connection must be available to the *afterConnect* function. They can be public or protected members of the base class. In the previous example the members were protected but the base classes were friend classes. This prevented inadvertent access when you use the plug, but allowed access when implementing it.

Unfortunately, friend status is not inherited, so making the base class members in the compound connection protected will prevent the subclass from accessing them. That's undesirable. On the other hand, making the members public allows unrestricted access, which is also undesirable. Documentation and comments can be used to caution about proper use if the members are public, but there is a way to avoid the whole problem. The following example shows how to gain access to protected members of another base class:

```
DECLARE_CONNECTION
  ( CompoundConnect3
  , PPlug
  , PSocket
  )

class PPlug : public CompoundConnect3::plug
{
  public:
    DECLARE_PLUG ()

  protected:
    int i ;
} ;

class PSocket : public CompoundConnect3::socket
{
  public:
```

```
        DECLARE_PLUG ()
   } ;


class MyPSocket ;

class MyPPlug : public PPlug
{
   friend MyPSocket ;
} ;

class MyPSocket : public PSocket
{
   public:
     void Sample ()

        ((MyPPlug *) pOther ) -> i = 1 ;

   } ;
```

A *friend* class for class X cannot be defined after X has been defined. The trick here is to define another class, *MyPPlug*. This class is based upon *PPlug*, which is based on *BaseClass* making *MyPSocket* a friend of *MyPPlug*, which gives it access to the protected members of *BaseClass*.

Now take a look at how to implement a more generic form of compound plugs. For simplicity in the following examples the compound connection plugs will be defined as public members, although they will be distinct from public members available for using with the compound plug. Replace the public statement for the compound connection members with protected and use the technique previously shown to gain access to them. Here are the class definitions:

```
// just something to work with
DECLARE_CONNECTION
   ( DummyConnection
   , Plug1
   , Socket1
   )
```

```
class Plug1 : public DummyConnection::plug
{
  public:
    DECLARE_PLUG ()
} ;


class Socket1 : public DummyConnection::socket
{
  public:
    DECLARE_PLUG ()
} ;



// ====  Compound Plug Definition  ====

DECLARE_CONNECTION
  ( CPlugConnection
  , CPlug
  , CSocket
  )

class CPlug : public CPlugConnection::plug
{
  public:
    DECLARE_PLUG ()

    // generally available members defined here

  public: // may be replaced with protected:
    Plug1::myEnd & plug1a () =  0 ;
    Plug1::myEnd & plug1b () =  0 ;
    // connected by CSocket to hidden socket
    Socket1::myEnd & socket1 () =  0 ;
} ;

class CSocket : public CPlugConnection::socket
{
  public:
    DECLARE_PLUG ()
```

```
      // generally available members defined here

    public: // may be replaced with protected:
      Plug1::myEnd & plug1 () = 0 ;
      // connected by CPlug to socket1
      Socket1::myEnd & socket1 () = 0 ;
      // connected by CPlug to plug1
  } ;



// ====  Implementation Definition  ====

class CPlugImplementation : public CPlug
{
  protected:
    Plug1 myPlug1a ;
    Plug1 myPlug1b ;
    Socket1 mySocket1 ;

  public:
    Plug1::myEnd & plug1a () { return myPlug1a ; }
    Plug1::myEnd & plug1b () { return myPlug1b ; }
    Socket1::myEnd & socket1 () { return mySocket1 ; }

    void afterConnect ( otherPlug * pOther )
    {
      plug1a <= pOther -> Socket1 () ;
      socket1 <= pOther -> Plug1 () ;
    }

    void beforeDisconnect ( otherPlug * )
    {
      -- myPlug1a ;
      -- myPlug1b ;
      -- mySocket1 ;
    }
  } ;

class CSocketImplementation : public CSocket
```

```
{
  public:
    CSocketImplementation ()
      {
        pPlug1 = & myPlug1 ;
        pSocket1 = & mySocket1a ;
      }

    Plug1::myEnd & plug1 () { return myPlug1 ; }
    Socket1::myEnd & socket1 () { return mySocket1a ; }

  protected:
    Plug1 myPlug1 ;
    Socket1 mySocket1a ;
    Socket1 mySocket1b ;

    void afterConnect ( otherPlug * pOther )
    {
      mySocket1b <= pOther -> plug1b () ;
    }

    void beforeDisconnect ( otherPlug * )
    {
      -- myPlug1 ;
      -- mySocket1a ;
      -- mySocket1b ;
    }
} ;
```

This example keeps the compound connection variables in a separate *public:* area. As mentioned earlier, this can be changed to *protected:* if you make corresponding adjustments to the code. Both the plug and socket are subclassed, although this is not a requirement of this approach. It is possible to have one side define all of the public plugs for one side of a compound connection defined, which requires the other side to perform the initial connection work in its *afterConnect* function. It is also possible that both sides will have public plugs that can be connected, but it should be indicated which side should initiate a particular connection. There may also be a mix of these two configurations. The example shows this type of mix.

The *CPlug* has three accessible plugs (one is named *socket1* but all are considered plugs). The plugs are all accessible as the results of pure virtual functions. This allows the plugs to be defined by subclasses instead of requiring them to be defined in *CPlug*. Note that the function return type is *Plug1::myEnd&* and *Socket1::myEnd&* instead of just *Plug1&* and *Socket1&*. The distinction makes little difference in our implementation, but it can make a difference in other implementations. *Plug1::myEnd &* can be a reference to either a plug or redirector while *Plug1 &* can only refer to a plug. Our example only uses plugs (and sockets), but a different implementation might use a redirector that points to a socket.

CPlug subclasses, such as *CPlugImplementation*, must initiate the connections of two of their public plugs, *plug1a* and *socket1*; although there are no comments in the example to indicate it. Comments should be added, or separate documentation must be supplied, for anyone building a subclass of these plugs. The comments and this type of documentation are not necessary if you are simply using the plugs, but some sort of documentation regarding the use of a plug class must be supplied in some form. A similar thing is done by the *CSocket* subclass, *CSocketImplementation*. However, in this case, the plug at the connection end, *mySocket1b*, is hidden from any access through the connection.

In this example, both sides perform a complete disconnect of all their plugs in their respective *beforeDisconnect* functions. A clean disconnect may also cause the plug to be deleted if it happens to be a dynamic plug.

The *CSocket* class also uses members that are pure virtual functions and return references to plugs. This allows the subclass to determine where the plug will actually be allocated. In this example, the plugs are still part of the overall compound object, but they could be dynamic plugs or parts of other components. Using pointers also makes it possible to assign values when the plug is constructed. Use redirectors if you need to use references. You can then assign to the redirector a pointer to a plug.

C++ conversion functions to be included in a class definition. The conversion functions are checked when an object of the class cannot be used in an expression. Only one conversion function can be selected or the compiler signals an error. The following definition includes a conversion function. The addition of the conversion function allows objects of this class to be connected to two different socket types.

```
class CPlugDuo : public CPlugImplementation
{
  protected:
    Plug1 myPlug1a ;
    Plug1 myPlug1b ;
    Socket1 mySocket1 ;

  public:
    operator Plug1 & () { return myPlug1a ; }
} ;
```

An object of this type is normally connected to a *CSocket* object. The addition of the conversion function allows a *CPlugDuo* object to be connected to a *Socket1* object. This can lead to very flexible plugs that can connect to a number of different socket types. Unfortunately, some problems may crop up. A function invocation cannot be ambiguous or the compiler will flag it as an error. Some plug connection functions will cause this type of problem with objects from this class because the compiler cannot determine the proper function to use. For example:

```
CSocket1 aSocket ;
CPlugDuo aPlugDuo ;

aSocket <= aPlugDuo ;
- aPlugDuo ;
```

The connection operation has no problems because the *Plug1* portion of *aPlug-Duo* can be connected to *aSocket* while the *CPlug* version cannot. Unfortunately, the disconnect operator will be the *CPlug* version. This will not be a problem if it breaks the connection made to the *Plug1* version, but it may not. Be careful if you do use conversion operators; they allow a plug to be more flexible but they can lead to some confusing results. For example, the *CPlug-Duo* class does not redefine functions such as *connected*. The result of the function with *aPlugDuo* will be *FALSE*, even after it is connected to aSocket, because its *connected* function checks the compound plug connection, not the internal connection made by the connection operation. Redefining the *connected* function to check internal connections is required for proper operation. The result should be *TRUE* if any of the connections are in place.

Compound plugs are as easy to define as normal plugs. The only major additions are redefinitions of the *afterConnect* and *beforeDisconnect* functions. Proper design of the base compound plug classes as abstract classes allows a variety of implementations to be built, just as with simple plugs. The great thing is that from the connection level, compound plugs work just like simple plugs. You only need to know the difference if you are building a new compound connection or subclassing an existing one.

The examples presented in this section make and break the same internal connections when a compound plug is connected or disconnected; however, this is not a requirement. A plug can make some connections and not others, depending upon plug-specific conditions. It is also possible to make and break internal connections while the compound plug connection is in force. This type of operation is application specific. The general rule for compound plugs is that new connections can be made after a compound plug is connected to a matching socket, and all connections should be broken when the compound plug is disconnected. No new connections should be made after the disconnect operation.

Standard Components: Filters and Tees

Components come in all shapes and sizes, but there are a number of component structures that lend themselves to standard implementations. Figure 7-6
shows the structure of some standard components discussed in this section. Filters are one of the most common types of standard components. They have the
same type of connection on both sides. The following is a basic filter definition:

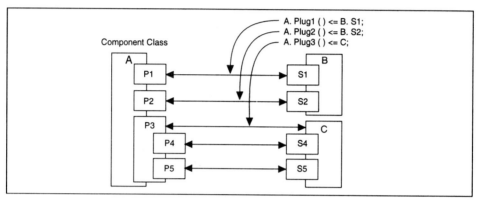

Figure 7-6. Component containing compound plug

```
class ConnectionFilter
{
  public:
    virtual Connection::plugA & Plug () = 0 ;
    virtual Connection::socketA & Socket () = 0 ;
} ;
```

This type of definition requires a subclass to implement the filter but allows
a number of subclass definitions. The use of *Connection::plugA&* and *Connection::socketA&* allows any kind of Connection plug or redirector to be
used in the implementation. A macro or template definition can be used to
easily define standard component abstract classes like this. For example:

```
// —- A macro version —

#define DECLARE_PLUG_FILTER(c,t)\
```

```
class c\
{\
  public:\
    virtual t::plugA & Plug () = 0 ;\
    virtual t::socketA & Socket () = 0 ;\
} ;

// example: DECLARE_PLUG_FILTER ( ConnectionFilter, Connection )

// — A template version —

template <class t>
class PlugFilter
{
  public:
    virtual t::plugA & Plug () = 0 ;\
    virtual t::socketA & Socket () = 0 ;\
} ;
// example: class ConnectionFilter : public PlugFilter < Connection
> {} ;
```

Filters are normally used to augment a connection by interposing the filter between a plug and socket that may already be connected. This can be done easily using the *addBefore* and *addAfter* plug protocol functions. The next example assumes that a set of classes is defined to implement the necessary compatible plug, socket, and filter objects. The *addAfter* function is used to insert the filter between an already connected plug and socket. The code looks like this:

```
// —- Some Connection subclass plugs —

Plug1 plug1 ;
Socket1 socket1 ;

Filter1 filter1 ;

plug1 <= socket1 ;              // make an initial connection
```

```
plug1.addAfter ( & filter1.Socket (), & filter1.Plug ()) ;
                    // insert filter
```

Note that *addAfter* requires pointers to its parameters; hence the use of the *&* operator. The operation of a filter is implementation specific, but normally information is passed from one side of the filter to the other, possibly with some modification of any data. The type of operations that can be performed depend on the connection definition. The simplest case is a filter that passes all function calls from one side to the other.

Filters are just one type of standard component. An adapter is simply a filter with a different connection type on each end. It is even possible to have plugs or sockets at either end. A filter tee is normally based on a filter class; it adds a third plug, which is usually different from the other two. A filter tee class definition looks like this:

```
class PlugFilterTee : public PlugFilter
{
  public:
    virtual AnotherConnection::plugA & TeePlug () = 0 ;
} ;
```

This type of definition also allows a subclass to be used where a *PlugFilter* is used. Filter tee components are often used for debugging, but general filter tee components can be defined. As with filters, the type and use of filter tee components is connection dependent.

Standard components are best defined like compound plugs; they should use pure virtual functions. These abstract classes can then be used to build inter-changeable subclasses.

Where to Use Components and Compound Plugs

Frequently, design and implementation are combined interactive processes. A compound plug is often initially designed as a component. Converting a component into a compound plug requires the addition of a connection definition and a matching socket class definition.

Components should be used when public portions of the component are available for general and possibly independent use. A component may have a number of public plugs and functions that must be used with a specified protocol. For example, a component may require that certain connections be made to its public plugs before certain functions can be used. In general, a component is viewed as a collection of plugs and functions.

On the other hand, compound plugs are viewed as a single item when used. Internally a compound plug is a component, but only an implementer need know about its construction. Someone using a compound plug only sees a plug. It can be connected and disconnected with a matching socket using the plug protocol functions and each may have additional functions defined, but the internal parts are hidden.

Connections to a component's plugs can be made at any time. A component may have a specified protocol but the connections are made explicitly. A compound plug must make its internal connections when it is connected, and internal connections are broken when the compound plug's connection is broken. That's the way the protocol works.

Can component and compound plug design be merged? Yes, but be careful. Making portions of a compound plug public can cause problems if internal connections can be manipulated independently of the compound plug connection.

This chapter has presented implementation and design particulars for components and compound plugs. In the next chapter you'll see how to design software using what you now know.

8 Dynamic Plugs

Dynamic plugs are allocated from the heap and automatically free themselves when all references to them are removed. The latter characteristic is what makes dynamic plugs especially useful. It's possible to manually allocate plugs from the heap; the manual allocation and deallocation of plugs from the heap does not make them dynamic. But dynamic plugs also automatically free themselves when all references to them are removed and, as a result, they tend to be easier to use.

Figure 8-1 shows the basics of how a dynamic plug works. A dynamic plug class usually includes a *static New* function that hides the C++ *new* function used to allocate an object from free space. The *New* function does the same thing, but sets up the plug object so it knows that it is a dynamic plug. The *New* function returns a pointer to the newly created object. This pointer is used to make a connection with a matching socket. The connection is broken when it is no longer needed. This may be done using the socket, or one of the internal protocol functions may break the connection. In any case, the dynamic plug deletes itself when the connection is broken. The original pointer will be invalid if it still exists. Normally the pointer is used only to make the initial connection.

The reason for using dynamic plugs becomes more apparent when you consider a program that includes a large number of components and connections. Keeping track manually of when to deallocate components can be a daunting task. Dynamic plugs make the job easier by performing the cleanup operations.

Dynamic plugs are not part of the basic plug definition; so how are they created? This is how it works. First, a set of dynamic plugs is allocated and connected together. This compound component is then connected to other plugs.

The compound component and all its parts are automatically deleted when the appropriate connections have been deleted.

This chapter starts out by defining a basic dynamic plug and addresses various trade-offs for different designs. The next section discusses how redirectors can be used with dynamic plugs and how they can be used to create dynamic components. Then a common type of dynamic plug, called a *generator*, is presented. Generator plugs normally do not get connected but are involved in creating a connection. A generator plug creates a new dynamic

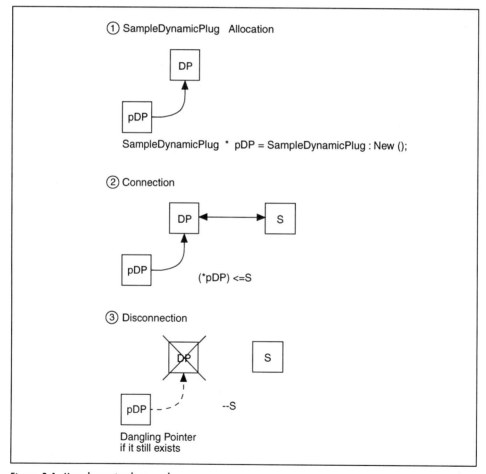

Figure 8-1. How dynamic plugs work

plug of the same connection type when a connection is attempted with the generator plug. The connection is then completed using the dynamic plug. The operation and use of generator plugs and their dynamic plug siblings are covered in detail. The final section, on dynamic components, combines the design methodology in the initial sections to present ways of building complex dynamic components.

Defining a Dynamic Plug

Dynamic plug support makes use of the *disconnectedFree* function included in each plug class declaration. The default definition does nothing, but a dynamic plug can use this function to deallocate itself.

Let's take a look at a simple dynamic plug to see how it works. The following definition assumes that the plug and socket will always be dynamically allocated.

```
DECLARE_CONNECTION
  ( DynamicSample
  , DynamicSamplePlug
  , DynamicSampleSocket
  )

class DynamicSamplePlug : public DynamicSample::plug
{
  protected:
    void * operator new ( size_t x )
    {
       return ::new char [ x ] ;
    }
    DynamicSamplePlug () {}

  public:
    void disconnectedFree (otherEnd*oldEnd)
    {
      delete this ;
    }

    static DynamicSamplePlug * New ()
```

```
        {
            return new DynamicSamplePlug ;
        }
    } ;

    class DynamicSampleSocket : public DynamicSample::socket
    {
      protected:
        void * operator new ( size_t x )
        {
            return ::new char [ x ] ;
        }
        DynamicSampleSocket () {}

      public:
        void disconnectedFree (otherEnd*oldEnd)
        {
          delete this ;
        }

        static DynamicSampleSocket * New ()
        {
          return new DynamicSampleSocket ;
        }
    } ;
```

There are a number of things defined in this example. First, dynamic allocation must be done using *DynamicSamplePlug::New* () instead of *new DynamicSamplePlug*. This is significant because the constructor function has been hidden. The *New* function is the only way to create an instance of this object. The *new* function is hidden by making it a protected member. The *disconnectedFree* function is defined to return the object's space to free space using the delete function. The *disconnectedFree* function is called only after the connection is broken using the -- operator. The *DynamicSampleSocket* definition is identical to the plug definition.

The problem with this type of definition is that the plug can only be used as a dynamic plug. There are a number of alternatives to this design. One is to make the base connection define a set of non-dynamic classes and then define dynamic subclasses. This approach presents a problem as well because you now have two sets of classes to contend with, which becomes difficult to manage if you need to subclass these classes. Another approach using redirectors will be discussed in the next section; the approach covered here is shown in Figure 8-2.

This case is very simple. The plug has only one connection, as in the previous example. The plug deletes itself when the single connection is broken, but only if the *bDynamic* variable is *TRUE*. The dynamic plug can be used as a

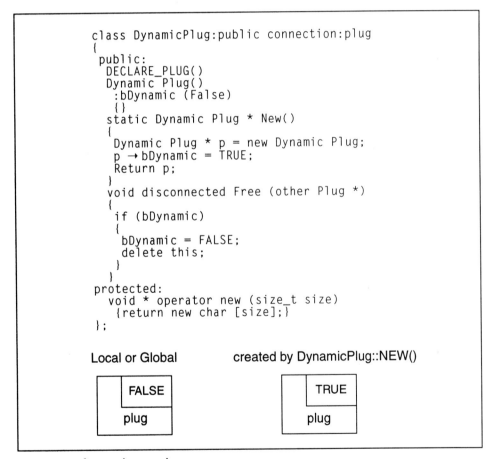

Figure 8-2. Defining a dynamic plug

normal plug too. The *bDynamic* variable will be set appropriately so it will not be deleted by a disconnection.

Actually, *new* can be made public if used properly. However, *new* does not create a dynamic plug. Instead, it creates a normal plug from the heap, which must be manually deleted using delete. This requirement is why dynamic plugs normally hide *new*. Otherwise, you might accidentally create a plug using *new* and assume it is a dynamic plug when it is not. Dynamic plug support is not included as part of the basic plug definition macro because it adds overhead that may not be necessary. Also, there is more than one way to implement dynamic plugs.

The only additional space required by the dynamic plug defined here is a boolean value. The *New* function must be used because the normal constructor is used regardless of whether the plug is created using *new* or not. The constructor initializes the *bDynamic* variable to *FALSE,* which prevents the object from being freed by *disconnectedFree.* The *New* function sets the variable to *TRUE* after the constructor sets it to *FALSE.* The same thing could have been tried in the *new* function, but *new* is called before the constructor, not afterward. Just in case you are wondering, the *new* function is called with a single parameter that is the size of the object in bytes. Returning a character array of the same size accomplishes the goal.

The approach presented in this section is applicable to simple plugs. The same approach can be extended to plugs used in dynamic components, but there are better ways to address dynamic component definition. It is also possible to use redirectors to create dynamic components, as mentioned earlier. The next section shows how redirectors can be used to do this, as well as how dynamic plugs can be created without using the intrinsic dynamic plug support in the examples in this section. There are trade-offs, however. The approach presented in this section is the most efficient in terms of space. The one presented next is more flexible but utilizes more space.

Dynamic Plugs and Redirectors

Another way to create a dynamic plug is to use redirectors. Figure 8-3 shows how a dynamic plug that was defined using the approach in the previous section works. Figure 8-4 shows how to do it using redirectors. There are really two differences between Figures 8-3 and 8-4. The first and most obvious is the addition of the redirector. The second is that the plug in Figure 8-4 is not a dynamic plug itself but rather a normal plug allocated from free space, which then has a special dynamic redirector associated with it. The dynamic redirector tracks the plug's operation and deletes the plug and then itself when the plug's connection is permanently broken using the -- operator.

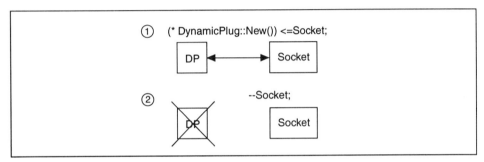

Figure 8-3. Dynamic plugs without redirectors

Two advantages the dynamic redirector has over implementing a special plug are that the requirement to imbed any special support in the plug class is eliminated and the redirector mechanism is the same one used to construct dynamic components.

Redirectors participate in any connection operations associated with the plug they redirect. They pass initial request function calls like the connection operator, <=, up to the plug they redirect. The requesters also receive status function calls from the plug as a connection is made or broken. This includes the *disconnectedFree* and *connectFailed* functions normally used to free a dynamic plug. A dynamic redirector deletes the plug and then itself when it receives either of these function calls. Therefore, it is very important to use only one dynamic redirector with a plug, since all redirectors in a redirector chain will receive the status messages, but a plug must only be deleted once. This is not to say that a dynamic redirector and plug cannot be part of a large redirector chain; only that at most, one of the redirectors in a chain can be a dynamic redirector associated with a particular plug. In fact, it is quite possible to have multiple dynamic redirectors in a single redirector chain to redirect a single plug, but each dynamic redirector is responsible for deleting its own unique plug. This type of configuration is possible using the *addBefore* function, which readjusts the redirector chains. The redirectors accumulate to the last plug if a number of *addBefore* function calls are made.

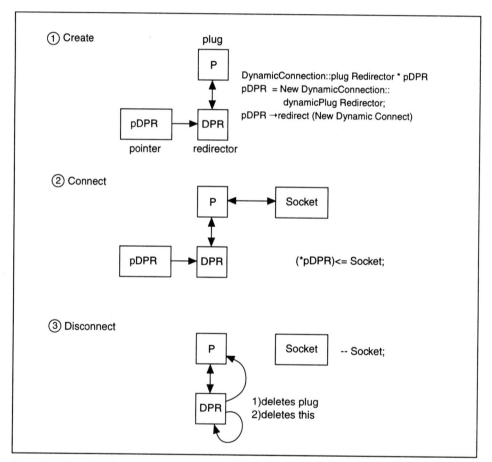

Figure 8-4. Dynamic plugs with redirectors

A dynamic redirector can only be created from free space. This is done by making the constructor protected and including a static *New* function that can access it. The *New* function takes one parameter: a pointer to a plug. The pointer should be obtained by allocating the plug using the *new* function. For example:

```
( SampleConnection::dynamicRedirectorPlug::New
  ( new SampleConnectionPlug ))
  <= ( SampleConnection::dynamicRedirectorSocket::New
        ( new SampleConnectionSocket )) ;
```

This allocates two dynamic plugs and connects them together. Note that the dynamic redirector classes are part of the main connection class while the plug and socket classes can be any subclass. This allows a single dynamic redirector class to support dynamic plugs for a host of different plug classes.

Although the dynamic redirector classes are not abstract classes, it is not possible to create an instance of the class except by using the *New* function. This is due to the fact that the constructor is protected. This is done on purpose because the redirector code always assumes that the object is allocated from free space and deletes itself when its plug is no longer in use.

The *dynamicRedirectorPlug* and *dynamicRedirectorSocket* classes are included with all connection class definitions, just like the normal *redirectorPlug* and *redirectorSocket* classes. The only difference between the two is in the *disconnectedFree* and *connectFailed* function operations. The normal redirector does nothing. The dynamic redirector deletes the plug initially associated with it and then itself.

There is one minor problem with this approach to using dynamic redirectors. The *addBefore* function will change which plug a redirector redirects. This means that the connection it is redirecting will not be the plug it is tracking but another plug. But it's not quite as bad as it sounds. The original plug will still be tracked and deleted when the connection to the new plug is broken. In general, this is what is desired since the connection to the new plug is logically connected to the original, and the original will not be needed when the connection is broken. One way to get around this problem is to redefine the *addBefore* function for the redirector. It is called after the connections are redone. The function can then use the redirector's pointer to the plug to change which plug it redirects.

Generator Plugs

Generator plugs are a special use of dynamic plugs. Figures 8-5 and 8-6 show two examples of generator plugs. Figure 8-6 shows a generator that tracks its children, while the one in Figure 8-5 does not. The children in both figures are dynamic plugs. References to the generator plug may be used to initiate a connection, but the generator plug will never be connected to another plug (that is, a matching socket). Instead, the generator plug lets another plug, which is a subclass of the same connection, be used to complete the connection. This new plug is often a dynamic plug, although it does not have to be, as noted at the end of this section. The dynamic plug is now connected with a socket and the generator is available for another connection. This can occur again and again with new plugs being created as necessary. The generator may track the plugs for a variety of reasons, including keeping the numbers below a partic-

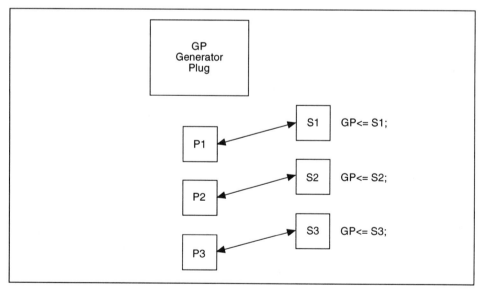

Figure 8-5. Dynamic plugs and generators

ular limit or to allow the siblings to communicate with themselves or with the generator plug, which is an ideal place to keep common information.

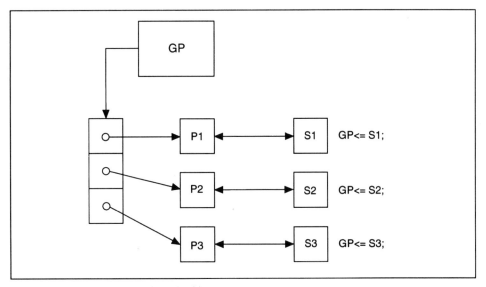

Figure 8-6. Dynamic plugs which track siblings

Defining a generator plug is not difficult if you don't track the objects you create. The following example shows how to define a generator that uses the dynamic plugs as its offspring. The generator plug does not track its children and the children do not track their siblings or parent. A list or array can be used to track the children from the parent by keeping a pointer to the plug when it is created. It is best to include a reference in the child to the generator plug so it can remove its reference within the list before the plug is deleted.

```
// — Class definition —

DECLARE_CONNECTION
    ( BasicConnection
    , BasicPlug
    , BasicSocket
    )
```

```
// — Basic plug class definitions —-

class BasicPlug : public BasicConnection::plug
{
  public:
    DECLARE_PLUG ()
} ;


class BasicSocket : public BasicConnection::socket
{
  public:
    DECLARE_PLUG ()
} ;

// — Plug Generator class definition —-

class BasicPlugGenerator : public BasicConnection::plug
{
  public:
    DECLARE_PLUG ()

    myEnd & getEnd ()
    {
      return * BasicConnection::dynamicPlugRedirector::New
                         ( new BasicPlug ) ;
    }
} ;
```

Note that the *BasicPlugGenerator* class is a subclass of *BasicConnection::plug* instead of *BasicPlug*. This means that the generator class need only include the functions required for the plug protocol support and not any extra functions associated with the *BasicPlug* class. Only a *BasicConnection::plug* generator is shown. A similar class for the socket side can be defined if necessary.

The generator only redefines the *getEnd* function. This function is called by the <= operator to obtain a new plug to connect to. The function here creates a new plug and passes a pointer to a newly created dynamic plug redirector. The latter makes the plug dynamic and handles deleting it when it is no longer needed. The reference to the dynamic plug is the one returned. The reference to the new plug will be obtained by a subsequent call to *getPlug* by the <= operator. The generator's *getEnd* function is where any tracking support would be included.

A more generic plug generator class can be constructed by adding a pointer to a creation function and using this instead of explicitly calling *new BasicPlug*. Likewise, the *dynamicPlugRedirector* can be subclassed. This class would create objects that included a pointer back to the generator plug. The pointer would be supplied to the redirector's constructor, which would save it as part of the redirector. The *disconnectedFree* function also needs to be redefined to remove the pointer to the redirector from the generator's tracking list before it calls the superclass *disconnectedFree* function, which deletes the plug and the redirector object.

Although this section describes generator plugs that can be dynamic and child plugs that are dynamic, this is not a requirement. It is possible to have generators that make connections from a fixed pool of objects that are part of the dynamic plug or from some other static structure or dynamic structure that is maintained using techniques other than dynamic plugs. The type of support required will be application specific, but the options are there for the choosing.

Dynamic Components

Dynamic components are a bit more complex than dynamic plugs, but the way you construct them is almost exactly the same. The main difference between a dynamic plug and a dynamic component is that a plug will delete itself when its only connection is broken. A component has more than one plug, and a dynamic plug may delete itself before all connections are broken by outside sources. A dynamic component may track some or all of its public or internal plugs depending upon the application. This section shows how these plugs can be tracked and how a dynamic component operates.

There are two alternatives to defining a dynamic component. The first uses multiple inheritance with a component class definition that includes the plugs that are to be tracked. The *disconnectedFree* function for each superclass is defined in the component class definition. These are distinguished by their parameter types, which are different for each plug, assuming a particular plug type is not replicated in the list of plugs to be tracked. The second alternative must be used if multiple plugs of the same type must be tracked by the dynamic component. The *disconnectedFree* functions must each check the status of the component and determine if it is to be deleted. Deleting the function normally causes all of the connections to it to be broken, assuming all of its plugs are defined within the object. Explicit deallocations must be done for any dynamically allocated resources used by the component, including plugs.

The second design alternative utilizes redirectors and a special aspect of redirectors. Each redirector can point to a *RedirectorNotify* object. The class definition is as follows:

```
class RedirectorNotify
{
  public
    virtual void connectFailed ( Plug * ) {}
    virtual void disconnected ( Plug * ) {}
    virtual void disconnectedFree ( Plug * ) {}
    virtual void afterConnect ( Plug * ) {}
    virtual void beforeDisconnect ( Plug * ) {}
};
```

A redirector will call the corresponding function of the *RedirectorNotify* object when the redirector's function is called. More than one redirector can refer to a notification object because, unlike the plug functions, the notification object functions do not contain parameters that are connection specific. Every plug is a subclass of *Plug* so the plug involved in the operation can be identified. Normally the notification functions will poll each plug and determine the appropriate action.

Figure 8-7 shows a component constructed with redirectors. The component class is based on *RedirectorNotify,* which allows the *disconnectedFree* function to be redefined. Three redirectors, of different connection classes, are used to track the three plugs included with the component object. This approach results in a class that looks like this:

```
class SampleDynamicComponent1 : public RedirectorNotify
{
    public:
      Connection1Plug plug1 ;
      Connection2Plug plug2 ;
      Connection3Plug plug3 ;
```

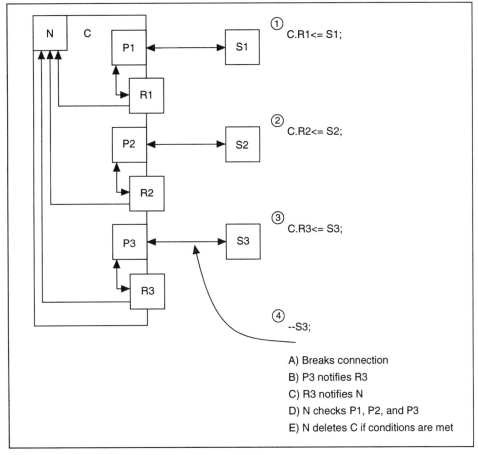

Figure 8-7. Dynamic component with redirectors

```
        SampleDynamicComponent1 ()
        {
          redirector1.redirect ( plug1 ) ;
          redirector2.redirect ( plug2 ) ;
          redirector3.redirect ( plug3 ) ;

          redirector1.setNotify ( this ) ;
          redirector2.setNotify ( this ) ;
          redirector3.setNotify ( this ) ;
        }

      protected:
        Connection1::redirector redirector1 ;
        Connection2::redirector redirector2 ;
        Connection3::redirector redirector3 ;

        void disconnectedFree ( Plug * )
        {
          if ((! plug1.connected ())
            && (! plug2.connected ())
            && (! plug3.connected ()))
          {
            delete this ;
          }
        }
    } ;
```

In this example, the main component deletes itself if all connections to its parts have been broken. This approach allows different types of tests to be performed as well as additional operations. For example, let's assume that only the first two connections are important. The new class definition looks like this:

```
    class SampleDynamicComponent2 : public RedirectorNotify
    {
      public:
        Connection1Plug plug1 ;
        Connection2Plug plug2 ;
        Connection3Plug plug3 ;
```

```
SampleDynamicComponent2 ()
{
    redirector1.redirect ( plug1 ) ;
    redirector2.redirect ( plug2 ) ;
    redirector3.redirect ( plug3 ) ;

    redirector1.setNotify ( this ) ;
    redirector2.setNotify ( this ) ;
    redirector3.setNotify ( this ) ;
}

protected:
    Connection1::redirector redirector1 ;
    Connection2::redirector redirector2 ;
    Connection3::redirector redirector3 ;

    void disconnectedFree ( Plug * )
    {
        if ((! plug1.isconnected ())
            && (! plug2.isconnected ()))
        {
            - plug3 ;
            delete this ;
        }
    }
} ;
```

Two changes have been made. The first is the removal of the connected check for *plug3* in *disconnectedFree*. The second is the addition of the disconnect operation in the same function. The first two plugs are already known to be disconnected. The disconnect operation forces the third plug to be disconnected, leaving no connections to the component; thereby allowing it to delete itself.

Dangling dynamic components are like dangling pointers; you don't want them in your program. A *dangling* dynamic component is one that is no longer needed but has not deleted itself because there are still sufficient connections to it. Figure 8-8 shows how a dangling dynamic component might remain after one of its connections is broken. The three remaining components are all dynamic and could free themselves, but two form a circular reference; therefore, the third does not delete itself. The way around this predicament is to define the overall construction as a component that includes its own set of redirectors. This component performs a higher level check of the connections when changes occur. In this case the designer would know to break down the constructed system when the single connection was broken. The components used in the construction would not be able to detect this situation. The use of a redirector to track this connection allows the support to operate without interfering with the operation of the connections and without subclassing the components used in the overall construction.

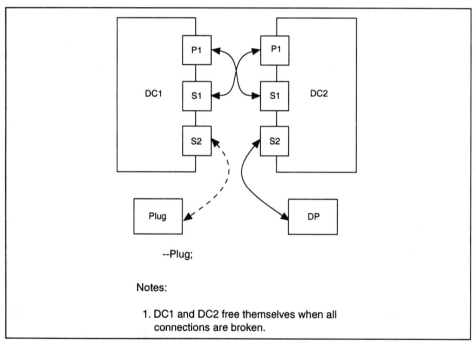

Figure 8-8. Dangling dynamic components

The techniques used to build and monitor dynamic plugs and components can also be used to monitor and debug. These techniques can be combined and enhanced to create larger components that are more powerful and flexible than the individual components.

Construction and Disassembly

Figure 8-9 shows how dynamic plugs and components, like those described in this chapter, can be used to build a larger system. The constructed component can be freestanding, or it might be part of a controlling component that includes redirectors to track the interior and exterior connections. The example in Figure 8-9 does not include redirectors. It depends solely on the operation of the internal components. Each component is dynamic and is freed under its own control. *Disconnecting plug P1* initiates the disassembly. Component *A* is only needed if both of its connections are intact. Component *B*, on the other hand, requires two of its connections to be broken before it goes away. This occurs when plug *P2* is disconnected from component *D*. Component *B* has only one remaining connection when *D* is gone. Component *C* goes away too, when its connection with *D* is gone. Luckily there are no dangling components.

The constructed component in Figure 8-9 does not exist except as the collection of its parts. Another possible configuration is to build an actual component with redirectors. This involves defining a class that can be used to allocate this type of object. This object tracks the other components using the redirectors, and it breaks an appropriate connection and deletes itself when no longer needed.

Another way to build a system of components like this is to build a general component that takes a list of redirectors. The general component would include or inherit from *RedirectorNotify*. A component function would link the redirectors to the general component. Additional functions would maintain two lists. One list contains plugs to be disconnected when all the plugs in the second list are disconnected. Notice how this would be possible because the -- disconnect operator and connected function are part of the *Plug* class from which all plugs are defined. The general component just proposed can therefore be very general, not just specific to a particular connection type.

279

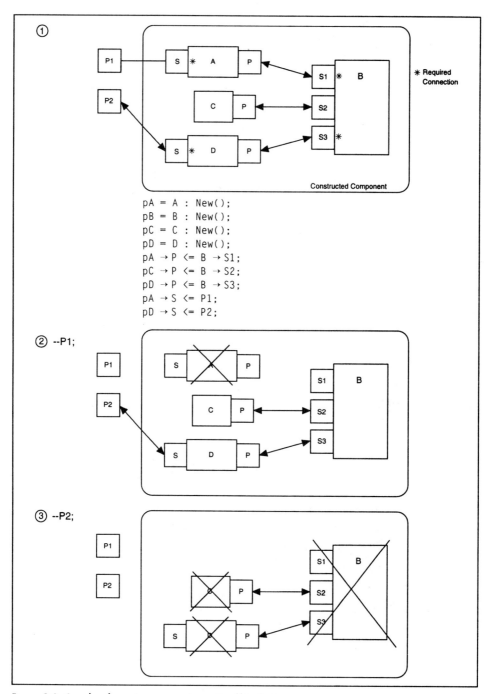

```
pA = A : New();
pB = B : New();
pC = C : New();
pD = D : New();
pA → P <= B → S1;
pC → P <= B → S2;
pD → P <= B → S3;
pA → S <= P1;
pD → S <= P2;
```

Figure 8-9. Complex dynamic component creation/dissolution

Summary

Dynamic plugs provide a way to build complex components that can dismantle themselves later. This advantage makes components easier to use because they can be built and given to another part of the program with the knowledge that they clean up after themselves. This cleanup can be more important than you might imagine.

Take a compound component built from other components, for instance. One aspect of this hypothetical design is the ability to access a component within the compound component. There also happens to be another component that you wish to use in its place. You use the standard plug operations to plug in the new component, which disconnects the old component. So where does the old one go? It stays around unconnected if it is not a dynamic plug, but it will free itself if it is a dynamic plug, assuming all its plugs have been appropriately disconnected.

The disadvantage is that dynamic plugs can be harder to design and implement. The simple examples already presented show the basic mechanism, but other issues present themselves as components become more complex. For example, circular linkages, such as feedback loops, can prevent a component from freeing itself because it still has a pair of connections. It may actually be one connection to a pair of its plugs, but the component will not be able to discern the difference between this situation and having a sequence of components connected between a pair of its plugs. Determining when to delete and disconnect is also important, and it is not always apparent when initially designing a component.

Overall, a well-designed dynamic plug can be a very valuable tool and well worth the trouble of implementing it accordingly.

9 Program Construction with Components

There are three basic techniques for constructing programs using components and plugs: *static, hierarchical,* and *dynamic.* These techniques can be combined, and most programs are a combination of techniques. This chapter describes these techniques and how you use plugs in *static, hierarchical,* and *dynamic* program construction. The last section of this chapter describes event-driven programming and its relationship to the three basic design techniques.

The focus here is on the mechanics of program construction. I will assume that the components used in the examples already exist, since the details of component construction have already been covered in earlier chapters of this book. I will not get into overall system design issues such as top-down versus bottom-up design. Any of these system design techniques can be applied to program construction using plugs.

For example, a top-down approach would start with a single large component, which would be broken down into small components with logical connections between them. Some of these components, in turn, would be broken down into additional collections of components. These design components and connections would then be implemented using program components and connections. This is where plugs come into play, and the software plugs and components should usually match the design components and connections in a one-to-one relationship.

A bottom-up approach would begin with the same type of logical design components and connections but start with a few components that would be connected. The system would grow as more components were added to the design.

Again, the plugs and components would then match the design connections and components.

In many cases the design components will simply be the available program components. This is especially true in a bottom-up design environment. The construction techniques addressed in this chapter deal with how the overall designs can be implemented. In many ways, this split between component design and system implementation is similar to the different tasks performed by an architect and an engineer or builder. Engineering is the focus here. Programmers and designers usually wind up being both architects and engineers, but this chapter only deals with the engineering or construction aspect.

The simplest technique is pure static construction. A structural diagram of static construction is shown in Figure 9-1. In this case, individual components are allocated at one time, usually as local variables, and connected together using their plugs. This structure remains intact while the program runs and is dismantled when the program terminates. Plug connections are automatically broken as each component is deleted. Static construction can be viewed as two-dimensional, with components placed on the plane and connected together much like a circuit board with its components. All components on the plane are deleted in one logical step when they are no longer needed. A three-dimensional view is required when the hierarchical technique is considered.

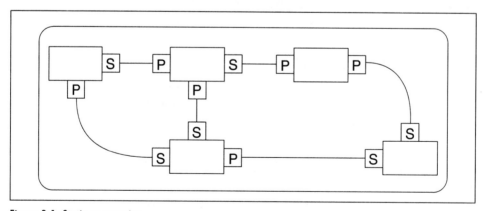

Figure 9-1. Static construction

The hierarchical technique, shown in Figure 9-2, builds on a statically constructed system by constructing layers of components. Each layer is constructed in a static fashion and the layers are then interconnected. Normally each layer is defined within a function as a set of local variables. The next layer is defined by calling a function, which in turn creates another layer of components, and the two can then be connected by the called function. The top layer goes away when the top function returns. The number and content of the layers changes as the program runs, but the base remains the same.

The dynamic technique utilizes dynamic components that automatically delete themselves when they are no longer needed, using a basic form of automatic

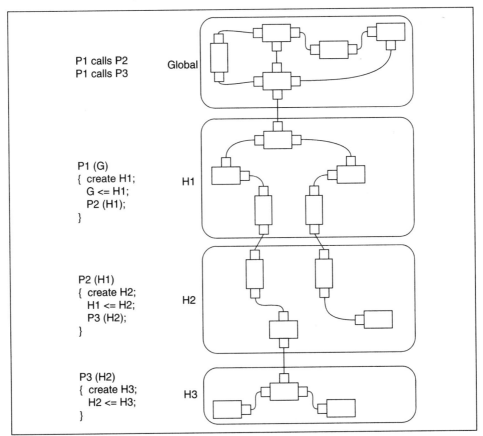

P1 calls P2
P1 calls P3   Global

P1 (G)
{ create H1;   H1
  G <= H1;
  P2 (H1);
}

P2 (H1)
{ create H2;   H2
  H1 <= H2;
  P3 (H2);
}

P3 (H2)
{ create H3;   H3
  H2 <= H3;
}

Figure 9-2. Hierarchical construction

garbage collection. Dynamic structures can also be created and maintained using explicit allocation and deallocation. Figure 9-3 shows how a particular structure is created through a number of procedure calls. Components are dynamically allocated from free space and connected with other components. References to dynamically allocated components, other than those used by the plug connections, may or may not be maintained by the program. Dynamic construction differs from static and hierarchical construction because the components and connections are not made at the same time. A portion of the overall system structure may be extended at a later time while another portion may be removed, either automatically or explicitly.

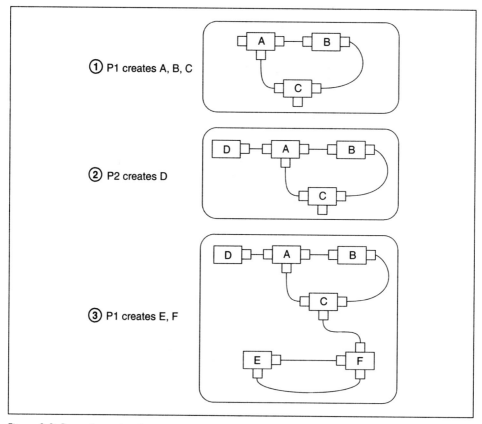

Figure 9-3. Dynamic construction

The following sections take a look at each construction technique in more detail and present the pros and cons associated with them. The examples include object definitions for components, plugs, and sockets. Component classes will be defined, but plug and socket classes will not. It is assumed that the appropriate base classes, plug declarations, and implementations are already done.

Static Construction

Static construction is the easiest construction method to implement and to understand. It has been used in most of the examples in previous chapters in this book. The idea is that all components are defined within the same scope: either global, local (within a function), or object (class-defined object variables). Connections can be made, changed, or broken arbitrarily as the program executes, but the components themselves are not continually being allocated and deallocated. All of the components and associated connections are deleted or broken when the associated scope is left. For global variables, this occurs when the program terminates. For local variables, this occurs when the function returns. For objects, this occurs when the object is deallocated. In particular, for global objects it is when the program terminates; for local objects it is when the function in which the object is defined returns; and for dynamically created objects it is when the object is freed using delete.

The following examples of global, local, and object-based static constructions use common plug definitions. These plug and component classes are used simply to show how static construction definitions look, so there is no additional explanation about what they do. The class and function names have been chosen to easily identify the relationship between the name and its associated object. For example, *PlugFunction1* is a function found in plug *Plug1*.

```
// ====  Connection1 connection definition  ====

DECLARE_CONNECTION
  ( Connection1
  , Plug1
  , Socket1
  )
```

```
class Plug1 : public Connection1::plug
{
  public:
    DECLARE_PLUG ()
    virtual void PlugFunction1 () {}
} ;

class Socket1 : public Connection1::socket
{
  public:
    DECLARE_PLUG ()
    virtual void SocketFunction1 () {}
} ;


// ====  Connection2 connection definition  ====

DECLARE_CONNECTION
  ( Connection2
  , Plug2
  , Socket2
  )

class Plug2 : public Connection2::plug
{
  public:
    DECLARE_PLUG ()
    virtual void PlugFunction2 () {}
} ;

class Socket2 : public Connection2::socket
{
  public:
    DECLARE_PLUG ()
    virtual void SocketFunction2 () {}
} ;
```

```
// ====   ComponentA Class Definition   ====

class ComponentA
{
  public:
    Plug1 plug1 ;
    Plug2 plug2 ;
    Socket2 socket2 ;

    void StartA ()
    {
      plug1.PlugFunction1 () ;
      plug2.PlugFunction2 () ;
      socket2.SocketFunction2 () ;
    }
} ;

class ComponentB
{
  public:
    Plug1 plug1 ;
    Socket1 socket1 ;
} ;

class ComponentC
{
  public:
    Socket1 socket1 ;
    Socket2 socket2 ;
} ;
```

A global definition using these plugs and components also requires a function definition to make connections. The *main* function is used for this purpose, but it could be any function in the program as long as it is called before the constructed system is used. The global example is structurally identical to the local and object definition examples. One instance of each component and a plug component (*plug2*) is declared. These components are then connected together and the *StartA* function is called which, in a real program, would set the program in motion to use the connections already in place. The lifetime of the components is that of the program. The connections, however, can be changed during that lifetime.

```
ComponentA componentA ;
ComponentB componentB ;
ComponentC componentC ;
Plug2 plug2 ;

void main ()
{
  componentA.plug1 <= componentB.socket1 ;
  componentA.plug2 <= componentC.socket2 ;
  componentA.socket2 <= plug2 ;

  componentB.plug1 <= componentC.socket1 ;

  componentA.StartA () ;
}
```

A local definition of this same structure is almost identical except that the data declarations are local to the function—*Sample* in this case. The operation and construction is the same as with the global definition; only the lifetime of the objects is different. The objects are created when the function is entered and destroyed when the function exits. Also upon exit, the connections created initially are broken before the objects themselves are destroyed.

```
void Sample ()
{
  ComponentA componentA ;
  ComponentB componentB ;
  ComponentC componentC ;
  Plug2 plug2 ;

  componentA.plug1 <= componentB.socket1 ;
  componentA.plug2 <= componentC.socket2 ;
  componentA.socket2 <= plug2 ;
```

```
componentB.plug1 <= componentC.socket1 ;

componentA.StartA () ;
}
```

A class definition adds, yet again, more syntactic sugar and moves the connection creation into the class constructor function. The components are created and initialized when an object of this class is created and initialized. The components are deleted when the object is deleted. The constructor function is called after the object is created.

```
class SampleClass
{
  public:
    ComponentA componentA ;
    ComponentB componentB ;
    ComponentC componentC ;
    Plug2 plug2 ;

  SampleClass ()
  {
    componentA.plug1 <= componentB.socket1 ;
    componentA.plug2 <= componentC.socket2 ;
    componentA.socket2 <= plug2 ;

    componentB.plug1 <= componentC.socket1 ;

    componentA.StartA () ;
  }
} ;
```

The only problem with this type of definition is that the *StartA* function is called when an object is created. This may or may not be desirable. Two alternatives exist if this function call is removed from the constructor function code: the *componentA.StartA* function can be called directly by the creator of the object since the component and the function are both public, or an additional function can be added to *SampleClass* that calls *componentA.StartA*.

The lifetime of the object-based static constructed structure is that of the object, which can be global, local, part of another object, or dynamically allocated from the heap. In the last case, the object must be explicitly freed, as there are no hooks into the plug connection mechanism to do so automatically.

Hierarchical Construction

Hierarchical construction is based on static construction techniques. Hierarchical construction requires more than one level of definition. The levels are the same as those used in the static construction method: global, local, and object. Note that a global level of definition can only occur once and can therefore only be at the base of a hierarchical design. An example of a global base will not be shown, since it is a simple transition from the local hierarchy shown next. The following example uses the same component class definitions presented in the previous section on static construction. The example also creates a structure that is identical and operationally the same. The difference is where the construction occurs and how it is taken apart. The example employs a pair of functions: *Hierarchical1* and *Hierarchical2*. The first function creates part of the structure, while the second creates the remaining portion and initiates the operation. Note the similarities and differences between this example and the examples in the static construction section. This is what the function definitions look like:

```
void Hierarchical2 ( ComponentA & componentA ) ;

void Hierarchical1 ()
{
  ComponentA componentA ;
  ComponentC componentC ;
  Plug2 plug2 ;

  componentA.plug2 <= componentC.socket2 ;
  componentA.socket2 <= plug2 ;

  componentB.plug1 <= componentC.socket1 ;

  Hierarchical2 ( componentA ) ;
```

```
    }

    void Hierarchical2 ( ComponentA & componentA )
    {
        ComponentB componentB ;

        componentA.plug1 <= componentB.socket1 ;

        componentA.StartA () ;
    }
```

The function call *componentA.StartA* must appear in the second function, *Hierarchical2*, and not in the first function, because *componentB* only exists when *Hierarchical2* is being executed. The component is deleted and all of its connections broken when the function returns. The difference between this version and the static version is the ability to call the *Hierarchical2* function repeatedly and have a new instance of *componentB* created each time. Also, *componentB* is only created when needed.

It is easy to see how the component hierarchy can be extended to a function calling depth greater than the two shown here. Likewise, increasing the number of function definitions and calls to incorporate other components and connections is also straightforward. This type of construction is useful where a base structure is built to support subsequent computation and new components are connected as needed and disconnected when they are no longer needed.

Hierarchical construction using objects differs from the hierarchical functional construction just described. The two functions are converted to classes from which objects can be defined, but the hierarchy is inverted in terms of definition. For example:

```
    class HierarchicalClass1
    {
      public:
        ComponentA componentA ;
        ComponentC componentC ;
```

```
      Plug2 plug2 ;

      HierarchicalClass1 ()
      {
        componentA.plug2 <= componentC.socket2 ;
        componentA.socket2 <= plug2 ;

        componentB.plug1 <= componentC.socket1 ;
      }
   }


class HierarchicalClass2
{
  public:
    HierarchicalClass1 hierarchical1 ;
    ComponentB componentB ;

    Hierarchical2 ()
    {
      hierarchical1.componentA.plug1 <= componentB.socket1 ;

      hierarchical1.componentA.StartA () ;
    }
}
```

In this case, *HierarchicalClass2* refers to *HierarchicalClass1* versus the *Hierarchical1* function calling the *Hierarchical2* function. The composition winds up being the same and the lifetimes are similar. A more complicated definition can be done, where *HierarchicalClass1* contains an instance of *HierarchicalClass2,* but this requires the use of constructors with parameters and separate function definitions outside the class definition.

You may have noticed that hierarchical construction using objects is the same type of construction that has been used for compound objects.

Dynamic Construction

Dynamic construction is only applicable to objects since dynamic objects are, by definition, allocated from the heap. This is shown in figure 9.4. Pointers to dynamically constructed structures can be defined globally, locally, or within an object, but the structure itself cannot be defined using a combination of methods. (This is discussed in the next section.) The advantage of dynamic over static or hierarchical construction is that one source, a function or class definition, can be used to create a structure, which can then be used by a different part of the program. In addition, the entire structure will free itself when the appropriate connections are broken. Dynamic plug and component construction is covered in more detail in Chapter 8.

For the next example, assume that the previous component class definitions have been augmented from static definitions to dynamic definitions. Com-

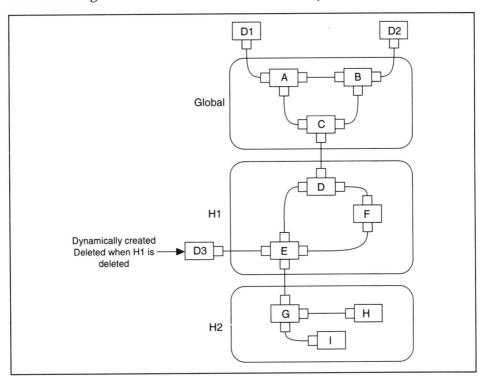

Figure 9-4. Combined construction

ponents will delete themselves when all connections to them are broken, and the *static New* function is included to allocate new objects.

The example creates, yet again, the same structure created in the two previous sections. The difference is that two functions, *DynamicCreate1* and *DynamicCreate2,* are used to create the structure. The structure is created from free space and is freed when it is no longer needed. A single reference to *componentA* is maintained but the other parts are only referenced by *componentA.*

```
ComponentA * DynamicCreate1 ()
{
   ComponentA & componentA  = ComponentA::New () ;
   ComponentC & componentC = ComponentC::New () ;
   Plug2 & plug2 = Plug2::New () ;

   componentA.plug2 <= componentC.socket2 ;
   componentA.socket2 <= plug2 ;

   componentB.plug1 <= componentC.socket1 ;

   return & componentA ;
}

void DynamicCreate2 ( ComponentA & componentA )
{
   ComponentB componentB ;

   componentA.plug1 <= componentB.socket1 ;
}

void DynamicCreateFunction ()
{
   ComponentA & componentA = DynamicCreate1 () ;

   DynamicCreate2 ( componentA ) ;

   componentA.StartA () ;
```

```
    delete & componentA ;
}
```

The creation function, *DynamicCreateFunction*, creates the structure in two steps: first by calling *DynamicCreate1* and then *DynamicCreate2*. The choice of parameter passing methods is arbitrary, and the connections between *componentA.plug1* and *ComponentB.socket1* could have been made in *DynamicCreateFunction* if *DynamicCreateFunction2* simply returned a pointer to *componentB*.

Dynamic construction has the advantage of automatic freeing of resources and the ability to create different sections of the structure in different functions and at different times. The disadvantage is the minor overhead of dynamic plugs, plus a possible problem. The problem is related to the automatic deallocation mechanism. The basic dynamic plug mechanism uses a simple reference count garbage collection scheme. It is not too difficult to create a structure with cycles, such as a circular linked list. This type of structure will never delete itself.

To avoid this problem, additional support must be included when designing the system. For example, the problem would not occur with the prior example because *componentA* is the center of the structure. It gets deleted when you are done; hence the connections to *componentB*, *componentC*, and *plug2* are broken. These components then delete themselves. But let's say that you had a pointer to *componentB* instead, and simply deleted it. In this case one connection to *componentA* would be broken but others to *componentA* would remain. This case is discussed in Chapter 8, but it is worth reiterating here because of its importance.

Combining Techniques

Most construction is a combination of the static, hierarchical, and dynamic construction methods. The base of an application may be a simple or complex static structure which is then augmented using hierarchical or dynamic construction techniques. The degree to which any technique is used will be based upon the application, and there is no requirement that any particular method be used. Static and hierarchical methods are very safe in terms of resource usage because the lifetime of the components and associated connections is well defined. Dynamic construction is a bit more complex, especially when combined with the other methods, because of the possibility of disconnected components floating around in free space unused and unable to deallocate themselves.

Figure 9-5 shows how the various techniques can be combined. Dynamic plugs are added to the global level and intermediate level. The latter will be freed when the function that created the level returns. This simple example will

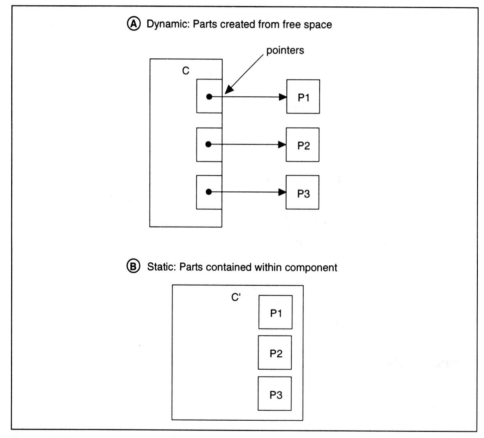

Figure 9-5. Construction via encapsulation

probably not result in disconnected dynamic components because the connections are limited and easily understood. The major difficulty with more complex designs is understanding where disconnected components might be created or where circular structures could exist. Luckily these are the same type of design considerations already encountered in data structure design.

Event-Driven Program Construction

Most of the graphical user interfaces in use today, such as Microsoft Windows, utilize an event-driven programming environment. Program construction using the methods outlined in previous sections is particularly applicable to these environments. Static global and object construction form the base of an application. These components are in turn available for use when an event invokes a function call, usually in conjunction with an object, such as a window object. This function can temporarily add to the overall program structure using local static or hierarchical construction methods already outlined in this chapter, or it can add to the structure in a more permanent fashion using dynamic construction methods.

For example, imagine an application with an underlying structure that presents a dialog box containing controls like buttons and list boxes. The underlying structure is globally or dynamically created before the dialog box is displayed. The dialog box interface normally starts with a dialog box object, which in turn would contain additional components and connections that could also be connected to the underlying structure. The individual controls could also contain components that are connected to the controls in the dialog box. The dialog box control operation, such as clicking on a button with a mouse, could in turn add a dynamic component to the underlying structure.

The window plugs defined in earlier chapters are used in just this fashion. A dialog box component would include a number of list box, combo box, and edit control sockets. A dialog box component object is required to present the dialog box. Connections to the sockets are made with plugs created elsewhere in the program. The dialog box component function to display the dialog box is then called. The dialog box then uses the connections to initialize the internal structures and objects that display the information on the screen.

Overall Program Construction

In general, overall program construction should be done as if it were a very large component. The *main* function should perform a minimal amount of creation and connection. Programming environments like Microsoft Foundation Class support for Microsoft Windows does its initialization in the *CWinApp::InitInstance* function. Keeping the initialization routine small makes it easier to understand what the program is doing. This is true for programs in general, but more so with components and plugs since the overall purpose of using these methods is for modular design and reuse.

10 Modification of Existing Programs Using Plugs

One of the strengths of the plug model is the ability to modify an existing program without studying the source code—the programmer can merely unplug and replug plugs. Not only does this get around the necessity of studying someone else's source code in order to make a simple modification, but it also makes it possible to modify programs when you do not have access to the source code.

This chapter describes how to design programs that can be modified after they are built, and also how to do this modification. Two plug functions, *addBefore* and *addAfter*, are described in more detail in this chapter, along with how they are used in program modification. These functions can be used after the fact, to modify existing programs, but they can also be used effectively when first building a program.

Although it is difficult to know ahead of time what kinds of modifications may be necessary in the future, it is often possible to know what areas of a program may be modified or what areas can be readily modified. For example, you might have a program that includes a connection that is a data stream. The connection definitions are provided and a pointer to the plug or socket of this connection is public. This allows you to insert a new component between these plugs that acts as a filter. You could also insert a component that has an additional plug, which you could use to tap into the information going through the component.

This type of modification becomes very handy if the connection descriptions come with a standard set of filters and taps and also provide the interface definition. The latter can be used to create new filters and taps, while the existing set can be used to modify programs using the corresponding type of connection.

The addBefore and addAfter Functions

First let's review how *addBefore* and *addAfter* work. They both take the same parameters, and the semantics are almost identical. Figure 10-1 shows graphically how the functions operate. In the first example some empty plugs and sockets are defined: *p1*, *p2*, *s1*, and *s2*. Initially *p1* is connected to *s1*. Using *addAfter*, *p1* is disconnected from *s1* and connected to *s2*, and *s1* is connected to *p2*. The code looks like this:

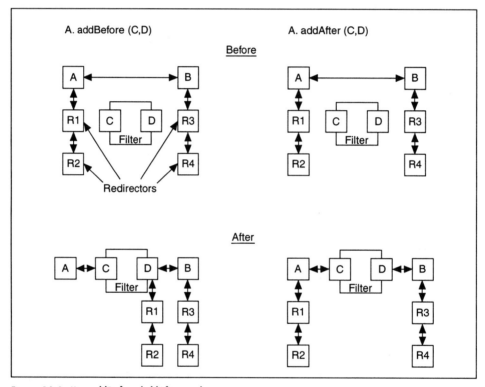

Figure 10-1. How addBefore/addAfter work

```
DECLARE_CONNECTION
  ( Sample
  , SamplePlug
  , SampleSocket
  )
```

```
class SamplePlug : public Sample::plug
{
  public:
    DECLARE_PLUG ()
} ;


class SampleSocket : public Sample::socket
{
  public:
    DECLARE_PLUG ()
} ;



SamplePlug p1, p2 ;
SampleSocket s1, s2 ;

p1 <= s1 ;      // starting with a connection in place

p1.addAfter ( s2, p2 ) ;      // plugs interposed

This example does the same thing as the next one:

p1 <= s1 ;      // starting with a connection in place

p2 <= (* - p1) ;      // reconnect socket to p2
s2 <= p1 ;            // reconnect socket to p1
```

The *addAfter* function simply shortens the operations; but it also makes it syntactically compatible with the *addBefore* function, which works a little differently. The *addBefore* example looks like this:

```
Sample::plugRedirector r1 ;

r1.redirect ( p1 ) ;  // p1 is redirected by r1

p1 <= s1 ;            // p1 connect to s1

p2 <= (* - p1) ;      // do the addBefore operation
```

```
s2 <= p1 ;

r1 = p2 ;                 // adjust the redirector
```

The difference between the *addAfter* and *addBefore* examples is the addition of the redirector, *r1*. It was not included with the *addAfter* example because there is no change if a redirector existed. The change only occurs when using addBefore. In fact, for program modification, the following example would be more common:

```
r1.addBefore ( s2, p2 ) ;
```

This function call simply replaces *p1* with *r1*, and it does the same thing. The reason a redirector is more commonly used with *addBefore* and *addAfter* is that subsequent changes can be made with respect to prior changes based upon what parts of the program are made public.

Let's look at these two functions a little more closely. There are two cases: a public plug or a public redirector for a plug. Using *addBefore* and *addAfter* directly with a public plug causes no change with respect to the public reference. For example:

```
SamplePlug p ;

class SampleComponent
{
  public:
    SamplePlug p ;
    SampleSocket s ;
} ;

SamplePlug s ;
SampleComponent a, b, c ;
SamplePlugRedirector r ;

r.redirect ( p ) ;        // r redirecting p
p <= s ;                  // p connected to s
```

```
p.addAfter  ( a.s, a.p ) ;     // r redirecting p
p.addBefore ( b.s, b.p ) ;     // r redirecting b.p
p.addAfter  ( c.s, c.p ) ;     // r redirecting b.p
```

Now you have a sequence of connections and references that look like Figure 10-2. Using components instead of individual plugs makes the purpose of *addBefore* and *addAfter* a bit clearer; especially compared to the next example, which again uses the redirector, *r*, in place of the plug, *p*, in the *addBefore* and *addAfter* function calls.

```
r.redirect ( p ) ;             // r redirects p
p <= s ;                       // p connected to s

r.addAfter  ( a.s, a.p ) ;     // r redirects p
r.addBefore ( b.s, b.p ) ;     // r redirects b.p
r.addAfter  ( c.s, c.p ) ;     // r redirects b.p
                      // c.s added after b.p
```

The sequence of connections and references now looks like Figure 10-3. This results in a completely different structure than the previous example! Component *b* is before the redirector and components *c* and *a* are after it. The dif-

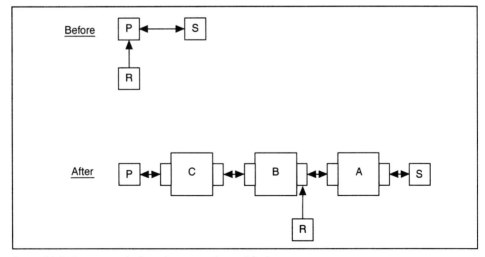

Figure 10-2. Program with plugs that cannot be modified

305

ference results from where the redirector is pointing at the time of the function call. For this example the difference occurs with the last *addAfter* function call. In the first example, the *c* component is added after plug *p*, but, in both cases, the redirector points to plug *b.p*. In the previous example, the redirector is used with the last *addAfter* function, which causes component *c* to be added after *b* instead of after *p*.

The value of this distinction between *addBefore* and *addAfter* is shown in the next two sections. In general, redirectors are a useful way of building a component or compound plug interface. The *addBefore* function allows changes to be made with respect to the redirector so the addition becomes part of the component after the change is made, whereas *addAfter* does not.

The next two sections address how to use *addBefore* and *addAfter*. Both sections present modifications to a component. The first section examines how to make changes to the internals of an existing component; the second section shows how to change a component at the interface level. There is a fine line between the two approaches. The methodology is the same, but each section also addresses how portions of a component should be designed to accommodate such modification.

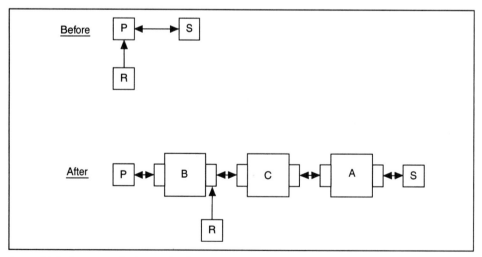

Figure 10-3. Program with plugs and redirectors

Changing Component Internals

Changing the internals of a component can be accomplished easily if the source code is available. However, the type of change addressed here assumes that the source code is not available but the component has been properly designed. How do you design a component for subsequent modification without giving away the source code? It is possible with plugs. Figure 10-4 shows the structure of a program built with plugs in a non-modifiable and modifiable form. The example assumes that items within the program are not available, but the redirectors added to the second (modifiable) part of the figure are available for use. You can use plugs and components to adjust the internal

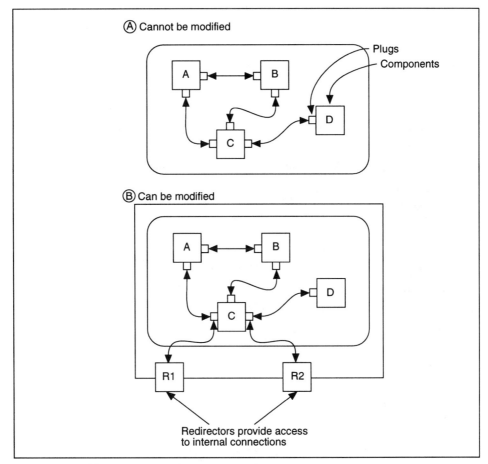

Figure 10-4. Modifying components/programs example

structure of the program using standard plug operations. You need to know the general structure and operation of the program, but not the source code, to make modifications with plugs.

The class definition for a component must be logically divided into the component interface and the customization interface. The component interface is the one that has been presented in this book thus far. Essentially it consists of the public functions and variables for use with the component. The variables are usually redirectors or pointers to plugs that are used to make connections when the component is used. The customization interface is also public, but it is not for general use. The customization interface is normally composed of redirectors or functions that return pointers to redirectors, although it does not have to be limited to this. However, any portion of the customization interface not utilizing plug connections is specific to that component.

The next example presents only the class interface of a component, which is all that is necessary for modifying an instance of the component. The class only contains enough code to demonstrate our example. The class also uses pure virtual functions, making it an abstract class. The interesting thing about this approach is that the basic object consists only of a pointer to the virtual function table regardless of the number of components added. Note that the size of the virtual function table does grow as more virtual functions are added. There are actually two abstract classes used in this example because the base class, *AbstractExtendableComponent*, is used in the next section too. It contains no customization interface section, only a component interface section. This is good practice in general because not all components need be customizable (unless, of course, that is the intended design).

```
class AbstractExtendableComponent
{
  public:
    // — Component Interface —

    virtual SamplePlug & p1 () = 0 ;
    virtual SamplePlug & p2 () = 0 ;
```

```
} ;

class AbstractCustomizableComponent
  : public AbstractExtendableComponent
{
  public:
    // — Customization Interface —

    virtual SamplePlug   & cp () = 0 ;
    virtual SampleSocket & cs () = 0 ;
} ;
```

The description of this abstract class must also indicate the purpose and oper-ation of the customization interface. In this example the functions have been delineated, but the purpose of the functions or their returned values has not been described. When you create your own programs, you should include this information elsewhere, for example, in the printed documentation. In this case, the documentation is right here. The plugs returned by the functions *cp* and *cs* point to both ends of an internal connection. The reason for provid-ing both ends is to allow any arbitrary addition to be easily removed.

For example, assume you have the following class defined so you can instan-tiate a new object:

```
class CustomizableComponent
  : public AbstractCustomizableComponent
{
  private:
    SamplePlug P1 ;
    SamplePlug P2 ;
    SamplePlug CP ;
    SampleSocket CS ;

  public:
    // — Component Interface —

    virtual SamplePlug & p1 () { return P1 ; }
    virtual SamplePlug & p2 () { return P2 ; }
```

```
// — Customization Interface —

virtual SamplePlug   & cp () { return CP ; }
virtual SampleSocket & cs () { return CS ; }
} ;
```

The *CustomizableComponent* would normally have a constructor that hooks together the plugs, but it's not needed for this example. Likewise, the plugs could be redirectors instead.

The following example shows how one of these component objects is created and modified.

```
CustomizableComponent Custom1 ;

SamplePlug p1 ;
SampleSocket s1 ;

Custom1.cp().addAfter ( s1, p1 ) ;

The original configuration can be restored using:

Custom1.cp() <= Custom1.cs () ;
```

Note that this does not guarantee a complete restoration if pointers to redirectors are returned by the functions. Remember that *addBefore* could be used instead of *addAfter*, which may leave some added components and connections intact. Note also that only one end of the connection is required for modification. Two are presented here to show how to restore a connection to its original configuration.

Modifying the internals of a component can be a bit hazardous, so the description of any customization points should be meticulously complete. The author of the component should discuss all possible implications of a modification.

The plugs used should be equally well documented. Figure 10-5 shows what a complex component might look like. It is possible to change a connection, between *C1* and *C2*, within an imbedded component, *C3*, using the redirector chain. The documentation for this complex component will definitely be extensive. Modifications can be made at clearly definable points.

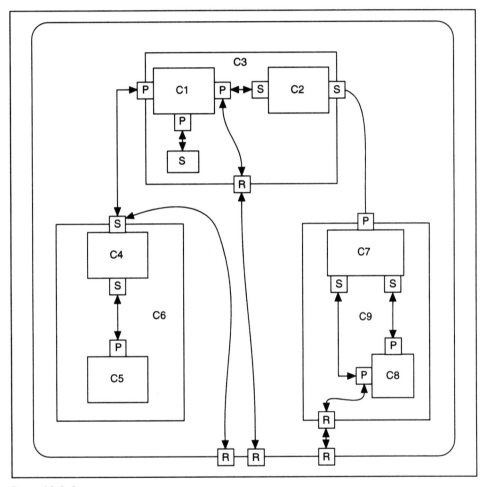

Figure 10-5. Programs as components

Figure 10-6 shows a simpler example. Two filter components are added before and after the redirector, which is the public part of the main component. This type of operation is quite common, which is why all plug classes include the *addAfter* and *addBefore* function definitions.

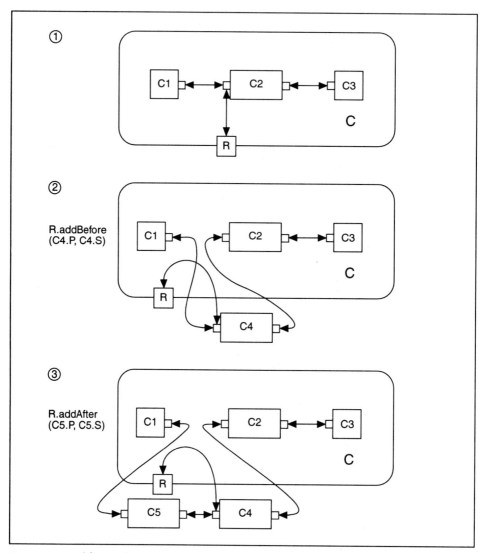

Figure 10-6. Modification by encapsulation

A modification can insert components between plugs, as the previous examples have shown, but you can also replace components. To replace a component you need access to one end of a connection. You then use the normal connection operator, as in:

```
SamplePlug ReplacementPlug ;

ReplacementPlug <= Custom1.cs () ;
```

Any prior connection to the plug returned by *Custom1.cs* will automatically be disconnected. The disconnected plug will free itself and its resources if it is a dynamic plug.

Modifications can be major or minor, but plugs can make the job easy. Let's take a big component as an example—a text editor. Some internal replaceable components might include a spell checker or grammar checker. These could each be a compound plug, which would in turn contain plugs for accessing the document and displaying results. Replacing a component is done by making a new connection. An example of a useful component to insert in a text editor might be a mail merge filter. This connection could be the data stream from the basic mail merge plug to the printer plug. The filter could replace a line with a syntax like this,

```
##graphic: c:\pictures\logo.pcx
```

with the printer code to display the graphic file. This may sound a bit archaic in this age of compound document processors, but it is easy to see how this would work. The data stream is scanned for the ##*graphic: keyword*, and the rest of the line is used to find the file containing the graphic image. The file is then opened and added to the data stream in place of the encoded line.

Filters can also be useful in debugging. They can be used to log the function calls and parameters made using a connection.

Extending a Component

Changing the internals of a component requires a public interface to the customization interface. Extending a component does not. Instead it uses the component interface. Modifications are made through the plugs that are available through this interface. It is at this interface that the use of redirectors becomes important. Redirectors do not have to be part of the base component design but it helps. First you'll take a look at how things should work, and then you'll look at how to make accommodations for modifying a component that does not incorporate redirectors.

The same sample plug and redirector definitions from the previous section are used. Also, the *AbstractExtendableComponent* class defined in the previous section is used as the base. It does not include the customizable interface as part of its definition. The new component class, *ExtendableComponent*, uses redirectors at its interface instead of plugs. The constructor for the class initializes the redirectors when an object is created. The *p1* and *p2* function return type is still *SamplePlug*, which means the redirectors cannot be changed directly. The *ExtendableComponent* definition looks like this:

```
class ExtendableComponent
  : public AbstractExtendableComponent
{
  private:
    SamplePlugRedirector R1 ;
    SamplePlugRedirector R2 ;

    SamplePlug P1 ;
    SamplePlug P2 ;

  public:
    ExtendableComponent ()
    {
      R1.redirect ( P1 ) ;
      R2.redirect ( P2 ) ;
    }
```

```
// — Component Interface —

virtual SamplePlug & p1 () { return R1 ; }
virtual SamplePlug & p2 () { return R2 ; }
} ;
```

Although direct changes to the redirectors are not possible from the outside, indirect changes can be made using *addBefore* in conjunction with the return values of *p1* and *p2*.

So how does the use of *addBefore* provide any benefit? Let's start by defining a new class that will be an extended component. The definition looks like this:

```
class ExtendedComponent
  : public ExtendableComponent
{
  private:
    SamplePlug    myPlug ;
    SampleSocket mySocket;

  public:
    ExtendedComponent
      : ExtendableComponent ()
    {
      p1().addBefore ( mySocket, myPlug ) ;
    }
} ;
```

Its constructor, which will be called after the *ExtendableComponent* constructor, adds a filter via two resident plugs, *myPlug* and *mySocket*. This adjusts the redirector returned by *p1* to point to *myPlug*.

Essentially the structure of the component has been modified with a minimal amount of work and without having to redefine any of the public component interface functions. Figure 10-7 shows a similar example, including a diagram of what the structure of the component looks like.

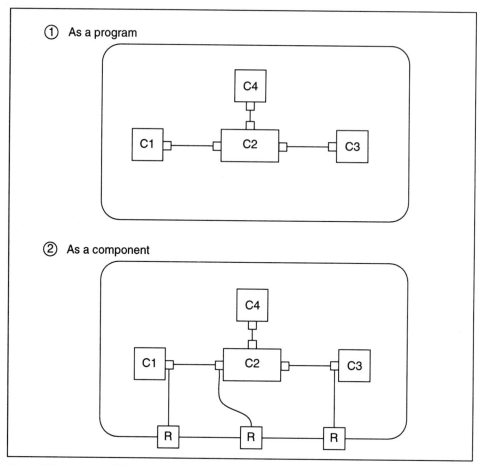

Figure 10-7. Structure of the component

The alternative is to include a new definition for *p1*.This returns a reference to a redirector, *R1*, which in turn points to *myPlug*. A new definition for *p2* and a matching redirector are also included for good measure. The new component now has redirectors on both plugs associated with its public component interface. The class constructor still adds the filter, but it must explicitly use the superclass version of *p1*.The code looks like this:

```
class ExtendedComponent2
   : public ExtendableComponent
   {
```

```
private:
  SamplePlug    myPlug ;
  SampleSocket mySocket;

  SamplePlugRedirector R1 ;
  SamplePlugRedirector R2 ;

public:
  ExtendedComponent2
    : ExtendedComponent ()
  {
    ExtendableComponent::p1()
      .addBefore ( mySocket, myPlug ) ;

    R1.redirect ( myPlug ) ;
    R2.redirect ( ExtendableComponent::p2()) ;
  }

  // — Component Interface —

  virtual SamplePlug & p1 () { return R1 ; }
  virtual SamplePlug & p2 () { return R2 ; }
} ;
```

This approach must be used if a redirector is not used by *ExtendableCompo-nent*. Otherwise, *p1* would still return a reference to the *ExtendableCompo-nent* plug and not the one added by the *ExtendedComponent2* constructor.

Programs Designed as Components

Designing a program as if it were a component allows the methods discussed in the previous sections to come into play when enhancing or including the program as part of another program. Having the program as one large component lets you address the program as a whole just as you would a smaller portion of the program, another component, or a group of components. Figure 10-8 shows how a design can start out as a program and wind up as a component.

The general rules for component and program construction are as follows:

1. Base the interface on an abstract class.

2. Include a customizable set of definitions as appropriate.

3. Use functions that return pointers or references to plugs.

4. Use redirectors when implementing interface plugs.

The use of virtual functions and redirectors entails added overhead when making connections, but this overhead is minimal. Plus, the resulting structures finally made will operate as efficiently as direct connections between plugs, because the resulting connections will be the same.

```
class foo : public bar
{
 public:
  foo ()
   :bar ()
   {
     A.addAfter (C.plug, C.Socket);
   }
 Protected:
    Sample Component C;
};
```

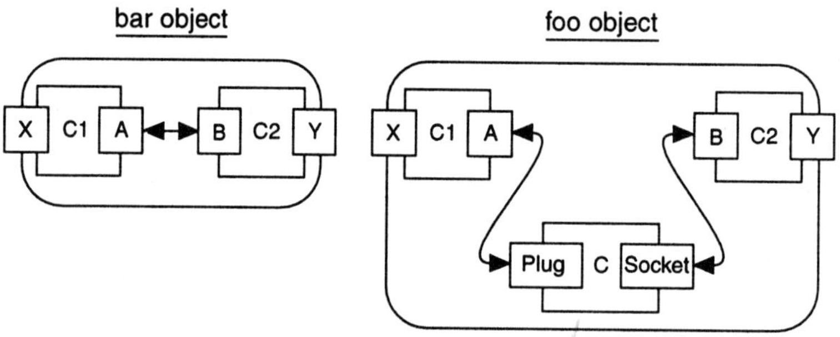

Figure 10-8. From program to component

More to Come

The search for the Holy Grail of reusable software is as old as programming itself. It has shown up in various forms and has been found to varying degrees in almost every programming language. Subroutine libraries were the first successful form of reuse that did not require the original source code. Unfortunately, extending or modifying an existing library is not an easy task.

Object-oriented programming has brought the idea of reusable software to the forefront but at the source code level. Classes, inheritance, and object-oriented programming are very good tools, but both using and extending objects require a good understanding of the classes involved.

Program design with plugs uses object-oriented techniques as a base, but the purpose of plugs and connections is different from that of classes and inheritance. The commonality when dealing with classes and inheritance is the programming language's syntax and semantics along with the functions and variables contained within a class definition. The programming language—pick your favorite—is very general, while the functions associated with the classes are very specific. Learning the programming language does not help understand how a particular class and its objects work. Okay, you need to know the language to read what the class defines, but you still must read the class definition. Any commonality between classes is up to the designer.

The commonality between plugs and components is the plug protocol. It applies to any plug. The standardization of the syntax and semantics for any plug is very important. Few object-oriented programming concepts are that consistent among classes—constructors, destructors, new, and delete come to mind.

Standardization is just one aspect of plug design. This book has presented many of the other concepts important to plug design, including dynamic plugs and components, compound connections, and the high-level/low-level view of plugs and connections.

Much of this book deals with how plugs work, how plugs and components can be designed, and the other details important to low-level programming. This has filled up most of the pages of this book, leaving some of the more interesting things for the future. Plugs and components are like wood, nails, and screws. When you can choose from an assortment of readily available parts rather than building your own, the use of plugs and components becomes more inviting.

I hope that the ideas presented in this book are intriguing enough to get programmers like you started on creating two things: plug interface standards and plug implementations to back them up. These plugs need to run the gamut from very simple text controls to very complex real-time control systems. Although plug connections are used to build structures, you should keep in mind that connecting plugs can be as dynamic as any conventional program.

A PLUGS.HPP

The file *Plugs.HPP* contains all the macro and class definitions required to define plugs and connections. It does not use C++ templates because these are currently available in only some of the popular C++ compilers on the market. For readers with access to one of these compilers, I have included a template version of *Plugs.HPP* in Appendix C. Functionally it is identical to this version. You will find no difference using the two if you look only at the plug functions and macros you use. The classes they define are essentially the same. The main reason to use the template version, if your compiler can handle it, is convenience in debugging.

I present the contents and operation of the *Plugs.HPP* file in this chapter. The first section is a quick overview of the basics: the class structure, the macro definitions, and how a connection is defined. The next section addresses general problems you may encounter using *Plugs.HPP* due to limitations or restrictions of the various C++ compilers. This version of Plugs.HPP is specifically designed for and tested with Borland C++ Version 3.1 and Microsoft C++ Version 7.0 and Version 8.0. (Version 8.0 is also sold as Visual C++.) The following section presents the contents of *Plugs.HPP* and discusses the various macros and functions in more detail. The final section examines the overhead imposed by plugs and connections, looking at the memory requirements for plugs and redirectors and the function calling overhead imposed by connections.

Plugs.HPP Class Structure

This section is a short synopsis of chapters 1 through 3. It provides a quick introduction to how a connection is defined, what classes are defined when defining a connection, and how the plug macros fit into this scheme of things. This should give you a better idea of just what it is that *Plugs.HPP* implements.

A connection definition uses the *DECLARE_CONNECTION* macro and requires a pair of class definitions after it that describe the plug and socket for the connection. These are normally abstract classes defining a general interface for the connection. Subclasses are used to implement plugs and sockets for the connection. The plug and socket classes utilize the *DECLARE_PLUG* macro. A simple connection definition looks like:

```
DECLARE_CONNECTION ( Simple, SimplePlug, SimpleSocket )

class SimplePlug : public Simple::plug
{
  public:
    DECLARE_PLUG ()

    virtual void InterfaceFunction1 () = 0 ;
} ;

class SimpleSocket : public Simple::socket
{
  public:
    DECLARE_PLUG ()

    virtual void InterfaceFunction2 () = 0 ;
} ;
```

Not shown in this example is the *Plug* class definition, which is also included in the *Plugs.HPP* file. The Plug class is the base class for all plug and socket classes. The *DECLARE_CONNECTION* macro expands into a connection class containing six nested classes, as shown in Figure 1. The eight classes that follow include the abstract plug and socket classes and the basic *plug* and *socket* classes, plus four redirector classes, two for the *plug* class and two for the *socket* class. One redirector class is for general use while the other is specifically designed for dynamic plugs. As shown in the last example, the *plug* and *socket* classes are used as the base class for the main plug and socket classes; in this case they are the *SimplePlug* and *SimpleSocket* classes.

This complex structure is used for a number of specific reasons. The use of a common *Plug* class allows some functions to be used with any plug and allows a general pointer type for any plug. (The plug and socket class hierarchy are identical so we will just examine one.) The abstract plug class is included so that the *plug* and *plugRedirector* classes have a common base. The *myEnd* type definition refers to this class; you will see this type used in a number of function definitions in *Plugs.HPP*. Another type definition is *myPlug*; it refers to the outer plug class, which is *SimplePlug* in the previous example. A *myEnd* pointer provides access to the plug connection functions, which can be applied to both a plug and its redirector. A *myPlug* pointer, on the other hand, provides access to a plug and cannot be used to refer to a redirector. This latter pointer does provide access to the functions defined in the outer plug class. The class definitions include complementary type definitions for the other end and plug and the redirector for this end.

The *plug* and *plugRedirector* classes are distinct: the *plug* class implements the connection support for plugs, while the redirector class implements the same functions from a redirector's perspective. Also, the *dynamicPlugRedirector* implements the *disconnectedFree* function differently from the normal *plugRedirector*: the dynamic redirector function is implemented so that it deletes the plug and then the redirector when the plug is no longer needed. The redirector classes are not abstract classes; redirector objects can be used directly. A redirector class object would be defined using the following syntax:

```
Simple::plugRedirector Redirector1 ;
```

A plug object may be allocated from the outer plug class but not from the inner; the inner plug class is an abstract class. Furthermore, the outer can be used only if it is not an abstract class, which it often is. The outer class also requires the use of the *DECLARE_PLUG* macro, which actually defines the *getPlug* function. You can eliminate the use of *DECLARE_MACRO* if you define the *getPlug* function yourself; note that it normally returns the value of *this*. Plug subclasses that do not use the *DECLARE_PLUG* macro are typically special classes for generator plug objects.

So that is how the macros are used and what the class structure looks like. The length of the *DECLARE_CONNECTION* macro is due to the number of complex classes defined. The *Plugs.HPP* file attempts to limit the length of the macro by eliminating any unnecessary white space because some compilers have limited macro expansion capabilities. The template version listed in appendix C is actually easier to read; so, since the explanation of the class functions presented in this appendix apply equally well to those in appendix C, you should check out appendix C if you find it difficult to understand the non-template version in this appendix.

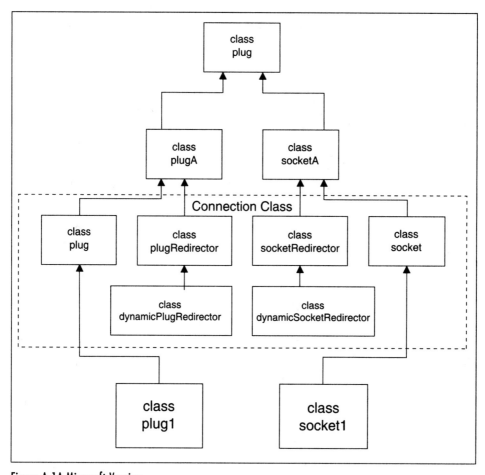

Figure A-1A Microsoft Version

Compiler Limitations and Possible Problems

I include this section specifically for the Microsoft C++ compilers but similar comments may be appropriate for other compilers. This version of *Plugs.HPP* is designed to work without templates but with C++. Nested classes must be supported. It is possible to define support for plugs without nested classes but additional changes will be required in the use of plugs. For example, a plug class requires a superclass from the connection class definition as in *Sample::plug*.

There are two limitations I encountered with Microsoft C++. The first, and most annoying, is the fixed and limited sized macro expansion buffer. The limit

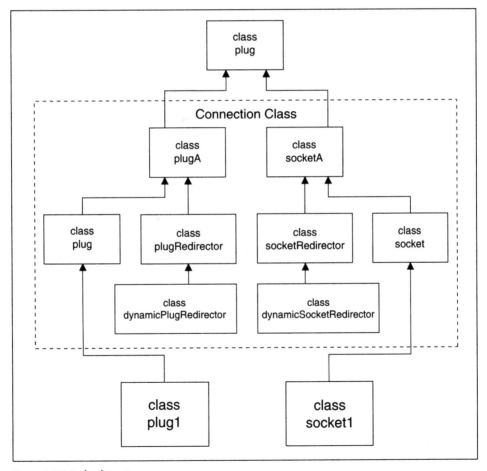

Figure A-1B Borland Version

forces you to effectively duplicate the connection definition macro each time you define a connection. The only difference between the two definitions is a single digit, so it is relatively easy to do using either a macro or a text editor.

The normal connection definition, as used in all the examples in this book, looks like:

```
DECLARE_CONNECTION ( Sample, SamplePlug, SampleSocket )
```

The Microsoft version looks like:

```
DECLARE_CONNECTION1 ( Sample, SamplePlug, SampleSocket )
DECLARE_CONNECTION2 ( Sample, SamplePlug, SampleSocket )
```

These two macros implement the same thing as the first one, except that each of the two expands to a size that fits in the Microsoft C++ compiler's macro expansion buffer. The part of the definition implemented by each macro is irrelevant, but you can check out the contents of *Plugs.HPP* if you want to know the details. This approach can be used with any other compiler that has a macro expansion limit.

The other limitation I found in Microsoft C++ has been classified as a bug but has yet to be fixed in the current compiler implementations. The bug has to do with nested class definitions. It seems that the compiler does not recognize a nested sibling class definition properly. For example, a class Outer contains two nested classes *Inner1* and *Inner2* as in:

```
class Outer
{
  class Inner1 {} ;
  class Inner2 {} ;
} ;
```

The two inner classes cannot refer to each other, which, unfortunately, is a requirement for our connection class definition. The Microsoft support in

Plugs.HPP gets around this limitation by defining hidden plug classes outside the Outer class and then using these to define the inner classes. This allows the inner classes to reference classes that are fully defined before the outer class is defined.

The macro definitions detect a Microsoft compiler using the predefined symbol *_MSC_VER*. The Borland-compatible version is used if this symbol is not found. Use the template version defined in Appendix C if you can. Use the Borland-compatible version if possible and if templates cannot be used. Use the Microsoft version as a last resort. Since the Borland compilers support templates you will probably want to use the version in Appendix C if you have a Borland compiler.

You will have to work up new macro definitions if none of the versions works with your C++ compiler. The next chapter describes what the macros and class definitions do and should provide sufficient information for a good C++ programmer to implement a version compatible with a different C++ compiler. If you must resort to this task, good luck. I found attempting workarounds for the Microsoft compiler to be annoying but the results were well worth the trouble.

Contents of Plugs.HPP

This section presents a full listing of *Plugs.HPP*. The latest version is contained on the diskette that goes with this book. I present the source code first so you can refer back to it; the rest of this section describes its contents, operation and use.

Here is what *Plugs.HPP* looks like.

```
// ====   PLUGS.HPP   ====

#if !defined(_PLUGS_HPP)
#define _PLUGS_HPP

// — Description of plug interface —
//
```

```
// Defining a plug class is not covered in these comments.
// A plug class uses the following operations:
//
// A <= B              connects A to B, does - A and - B first
// - A                 disconnects A, but will not free otherEnd
//                        returns otherEnd
// -- A                disconnects A, will free otherEnd
// A.connected()    returns 0 if A is disconnected
// A.usable()       returns 0 if not usable
//                     (i.e. uninitialized redirector)
//
// A -> V              access a member of the object at
//                     the other end of A, normally assumes there
//                     is something at the other end
//
// R.redirect(A)       change redirector R's reference to A
//                        returns prior reference
//
// A.addBefore(B,C)  connects A to B and C to what A was con-
nected //                          to if A has a redirector then
it points to C
// A.addAfter (B,C)  like addBefore
//                       if A has a redirector it does not change
//
// - Plug Class Definition Macros -
//
//
// DECLARE_CONNECTION (connection,plugBase,socketBase)
//
// class plugBase : public connection::plug
// {
// public:
//    DECLARE_PLUG ()
//
//    /* specifics here */
// } ;
//
//
// class plugBase : public connection::plug
// {
```

```
//    public:
//      myEnd * getPlug () { return this ; }
//
//      /* specifics here */
// } ;
//
//
// ─ plugCheck alternate definition ─
//
// Define a check macro if you want to check for invalid access
// using ->.

#if !defined(plugCheck)
#define plugCheck(ptr)
#endif


// ─ Simple plug macro definitions ─

#if !defined(BOOL)
typedef int BOOL ;
#endif
#if !defined(FALSE)
#define FALSE 0
#endif
#if !defined(TRUE)
#define TRUE 1
#endif


#define DECLARE_PLUG() myPlug*getPlug(){return this;}

class Plug
{
  public:
    virtual ~Plug () {}
    virtual BOOL usable        () {return TRUE;}
    virtual BOOL isRedirector  () {return FALSE;}
    virtual BOOL connected     () = 0 ;
    virtual void operator -    () = 0 ;
```

```
      virtual void connectFailed (){}
} ;


class RedirectorNotify
{
  public:
    virtual void connectFailed    ( Plug * ) {}
    virtual void disconnected      ( Plug * ) {}
    virtual void disconnectedFree ( Plug * ) {}
    virtual void afterConnect     ( Plug * ) {}
    virtual void beforeDisconnect ( Plug * ) {}
} ;


#define DPLUG(c,dp)\
class c:public dp\
{protected:myPlug*pMyPlug;\
 c(myPlug*p):pMyPlug(p){redirect((myEnd*)p);}\
 void*operator new(size_t s){return new char[s];}\
public:\
 static myEnd*New(myPlug*p){return new c(p);}\
 void disconnectedFree(myPlug*)\
 {delete(Plug*)pMyPlug;delete this;}};\

#if defined(_MSC_VER)
#define DECLARE_CONNECTION1(c,bp,bs)\
class bp;class bs;\
class c##xpr;class c##xsr;class c##xs;\
DO_PLUGA(c##xp,c##xs,bp,bs,c##xpr)\
DO_PLUGA(c##xs,c##xp,bs,bp,c##xsr)\
DO_REDIRECTOR(c##xpr,c##xp)\
DO_REDIRECTOR(c##xsr,c##xs)

#define DECLARE_CONNECTION2(c,bp,bs)\
class c{public:\
DO_PLUG(plug,c##xp)\
DO_PLUG(socket,c##xs)\
class plugRedirector:public c##xpr{};\
class socketRedirector:public c##xsr{};\
```

```
DPLUG(dynamicPlugRedirector,c##xpr)\
DPLUG(dynamicSocketRedirector,c##xsr)\
};

#define DECLARE_CONNECTION(c,bp,bs)\
DECLARE_CONNECTION1(c,bp,bs)\
DECLARE_CONNECTION2(c,bp,bs)\

#else
#define DECLARE_CONNECTION1(c,bp,bs) DECLARE_CONNECTION(c,bp,bs)

#define DECLARE_CONNECTION2(c,bp,bs)

#define DECLARE_CONNECTION(c,bp,bs)\
class bp;class bs;\
class c{public:\
class plugRedirector;class socketRedirector;class socketA;\
DO_PLUGA(plugA,socketA,bp,bs,plugRedirector)\
DO_PLUGA(socketA,plugA,bs,bp,socketRedirector)\
DO_REDIRECTOR(plugRedirector,plugA)\
DO_REDIRECTOR(socketRedirector,socketA)\
DO_PLUG(plug,plugA)\
DO_PLUG(socket,socketA)\
DPLUG(dynamicPlugRedirector,plugRedirector)\
DPLUG(dynamicSocketRedirector,socketRedirector)\
};
#endif

#define DO_PLUGA(ap,as,bp,bs,r)\
class ap:public Plug{public:\
typedef bs otherPlug;\
typedef as otherEnd;\
typedef bp myPlug;\
typedef ap myEnd;\
typedef r redirector;\
protected:union{myEnd*pMyEnd;otherPlug*pOther;};\
redirector*pRedirector;\
public:\
ap():pRedirector(0){pOther=0;}\
virtual myPlug*getPlug()=0;\
```

```
virtual myEnd*getEnd(){return(myEnd*)getPlug();}\
virtual void operator<=(otherEnd&)=0;\
virtual otherPlug*operator->(){plugCheck(pOther);return pOther;}\
virtual otherPlug&operator*(){plugCheck(pOther);return*pOther;}\
virtual otherPlug*operator-()=0;\
virtual void addBefore(otherEnd*,myEnd*)=0;\
virtual void addAfter(otherEnd*,myEnd*)=0;\
virtual BOOL connected(){return pOther!=0;}\
virtual void connectto(otherPlug*p){pOther=p;}\
virtual redirector*getRedirector(){return pRedirector;}\
virtual redirector*setRedirector(redirector*pR)\
 {redirector*pOld=pRedirector;pRedirector=pR;return pOld;}\
virtual void setMyEnd(myEnd*p){pMyEnd=p;}\
virtual void disconnectedFree(otherPlug*){}\
virtual void disconnected(otherPlug*){}\
virtual void afterConnect(otherPlug*){}\
virtual void beforeDisconnect(otherPlug*){}\
};

#define DO_PLUG(c,a)\
class c:public a{public:\
~c(){if(pOther)-*(otherEnd*)pOther;\
if(pRedirector)pRedirector->redirect(0);}\
void operator<=(otherEnd&p)\
 {otherEnd*prior=(otherEnd*)-*this;\
 if(prior)--*prior;\
 if(&p){otherEnd*pp=(otherEnd*)-p;\
 if(pp)--pp;\
 myEnd*e1=getEnd();\
  if(e1){otherEnd*e2=p.getEnd();\
   if(e2){myPlug*p1=e1->getPlug();\
    otherPlug*p2=e2->getPlug();\
    e1->connectto(p2);\
    e2->connectto(p1);\
    e1->afterConnect(p2);\
    e2->afterConnect(p1);}\
   else e1->connectFailed();}}\
  else connectFailed();}\
otherPlug*operator-()\
 {otherPlug*prior=pOther;\
```

```
 if(prior){myPlug*mp=getPlug();\
  beforeDisconnect(prior);\
  ((otherEnd*)prior)->beforeDisconnect(mp);\
  disconnected(prior);\
  ((otherEnd*)prior)->disconnected(mp);}\
 return prior;}\
void operator-()\
 {otherPlug*prior=-*this;\
 if(prior)-*(otherEnd*)prior;\
 disconnectedFree(prior);}\
void addBefore(otherEnd*inner,myEnd*newEnd)\
 {addAfter(inner,newEnd);\
 if(pRedirector)pRedirector->redirectBefore(newEnd);}}\
void addAfter(otherEnd*inner,myEnd*newEnd)\
 {if(pOther&&newEnd)(*newEnd)<=(*(otherEnd*)-*this);\
 (*this)<=(*inner);}\
void afterConnect(otherPlug*p)\
 {if(pRedirector)pRedirector->afterConnect((myPlug*)this);}\
void beforeDisconnect(otherPlug*p)\
 {if(pRedirector)pRedirector->beforeDisconnect((myPlug*)this);}\
void disconnectedFree(otherPlug*p)\
 {if(pRedirector)pRedirector->disconnectedFree((myPlug*)this);}\
void disconnected(otherPlug*p)\
 {pOther=0;if(pRedirector)\
  pRedirector->\
disconnected((myPlug*)this);}\
void connectFailed()\
 {if(pRedirector)pRedirector->connectFailed((myPlug*)this);}\
} ;



#define DO_REDIRECTOR(c,pc)\
class c : public pc\
{protected:RedirectorNotify*pNotify;\
public:\
c():pNotify(0){}\
~c(){remove();}\
virtual void setNotify(RedirectorNotify*p){pNotify=p;}\
```

```
virtual void setNotify(RedirectorNotify&p){pNotify=&p;}\
virtual void reset(myEnd*){pMyEnd=0;}\
virtual void remove ()\
{if(pMyEnd)pMyEnd->setRedirector(pRedirector);\
 if(pRedirector)pRedirector->setMyEnd(pMyEnd);}\
virtual void redirectBefore(myEnd*pNew)\
{redirector*pOld=pRedirector;\
 redirect(pNew);\
 if(pOld)pOld->redirectBefore(pNew);}\
virtual void redirect(myEnd&NewPlug){redirect(NewPlug);}\
virtual void redirect(myEnd*pNew)\
{remove();\
 if(pNew){pMyEnd=pNew;\
  pRedirector->redirect(pNew->setRedirector(this));}}\
myPlug*getPlug(){return pMyEnd?pMyEnd->getPlug():0;}\
myEnd*getEnd(){return pMyEnd?pMyEnd->getEnd():0;}\
void operator<=(otherEnd&p){if(pMyEnd)(*pMyEnd)<=p;}\
otherPlug*operator->(){return&(*(*pMyEnd));}\
otherPlug&operator*(){return(*(*pMyEnd));}\
otherPlug*operator-(){return pMyEnd?-*pMyEnd:0;}\
void operator—(){if(pMyEnd)—*pMyEnd;}\
void addBefore(otherEnd*inner,myEnd*newEnd)\
{pMyEnd->addBefore(inner,newEnd);}\
void addAfter(otherEnd*inner,myEnd*newEnd)\
{pMyEnd->addAfter(inner,newEnd);}\
BOOL connected(){return pMyEnd?pMyEnd->connected():0;}\
BOOL usable(){return pMyEnd?pMyEnd->usable():0;}\
BOOL isRedirector(){return 1;}\
virtual void afterConnect(myPlug*p)\
 {if(pRedirector)pRedirector->afterConnect(p);\
  if(pNotify)pNotify->afterConnect((Plug*)p);}\
virtual void beforeDisconnect(myPlug*p)\
 {if(pRedirector)pRedirector->beforeDisconnect(p);\
  if(pNotify)pNotify->beforeDisconnect((Plug*)p);}\
virtual void disconnectedFree(myPlug*p)\
 {if(pRedirector)pRedirector->disconnectedFree(p);\
  if(pNotify)pNotify->disconnectedFree((Plug*)p);}\
virtual void disconnected(myPlug*p)\
 {if(pRedirector)pRedirector->disconnected(p);\
  if(pNotify)pNotify->disconnected((Plug*)p);}\
```

```
virtual void connectFailed(myPlug*p)\
 {if(pRedirector)pRedirector->connectFailed(p);\
if(pNotify)pNotify->connectFailed((Plug*)p);}\
};

#endif

// ====  End of PLUGS.HPP  ====
```

The order of the items in *Plugs.HPP* is irrelevant, because, with two exceptions, the items are all macro definitions that do not depend upon each other until invoked. The two exceptions are the *Plug* and *RedirectorNotify* classes. This section examines each item in order of its appearance in the *Plugs.HPP* file and describes how it is used.

The file starts out with a set of comments describing the general nature of plugs and plug functions. It is really more of a reminder because the description is rather short.

The first macro in the file is *plugCheck*. It is used in the -> operator and * operator of the *plug* class. The macro only gets defined if it is undefined. This allows you to define the macro before including the *Plugs.HPP* file and use your definition instead of the default definition. The chapter on debugging examines the use of *plugCheck*. The default definition does nothing, on the assumption that any invalid pointer bugs will be caught using a conventional debugger or that there are no plug-access-related bugs in the program.

The *plugCheck* macro definition is followed by conditional definitions for *BOOL, TRUE* and *FALSE*. These are relatively standard definitions normally included in *STDDEF.H*. They are included here just in case you did not include *STDDEF.H* or some similar set of definitions. These particular definitions are used in the subsequent class definitions in *Plugs.HPP*.

The *DECLARE_PLUG* macro comes next. This is the macro that must be included in any outer plug class definition. It declares the default case for the *myPlug* function; the default case simply returns *this*, which is a pointer to the plug object. Its use is described in the first two chapters of the book.

The *Plug* class and *RedirectorNotify* class come next. The *Plug* class is an abstract class that is the basis for all *plug* classes. There can never be a Plug object because the class is abstract but there can be pointers to the class. The *Plug* class defines a minimum number of plug-related functions, essentially those that do not refer to a plug subclass. The pure *virtual* functions like *connected* and the - - operator are defined by the *DECLARE_CONNECTION* macro when it is invoked. The overhead introduced by the Plug class is the initial virtual dispatch table and the pointer to it. Subsequent subclasses can share the pointer because each subclass has its own virtual dispatch table which includes pointers at the beginning to the table for the functions defined in the superclass, which, in this case, is the *Plug* class.

The *RedirectorNotify* class is not abstract although all the functions are *virtual*. An instance of this class can be created although it is normally used in a subclass, which is often a component utilizing redirectors. Check out the chapter on *Dynamic Plugs* for more details on the use of this class.

Next come the macro definitions for *DPLUG, DECLARE_CONNECTION, DO_PLUGA, DO_PLUG,* and *DO_REDIRECTOR*. The *DECLARE_CON-NECTION* definition includes support for *DECLARE_CONNECTION1* and *DECLARE_CONNECTION2 which are needed to address limitations of* some compilers. See the prior section for details on those limitations and the description of these macros later in this section for how the macros works.

The macros are used to define the plug and connection classes. Only the *DECLARE_CONNECTION* macro is used in this book. The other macros simply make it easier to define because much of the class definitions for a connection are essentially identical. Here is a quick overview of the macros and the kind of class they are used to define when the macro is invoked. The

DPLUG macro is used to define the dynamic redirector class. The *DO_PLUGA* is used to define the abstract plug or socket classes while *DO_PLUG* is used to define the basic plug and socket classes. Finally, *DO_REDIRECTOR* is used to define the basic redirector class for plugs and sockets.

The macro names, with the exception of *DECLARE_CONNECTION*, are irrelevant. The actual names are arbitrary and can be changed without affecting the plug and connection definition and use. The *DECLARE_CONNECTION* macro is used in the template version of *Plugs.HPP* which described in appendix C but you will see that all the other macros are gone. They are replaced by template definitions. The one exception is the *plugCheck* macro, but its operation is slightly different, as noted in appendix C.

We start with a discussion of the *DECLARE_CONNECTION* macro since it uses all the other macros just mentioned. There are two major items to note about the macro definition. First, it is conditionally defined based on the existence of the *_MSC_VER* symbol. Second, it can be defined as a combination of the *DECLARE_CONNECTION1* and *DECLARE_CONNECTION2* macros. The reason for this mess was presented in the previous section and is due to various limitations encountered in the Microsoft C++ compilers (versions 7 and 8). The conditional definition allows the *DECLARE_CONNECTION* macros to be defined properly for a particular compiler. In this case, the tested compilers were Microsoft C++ and Borland C++. We take a look at both definitions here and highlight the differences. Luckily, both definitions use the other macros in the same way, so this is the only part of the file that is compiler-dependent. If you encounter another compiler that does not work properly with these macros, look for problems and fixes in the *DECLARE_CONNECTION* macros first.

The version of *DECLARE_CONNECTION* for the Microsoft compiler comes first. It defines the *DECLARE_CONNECTION1* and *DECLARE_CONNECTION2* macros and then defines the *DECLARE_CONNECTION* macro as a combination of the two. It is assumed that the *DECLARE_CONNECTION1* macro will be invoked first and then the *DECLARE_CONNEC-*

TION2 macro will be invoked next with the exact same parameters. This allows the macro to define class definitions using a smaller macro expansion buffer, as for the Microsoft compilers. The split is about even in terms of space required to expand the two macros. The macros utilize the C token-passing operator, ##. The operator works when the macro is invoked and essentially concatenates the text to its left and right after other macro parameter replacements are made. Check out appendix E for details on macros.

All the macros discussed here are multiline macros. The backslash, \, at the end of the line tells the compiler (actually the preprocessor portion of the compiler) that the macro is continued on the next line. The last line of the multiline macro does not contain a backslash. The second line of the macro uses the ## operator. The first macro parameter is c and it appears to the left of the first instance of the ## operator. The c will be replaced by the value of the parameter. The *xpr* that appears after the ## operator is not a parameter so it remains as a literal. The two are combined, with the ## operator being removed when the macro is expanded. As an example, the *DECLARE_CONNECTION1* macro is listed next so you don't have to scan the file listing for it. It is followed by an example of the macro invocation.

```
#define DECLARE_CONNECTION1(c,bp,bs)\
class bp;class bs;\
class c##xpr;class c##xsr;class c##xs;\
class plugRedirector;class socketRedirector;class socketA;\
DO_PLUGA(c##xp,c##xs,bp,bs,c##xpr)\
DO_PLUGA(c##xs,c##xp,bs,bp,c##xsr)\
DO_REDIRECTOR(c##xpr,c##xp)\
DO_REDIRECTOR(c##xsr,c##xs)
```

```
DECLARE_CONNECTION1 ( Sample, SamplePlug, SampleSocket )
The macro invocation is expanded by the preprocessor into:
class SamplePlug;class SampleSocket;
class Samplexpr;class Samplexsr;class Samplexs;
DO_PLUGA(Samplexp,Samplexs,SamplePlug,SampleSocket,Samplexpr)
```

```
DO_PLUGA(Samplexs,Samplexp,SampleSocket,SamplePlug,Samplexsr)
DO_REDIRECTOR(Samplexpr,Samplexp)
DO_REDIRECTOR(Samplexsr,Samplexs)
```

The macros *DO_PLUGA* and *DO_REDIRECTOR* are then expanded. Note how the ## operator disappears and the literal suffixes are added to the end. You will also note that the classes defined by this macro are global, not nested. The nested definitions come next in the *DECLARE_CONNECTION2* macro. The reason for this is a bug in the Microsoft C++ compiler. It does not properly handle forward definitions of nested classes. Luckily it properly handles forward class definitions at the global level. The suffix characters are added to make the names unique and to avoid conflicts with similar names that might be used elsewhere in the program. The suffixes and their related class definitions are:

```
xs  abstract socket
xp  abstract plug
xsr socket redirector
xpr plug    redirector
```

The defined classes use pointers to each other, which is why they must be defined globally when using the Microsoft compiler. These classes are then used in the *DECLARE_CONNECTION2* macro which defines the nested classes within the main connection class. Lets take a look at the rest of *DECLARE_CONNECTION1* before we examine what *DECLARE_CON-NECTION2* does.

The first part of the expanded *DECLARE_CONNECTION1* macro consist of forward class definitions. This allows pointers or C++ references to be used in other class definitions and type definitions. The abstract plug and socket class definitions come next, with the help of the *DO_PLUGA* macros. We will take a look at what these class definitions look like when we cover the *DO_PLUGA* macro later in this section. Essentially, the first parameter to the macro is the class name and the other parameters are the various types used within the class definition. The plug and socket definitions are complementary. The *DO_REDIRECTOR* macro is invoked next with the same type of parameter list. The first parameter is the class name; it only needs a second abstract class name parameter because that class contains the necessary type definitions as part of its class definition.

The global classes necessary for a connection are defined once the *DECLARE_CONNECTION1* macro has been expanded. The following *DECLARE_CONNECTION2* macro invocation defines the connection class. For our previous example we need a source line that looks like:

```
DECLARE_CONNECTION2 ( Sample, SamplePlug, SampleSocket )
```

The following is a cleaned-up version of the macro expansion of *DECLARE_CONNECTION2*.

```
class Sample
{
  public:
    DO_PLUG ( plug, Samplexp )
    DO_PLUG ( socket, Samplexs )

    class plugRedirector : public Samplexpr {};
    class socketRedirector : public Samplexsr {};

    DPLUG ( dynamicPlugRedirector, Samplexpr )
    DPLUG ( dynamicSocketRedirector, Samplexsr )
};
```

This class definition includes six class definitions. Four are defined using macros, the first two using the *DO_PLUG* macro. The first macro parameter is the class name, which are the notable plug and socket classes. These are based upon the global plug and socket classes defined using *DECLARE_CON-NECTION1*. The nested redirector classes are the same as the global redirector classes. This mechanism works better with the Microsoft C++ compilers instead of using a nested *typedef* because of another limitation of the compiler. The *DPLUG* macro is used to define the two dynamic redirector classes, and again the first parameter is the class name.

So we now have defined the six nested classes used in this *book: plug, socket, plugRedirector, socketRedirector, dynamicPlugRedirector,* and *dynamicSocketRedirector.* The classes are nested in the connection class, which is *Sample* in our previous examples. The *DECLARE_CONNECTION* macro wraps up this section of the conditional definition. It simply uses the two macros with the same set of parameters. Unfortunately, this approach cannot be used with Microsoft's compiler because of the limited and fixed macro expansion buffer.

We now take a look at the cleaner alternate to this conditional macro definition. This starts after the *#else* and begins with the *DECLARE_CONNECTION1* macro definition. The *DECLARE_CONNECTION1* macro is simply defined as *DECLARE_CONNECTION.* The *DECLARE_CONNECTION2* macro expands to nothing. This allows the dual macro invocation mechanism (1/2) to be used even if you have a compiler which is capable of handling the single macro version.

The expanded version of this *DECLARE_CONNECTION* macro definition for our previous Sample example winds up like the following cleaned-up source code.

```
class SamplePlug ;
class SampleSocket ;

class Sample
{
  public:
    class plugRedirector ;
    class socketRedirector ;
    class socketA;

    DO_PLUGA(plugA,socketA,SamplePlug,SampleSocket,plugRedirector)
    DO_PLUGA(socketA,plugA,SampleSocket,SamplePlug,
      socketRedirector)

    DO_REDIRECTOR(plugRedirector,plugA)
    DO_REDIRECTOR(socketRedirector,socketA)
```

```
            DO_PLUG(plug,plugA)
            DO_PLUG(socket,socketA)

            DPLUG(dynamicPlugRedirector,plugRedirector)
            DPLUG(dynamicSocketRedirector,socketRedirector)
    } ;
```

This is very similar to the Microsoft support except that all classes are nested so there is no need for the global classes defined with the suffixes. There are five forward class definitions: two global and three nested. The two global are the same defined in the Microsoft support. They are the plug and socket classes that use the *DECLARE_PLUG* macro. The three forward nested class definitions include the two redirectors and the abstract socket class which must be defined but which is never used directly. The abstract plug class does not have to be defined in this manner because it is defined next. The *DO_PLUGA* macro will be expanded twice to define the plug and socket abstract classes: *plugA* and *socketA*. This is followed by the redirector class definitions via *DO_REDIRECTOR* and then the *plug* and *socket* class definitions. The dynamic redirector class definitions are last.

This ends the compiler-dependent portion of *Plugs.HPP*. Both versions wind up defining a similar nested class structure. The macros completely hide the various differences and limitations of the compiler, with the exception of the *DECLARE_CONNECTION1* and *DECLARE_CONNECTION2* macros, which must be used to overcome the Microsoft macro expansion buffer size limitation.

We now take a look at the support macros: *DO_PLUGA, DO_PLUG, DO_REDIRECTOR* and *DPLUG*. These are presented as conventional class definitions, which should make them easier to read and understand. The class definitions retain the macro parameters, but the initial definition line will also be listed as a comment. A description of the class definition follows the source code. For example, here is the cleaned-up version of *DO_PLUGA*.

```
// #define DO_PLUGA(ap,as,bp,bs,r)

class ap : public Plug
{
  public:
    typedef bs otherPlug;
    typedef as otherEnd;
    typedef bp myPlug;
    typedef ap myEnd;
    typedef r redirector;

  protected:
    union
    {
      myEnd*pMyEnd;
      otherPlug*pOther;
    };
    redirector*pRedirector;

  public:
    ap()
      : pRedirector(0)
      {pOther=0;}
    virtual myPlug*getPlug()=0;
    virtual myEnd*getEnd(){return(myEnd*)getPlug();}
    virtual void operator<=(otherEnd&)=0;
    virtual otherPlug*operator->(){plugCheck(pOther);
     return pOther;}
    virtual otherPlug&operator*(){plugCheck(pOther);return*pOther;}
    virtual otherPlug*operator-()=0;
    virtual void addBefore(otherEnd*,myEnd*)=0;
    virtual void addAfter(otherEnd*,myEnd*)=0;
    virtual BOOL connected(){return pOther!=0;}
    virtual void connectto(otherPlug*p){pOther=p;}
    virtual redirector*getRedirector(){return pRedirector;}
    virtual redirector*setRedirector(redirector*pR)
     {redirector*pOld=pRedirector;pRedirector=pR;return pOld;}
    virtual void setMyEnd(myEnd*p){pMyEnd=p;}
    virtual void disconnectedFree(otherPlug*){}
    virtual void disconnected(otherPlug*){}
```

```
          virtual void afterConnect(otherPlug*){}
          virtual void beforeDisconnect(otherPlug*){}
    };
```

DO_PLUGA is used to define the abstract plug and socket classes. The class definition is based upon the *Plug* class. The definition starts with a set of *type-def* definitions. These are used in this class definition and in subclass definitions so the connection, plug and socket class names do not have to be used explicitly. It comes in handy if you ever try to change from a plug to a socket. The *myEnd* type is the abstract plug for a plug and the abstract socket for a socket. You will notice that the explicit class names are only used in the *type-def* statements while these type definition names are used in the rest of the class definitions.

The public type definitions are followed by two protected pointer definitions. The first pointer is implemented as a union. This is done so the same space can be used by plugs or redirectors with the proper type being used. The plug support uses *pOther* while the redirector uses *pMyEnd*. The pRedirector pointer is used by both plugs and redirectors. The *union* is unnamed so the elements can be referenced without a prefix.

The next public section contains the function definitions for the abstract plug class. All function definitions are *virtual* except the constructor, which comes first. The constructor initializes the two pointers to 0. The union pointer must be initialized using an assignment statement. The rest of the functions can be divided into three categories: pure virtual functions, empty functions, and implemented functions. The pure virtual functions must be defined by the subclasses such as the plug classes defined by *DO_PLUG*. These functions require support specific to the type of subclass. The *getPlug* function is a pure virtual function in this class definition. The empty functions contain a function body definition which looks like {}. This defines a function that does nothing. One of the empty function definitions is *disconnectedFree*. The implemented functions provide a definition suitable for both plugs and redirectors. These functions are divided into three groups: the first group is related to redirector support and is common to both plugs and redirectors and includes *setRedirector* and *getRedirector*. The next group is *setMyEnd*, which is specific to redirectors. The third group covers the remaining functions and is related to plug operations like the -> operator. A redirector subclass will redefine these functions. Their use and semantics is covered in chapter 2.

The plug and socket classes are subclasses of the abstract plug and socket classes. The former are defined using the *DO_PLUG* macro. The following is the cleaned-up class definition, which will be followed by a commentary on the class and its functions.

```
// #define DO_PLUG(c,a)

class c : public a
{
  public:
    ~c()
    {
      if (pOther)
        -*(otherEnd*)pOther;
      if (pRedirector)
        pRedirector->redirect(0);
    }

    void operator<=(otherEnd&p)
    {
      otherEnd*prior=(otherEnd*)-*this;
      if (prior)
        --*prior;
      if (&p)
      {
      otherEnd*pp=(otherEnd*)-p;
      if (pp)
        --pp;
        myEnd*el=getEnd();
        if (el)
        {
          otherEnd*e2=p.getEnd();
          if (e2)
```

```
      {
        myPlug*p1=e1->getPlug();
        otherPlug*p2=e2->getPlug();
        e1->connectto(p2);
        e2->connectto(p1);
        e1->afterConnect(p2);
        e2->afterConnect(p1);
      }
    else
      e1->connectFailed();
  }
 }
 else
   connectFailed();
}


otherPlug*operator-()
{
  otherPlug*prior=pOther;
  if (prior)
  {
    myPlug*mp=getPlug();
    beforeDisconnect(prior);
    ((otherEnd*)prior)->beforeDisconnect(mp);
    disconnected(prior);
    ((otherEnd*)prior)->disconnected(mp);
  }
  return prior;
}


void operator--()
{
  otherPlug*prior=-*this;
  if (prior)
    --*(otherEnd*)prior;
  disconnectedFree(prior);
}


void addBefore(otherEnd*inner,myEnd*newEnd)
{
```

```
    addAfter(inner,newEnd);
    if (pRedirector)
      pRedirector->redirectBefore(newEnd);
}

void addAfter(otherEnd*inner,myEnd*newEnd)
{
    if (pOther&&newEnd)
      (*newEnd)<=(*(otherEnd*)-*this);
    (*this)<=(*inner);
}

void afterConnect(otherPlug*p)
{
    if (pRedirector)
      pRedirector->afterConnect((myPlug*)this);
}

void beforeDisconnect(otherPlug*p)
{
    if (pRedirector) pRedirector->
      beforeDisconnect((myPlug*)this);
}

void disconnectedFree(otherPlug*p)
{
    if (pRedirector)
      pRedirector->disconnectedFree((myPlug*)this);
}

void disconnected(otherPlug*p)
{
    pOther=0;
    if (pRedirector)
      pRedirector->disconnected((myPlug*)this);
}

void connectFailed()
{
    if (pRedirector)
```

```
                         pRedirector->connectFailed((myPlug*)this);
             }

      } ;
```

This class definition implements most of the plug protocol for plugs and sockets. It uses the *pOther* and *pRedirector* pointers defined in the abstract plug class, and a destructor is included to disconnect the plug and its redirector. The more complicated functions of the bunch are the main connection and disconnection operators: <=, - and --. Their protocol is described in chapter 2 so we will not try to analyze the functions in detail. The same is true for the *addBefore* and *addAfter* functions. The remaining functions are defined to notify the redirector, if *pRedirector* is not zero, by calling the matching redirector function with the *this* pointer. Casts are used to get the proper pointer type.

The *DO_REDIRECTOR* macro is used to define the basic redirector classes. The cleaned-up version is next, followed by a few comments about the class definition.

```
// #define DO_REDIRECTOR(c,pc)

class c : public pc
{
  protected:
    RedirectorNotify*pNotify;

  public:
    c() : pNotify(0) {}
    ~c()
    {
      remove();
    }

    virtual void setNotify(RedirectorNotify*p)
    {
      pNotify=p;
    }
```

```
virtual void setNotify(RedirectorNotify&p)
{
  pNotify=&p;
}

virtual void reset(myEnd*)
{
  pMyEnd=0;
}

virtual void remove ()
{
  if (pMyEnd)
    pMyEnd->setRedirector(pRedirector);
  if (pRedirector)
    pRedirector->setMyEnd(pMyEnd);
}

virtual void redirectBefore(myEnd*pNew)
{
  redirector*pOld=pRedirector;
  redirect(pNew);
  if (pOld)
    pOld->redirectBefore(pNew);
}

virtual void redirect(myEnd&NewPlug)
{
  redirect(NewPlug);
}

virtual void redirect(myEnd*pNew)
{
  remove();
  if (pNew)
  {
    pMyEnd=pNew;
    pRedirector->redirect(pNew->setRedirector(this));
  }
```

```
      }

    myPlug*getPlug()
    {
      return pMyEnd?pMyEnd->getPlug():0;
    }

    myEnd*getEnd()
    {
      return pMyEnd?pMyEnd->getEnd():0;
    }

    void operator<=(otherEnd&p)
    {
      if(pMyEnd)
        (*pMyEnd)<=p;
    }

    otherPlug*operator->()
    {
      return&(*(*pMyEnd));
    }

    otherPlug&operator*()
    {
      return(*(*pMyEnd));
    }

    otherPlug*operator-()
    {
      return pMyEnd?-*pMyEnd:0;
    }

    void operator--()
    {
      if (pMyEnd)
        --*pMyEnd;
    }

    void addBefore(otherEnd*inner,myEnd*newEnd)
```

```
{
  pMyEnd->addBefore(inner,newEnd);
}

void addAfter(otherEnd*inner,myEnd*newEnd)
{
  pMyEnd->addAfter(inner,newEnd);
}

BOOL connected()
{
  return pMyEnd?pMyEnd->connected():0;
}

BOOL usable()
{
  return pMyEnd?pMyEnd->usable():0;
}

BOOL isRedirector()
{
  return 1;
}

virtual void afterConnect(myPlug*p)
{
  if (pRedirector)
    pRedirector->afterConnect(p);
  if(pNotify)
    pNotify->afterConnect((Plug*)p);
}

virtual void beforeDisconnect(myPlug*p)
{
  if (pRedirector)
    pRedirector->beforeDisconnect(p);
  if (pNotify)
    pNotify->beforeDisconnect((Plug*)p);
}
```

```
virtual void disconnectedFree(myPlug*p)
{
  if (pRedirector)
    pRedirector->disconnectedFree(p);
  if (pNotify)
    pNotify->disconnectedFree((Plug*)p);
}

virtual void disconnected(myPlug*p)
{
  if (pRedirector)
    pRedirector->disconnected(p);
  if (pNotify)
    pNotify->disconnected((Plug*)p);
}

virtual void connectFailed(myPlug*p)
{
  if (pRedirector)
    pRedirector->connectFailed(p);
  if (pNotify)
    pNotify->connectFailed((Plug*)p);
}
};
```

The redirector class adds a pointer to a notification object. The notification object status functions are called when corresponding redirector functions are called. These are normally called by a plug or a plug's redirector. The redirector protocol is covered in chapter 2 and will not be presented again here. The functions in this class are used to maintain the redirector in a redirector list, forward functions to a plug at the end of a redirector list, or forward notification functions down the redirector list and to the notification object if the *pNotify* pointer is not zero.

We finally come to the last macro, *DPLUG*. It is used to define a dynamic redirector plug class, which is used in the Dynamic Plug chapter. The cleaned-up version looks like:

```
// #define DPLUG(c,dp)

class c : public dp
{
  protected:
    myPlug*pMyPlug;

    c (myPlug*p)
    : pMyPlug(p)
    {
      redirect((myEnd*)p);
    }

    void*operator new(size_t s)
    {
      return new char[s];
    }

  public:
    static myEnd*New(myPlug*p)
    {
      return new c(p);
    }

    void disconnectedFree(myPlug*)
    {
      delete(Plug*)pMyPlug;
      delete this;
    }
};
```

This class adds a pointer to the object definition, which is used to track a plug (which must be created using *new*). The constructor is *protected* so it can only be accessed from the static *New* function, which is *public*. The *new* operator is also protected, so an instance of this object can only be defined using *New*. The redefined *disconnectedFree* function handles the release of the plug and the redirector to free space once the plug is no longer needed.

This wraps up the description of the *Plugs.HPP* file.

Memory Requirements and Overhead

There are two major types of classes defined in *Plugs.HPP:* plugs and redirectors. The basic object structures are used when building subclasses. Useful plugs and special redirectors are always subclasses. Conventional redirectors all have the same structure and are normally used as is.

This section describes the memory requirements and overhead in general terms as well as specific terms for 80x86 class machines. In this section only, I refer to plugs as meaning the base structure of all plugs. Subclasses can include additional overhead, in both the number of functions provided and the number of variables that may be part of an object.

Plugs and redirectors both use virtual functions, which means that these objects include a pointer to a virtual dispatch table containing pointers to the code that implements a virtual function for a particular class. The start of a virtual dispatch table is used for the same functions if the objects are associated with two different subclasses that inherit from the same superclass. For example, class *A* has virtual functions *F1*, *F2* and *F3*. Class *B* and *C* inherit from *A*. The contents of the start of the virtual function tables for B and C refer to the same functions if *B* and *C* do not redefine *F1*, *F2 or F3*. The pointers are different if one or more of the functions are redefined. The size of the function table does not affect the size of the pointer to the virtual dispatch table.

A plug contains two pointers: one to the plug/socket at the other end of a connection and the other to the plug's redirector. The pointer values are 0 if the pointer does not refer to another object. Redirectors have three pointers: one to the object being redirected, one to the redirector's redirector and one to a *RedirectorNotify* object. Like the plug pointers, these refer to the appropriate kind of object or they are *0*.

The size, in bytes, of all pointers is machine- and compiler-specific. The sizes of the virtual table pointers are often independent of the other pointers. Some compilers even allow different size pointers within an object. The plug definitions in *Plugs.HPP* use the default pointer size for all pointers, including the virtual table pointer.

On an 80x86 CPU, the pointers may be 2, 4, or 6 bytes, depending upon the mode used. A 2-byte pointer is a simple 16-bit offset. A 4-byte pointer may be a 16-bit segment/offset pair when using the 80x86 segmented mode or a 32-bit absolute address when using a 32-bit environment like UNIX. A 6-byte pointer is a 16-bit segment/32-bit offset, which is rarely encountered.

For some simple estimate of size, let's look at the 2-byte and 4-byte pointers. The smallest case for a plug object uses only 2-byte pointers. This leads to a minimum size of 6 bytes for 3 pointers and a maximum size of 12 bytes. A redirector weighs in at minimum of 8 bytes or a maximum of 16 bytes. Neither is excessively large.

In terms of function-call overhead we have the initial overhead of virtual functions. An object function includes a hidden parameter, which is the pointer to the object. A virtual function call requires this as well as an indirect reference to the object to obtain the pointer to the virtual dispatch table, and then a table reference to get the function's address. The calling overhead for a plug function call using a plug is the same as for a virtual function call. The overhead for using a virtual function at the other end of the connection is the same, plus a pointer reference. The overhead is not quite as bad when you consider the difference in overhead between a normal virtual function call and one using a connection.

B PLUG-Based Class Libraries

Plug-based class libraries can be divided into three types:

- ❍ Reusable software
- ❍ Existing libraries with plugs added
- ❍ Libraries designed using plugs
- ❍ Libraries that are completely plug-based

All three are valid ways of using plugs to share resources. The differences among the three approaches are like the differences encountered when dealing with C++ class libraries that started out as C libraries. For example, the first conversion from a C to a C++ library usually results in a set of classes embodying the original set of functions and data structures. The next iteration may use classes and inheritance in a more complex manner, such as breaking functionality into multiple classes and having them combined by the programmer using multiple inheritance or templates. This process continues as the library designer and the users learn more and demand more from their tools.

The use of plugs in class libraries normally starts by adding plug connection definitions to existing C++ libraries. The next iteration of the library starts to add member functions to both sides of a connection, allowing the plugs to be used at a higher level. However, at this point plugs will be used for external connections only, not within the library itself. Finally, the libraries themselves will be designed using plugs internally, permitting some of the internal construction to be available for modification.

A basic plug-based library is divided into two sections: an interface class specification section and an implementation section. The interface section contains one or more .HPP header files with base class definitions and plug connection definitions that describe the generic version of the plug interface supplied by the implementation section. The class definitions in the interface section are usually abstract classes and cannot be used to create objects; only to define new classes. The interface classes provide the base for the implementation section and also allow new implementations to be created that may be used in place of the ones supplied by the library's implementation section.

The implementation section consists of one or more .HPP files that use one or more of the .HPP files from the interface section. The interface section files define the plug classes that can be used to allocate objects; these objects are the plugs and components that are provided by the library.

Each section should include written and electronic documentation. The latter can be provided as .DOC files in a basic text format. Files or chapters should be dedicated to the individual files and classes defined in each file contained in the interface and implementation sections.

Source code is optional for both the interface and implementation sections. The interface section often requires no additional source code because the definitions within the .HPP files are sufficient. Object files or object file libraries can be supplied in lieu of or in addition to source code.

A Sample Library

A sample library is described in this appendix. Two connections are defined, each in its own header file. The implementation section contains individual plug implementations for each type of plug defined in the interface section, and one plug has an additional implementation to show how additional plugs might be defined. The example follows the general recommendations for how a library interface and implementation should be done. The file names have been chosen to reflect the type of file rather than the type of component or plug. In general, the latter is preferable.

The sample library implements two basic string stream-oriented connections. One set is unidirectional, one bidirectional. The actual implementations use disk files as the source and sink. A tee filter component for the bidirectional connection is defined. The component contains three plugs. Two are for the filter connections and a third is used to distribute an annotated copy of what passes through the filter.

The files used with this library definition are listed in the following table.

Table B.1

Interface Section
BaseA.HPP	ConnectionA unidirectional connection interface definition
BaseB.HPP	ConnectionB bidirectional connection interface definition
CompC.HPP	ComponentC filter interface definition

Implementation Section
ActualPA.HPP	ConnectionA plug definition
ActualSA.HPP	ConnectionA socket definition
ActualPB.HPP	ConnectionB plug definition
ActualSB.HPP	ConnectionB socket definition
ActualC1.HPP	ComponentC type 1 definition
ActualC2.HPP	ComponentC type 2 definition

These files are augmented with the following documentation files:

Table B.2

BaseA.DOC	ConnectionA interface definition
BaseB.DOC	ConnectionB interface definition
CompC.DOC	ComponentC interface definition
ActualPA.DOC	ConnectionA plug definition
ActualSA.DOC	ConnectionA socket definition
ActualPB.DOC	ConnectionB plug definition
ActualSB.DOC	ConnectionB socket definition
ActualC1.DOC	ComponentC type 1 definition
ActualC2.DOC	ComponentC type 2 definition

The implementation files are listed next. The resulting object files may be supplied with the library source code or in place of the .CPP files. A single object library could be provided instead of individual object files.

Table B3

CompC.CPP	ComponentC interface definition
ActualPA.CPP	ConnectionA plug definition
ActualSA.CPP	ConnectionA socket definition
ActualPB.CPP	ConnectionB plug definition
ActualSB.CPP	ConnectionB socket definition
ActualC1.CPP	ComponentC type 1 definition
ActualC2.CPP	ComponentC type 2 definition

File Contents

The contents of the files are presented and described in the next two sections; first the unidirectional connections, then the bidirectional. The documentation files are presented first because they provide the description of connections, plugs, and components defined in the .HPP files and implemented in the .CPP files. The documentation files are also grouped with their associated .HPP and .CPP files.

Note that the documentation and comments within the definition and implementation source files are almost nonexistent. This is because the documentation and associated commentary are more than adequate to describe their content and operation. This would not be true on a more extensive implementation. The use of documentation or .DOC files should not preclude the proper use of comments and naming conventions. Likewise, good code-commenting procedures should not preclude decent documentation or .DOC files.

This set of files does not require any common constant or structure definitions that may be required with a more complex connection. Normal C documentation and coding practices can be used to handle such requirements.

Unidirectional String Stream Connections

The unidirectional string stream connection class, *StrStream1,* allows a single C string pointer to be passed from the plug end of the connection to the socket end. The string stream class provides a basic set of abstract plug classes to support this type of exchange. A pair of plugs is used to implement a bidirectional connection, which is described in the next section.

The connection provides the mechanism to move lines of text from one point to another. It does not impose any other restrictions on the ordering or content of the data. Actual implementations of the plugs or components using this connection interface may impose both content and ordering restrictions. One possible source, and the one implemented in this section, is a C text file. An alternative could be a command line input from the keyboard or a line of data from an interface to a laboratory instrument connected to the computer. The destination socket is also a C text file, where each line received will be written to the file. The next set of listings describes the basic interface for the connection.

```
// File: BaseA.DOC    ConnectionA interface definition
/*
```

The StrStream1 connection class uses *StrStreamSource* and *StrStreamDestination* base classes for the plug and socket, respectively. The *StrStream1* connection allows a C string pointer to be passed across the connection. There is no restriction on the contents or ordering with respect to this connection definition. A particular implementation of the plug or socket class may impose either.

The *StrSteam1* class is useful for implementing line-at-a-time interfaces that are driven by the source. A corresponding connection can be defined that works in the opposite direction.

The public interface can be used by anyone using a plug based on this connection. In addition, all public plug functions can be used. The internal interface is to be used only when implementing new plugs based on these classes.

```
====  Public Interface   ====
Connection: StrStream1
   Plug: StrStreamSource
      Process ( const char * )

   Socket: StrStreamDestination
      none


====  Internal Interface   ====
Connection: StrStream1
   Plug: StrStreamSource
      none

   Socket: StrStreamDestination
      Process ( const char * )
```

StrStreamSource and *StrStreamDestination* both implement the *Process* function. The *StrStreamSource* version assumes that a connection is in place and calls the *Process* function at the other end. The *StrStreamSource OtherEnd* function is defined in the connection plug class. It provides access to the other end of the connection.

Note that the *StrStreamDestination Process* function is protected. Any plug subclass can access it using the *Process* function defined by the plug base class.

```
*/


// ===================================
// File: BaseA.HPP    ConnectionA interface definition

#ifndef ( _BaseA )
#define _BaseA

DECLARE_CONNECTION
  ( StrStream1
  , StrStreamSource
  , StrStreamDestination
  )

class StrStreamSource : public StrStream1::plug
{
  public:
    DECLARE_PLUG ()

    virtual void Process ( const char * buffer ) ;
} ;

class StrStreamDestination : public StrStream1::socket
{
  public:
    DECLARE_PLUG ()

  protected:
```

```
       friend StrStreamSource ;

       virtual void Process ( const char * buffer ) = 0 ;
    } ;



    #endif


    // File: BaseA.CPP     ConnectionA interface definition

    #include "BaseA.HPP"

    void StrStreamSource::Process ( const char * buffer )
    {
      pOther->Process ( buffer ) ;
    }
```

The next set of files defines and implements one possible version of the *StrStream1* plug. The *FileStrStreamSourcePlug* class can be used to define a plug object. This plug can be used and connected to a corresponding socket. The *Process* function can be called directly. The *FileStrStreamSource* plug class adds the *Send* function to its public repertoire. The *Process* function can still be used. The *Send* function uses the *Process* function to operate on all the lines it can read from the named text file. This version is not very sophisticated— there are no error indications if the file cannot be opened, and the only other check is to make sure that the connection exists. Even this could be eliminated with the proper documentation, placing the burden on the plug's user. This is not unreasonable, given that the *Process* function also has this restriction.

The *FileStrStreamSourceBase* class was included so that additional plug classes could be defined based upon it. Note that this class does not contain a *FILE* pointer, whereas the *FileStrStreamSource* class does.

```
    // File: ActualPA.DOC ConnectionA plug definition
    /*
```

The *FileStrStreamSourcePlug* class implements the basic *StrStream1* plug class. It is usable by itself and objects of this type can be connected to the corresponding socket. The base *Process* function should only be used after the plug is connected to a socket. No connection check is made when the *Process* function is used.

The *FileStrStreamSourceBase* abstract class defines a higher-level interface that allows a named text file to be sent to a socket using the *Process* function; one line from the text file per function call. The entire file is copied by a single *Send* function call. The *Process* function can be used before and after a *Send* function call. Unlike the *Process* function, the *Send* function checks for a connection prior to using the *Process* function. There is no indication of an error if the file cannot be opened or an error occurs while the file is being read.

```
====  Public Interface  ====
   Connection: StrStream1
     Plug Base: StrStreamSource
        Process ( const char * )

     Plug: FileStrStreamSourcePlug

     Abstract Plug: FileStrStreamSourceBase
        void Send ( const char * fileName )

     Plug: FileStrStreamSource
        void Send ( const char * fileName )
```

The functions would normally be described in more detail in this section of the file, but here they are not because the number of functions is so small and the previous discussion covers their operation. The parameters and their use are also limited and should be obvious.

```
====  Internal Interface  ====
   none

*/
```

```
// =====================================
// File: ActualPA.HPP  ConnectionA plug definition

#include "BaseA.HPP"

class FileStrStreamSourceBase : public FileStrStreamSource
{
  public:
    virtual void Send ( const char * fileName ) = 0 ;
} ;

class FileStrStreamSource : public FileStrStreamSourceBase
{
  protected:
    FILE * file ;

  public:
    virtual void Send ( const char * fileName ) ;
} ;

// File: ActualPA.CPP  ConnectionA plug definition

#include "stdio.hpp"
#include "ActualPA.HPP"

void FileStrStreamSource::Send ( const char * fileName )
{
  if ( connected ())
  {
    FILE * file = fopen ( fileName, "rt" ) ;
    if ( file != NULL )
    {
      char buffer [ 256 ] ;

      while ( fgets ( buffer, file ))
      {
        Process ( buffer ) ;
      }
    }
```

```
        }
    }
```

The next set of files defines and implements the socket end of the *StrStream1* connection. The data is placed into a file, which must be opened prior to the sockets use; otherwise, the data is simply ignored.

```
// File: ActualSA.DOC  ConnectionA socket definition
/*
```

The *FileStrStreamDestinationSocket* class implements the plug functions but does not define the *Process* function specified in the connection's socket base class.

```
====  Public Interface  ====
   Connection: StrStream1
     Socket Base: StrStreamDestination

     Socket: FileStrStreamDestinationSocket

     Abstract Socket: FileStrStreamDestinationBase
       void BeginReceive ( const char * fileName )
       void EndReceive ()

     Socket: FileStrStreamDestination
       void BeginReceive ( const char * fileName )
       void EndReceive ()

====  Internal Interface  ====
   none

*/


// ===================================
// File: ActualSA.HPP  ConnectionA socket definition

#ifndef ( _ACTUALSA )
#define _ACTUALSA
```

```
#include "stdio.hpp"
#include "BaseA.HPP"

class FileStrStreamDestinationBase : public FileStrStreamDestina-
tion
{
  public:
    virtual void BeginReceive ( const char * fileName ) = 0 ;
    virtual void EndReceive () = 0 ;
} ;

class FileStrStreamDestination : public FileStrStreamDestination-
Base
{
  protected:
    FILE * file ;
    virtual void Process ( const char * buffer ) ;

  public:
    virtual void BeginReceive ( const char * fileName ) ;
    virtual void EndReceive () ;
} ;

#endif

// File: ActualSA.CPP  ConnectionA socket definition

#include "ActualSA.HPP"

void FileStrStreamDestination::Process ( const char * buffer )
{
  if ( file != NULL )
  {
    fputs ( buffer, file ) ;
  }
}


void FileStrStreamDestination::BeginReceive ( const char * fileName
)
```

```
  {
    if ( file != NULL )
    {
      EndReceive () ;
    }

    file = fopen ( fileName, "wt" ) ;
  }

  void FileStrStreamDestination::EndReceive ()
  {
    if ( file != NULL )
    {
      fclose ( file ) ;
      file = NULL ;
    }
  }
```

The *StrStream1* connection class is by design a very limited connection. The purpose of this appendix is to show how the files are configured, not how the classes or connections are constructed. The next section defines and implements another connection class whose implementations utilize the classes and components implemented for the *StrStream1* connection. There is no requirement that another plug library must use this same scheme, but it is often the case that a library defines and provides numerous connection definitions and associated implementations.

Bidirectional String Stream Connections

A pair of the unidirectional *StrStream1* connections are used to implement a bidirectional connection. The basic bidirectional connection is a compound plug composed of two unidirectional plugs (actually a *StrStream1::plug* and a *StrStream1::socket*). Both ends of this bidirectional connection are the same. This is not a requirement; it is actually more typical to have the ends different, as in the *StrStream1* connection. Note, however, that the plug and socket connections are distinct. They are not interchangeable, even though their base class is the same. This is also true for connections that may use common base class definitions. For example, connections *C1* and *C2* both use a plug whose base class is *B*. A *C1::plug* can be connected to a *C1::socket* but not to a *C2::socket*.

```
// File: BaseB.DOC    ConnectionB interface definition
/*
```

StrStream2 is a compound connection class using a pair of *StrStream1* plugs, a *StrStream1::plug* and a *StrStream1::socket*. The pair are internal to the *StrStream2* connection. In fact, the base connection does not include a public interface. The only public interface is the plug protocol.

Any public interface must be defined by plug subclasses of this connection. The connection, like most compound connections, is treated as a whole, with the individual internal connections kept out of the public eye.

Note: The plug and socket interfaces are identical, but the plug and socket classes are not interchangeable using this definition. Is it possible to define a connection with the same type of plug at both ends? Yes. Unfortunately, there is no macro defined to do this, so you will have to resort to defining it explicitly.

```
====  Public Interface  ====
   none

====  Internal Interface  ====
Connection: StrStream2
  Plug: StrStream2Plug
    StrStream1::plug & Plug1 ()
    StrStream1::socket & Socket1 ()

  Socket: StrStream2Socket
    see Plug1 functions.
```

The *afterConnect* and *beforeDisconnect* functions are also implemented to handle the compound plug's connection protocol. Each side connects and disconnects its own StrStream::plug, which causes the other side to connect or disconnect the associated socket.

The *Plug1* and *Socket1* functions provide access to the internal *StrStream1::plug* and socket objects. The base class does not define any particular implementation, so these may be plugs or redirectors that are part of a subclassed object, or they may be objects located outside the subclassed object.

```
*/


// ===================================
// File: BaseB.HPP     ConnectionB interface definition

#ifndef ( _BaseB )
#define _BaseB

#include "BaseA.HPP"

DECLARE_CONNECTION
  ( StrStream2
  , StrStream2Plug
  , StrStream2Socket
  )

class StrStream2Plug : public StrStream2::plug
{
  public:
    DECLARE_PLUG ()

    virtual void AfterConnect ( otherPlug * pOther )
    {
      Plug1 () <= pOther -> Socket1 () ;
    }

    virtual void BeforeConnect ( otherPlug * pOther )
    {
      -- Plug1 () ;
```

```
        }

        virtual StrStream1::plug::myEnd & Plug () = 0 ;
        virtual StrStream1::socket::myEnd & Socket () = 0 ;
    } ;



    class StrStream2Socket : public StrStream2::socket
    {
      public:
        DECLARE_PLUG ()

        virtual void AfterConnect ( otherPlug * pOther )
        {
          Plug1 () <= pOther -> Socket1 () ;
        }

        virtual void BeforeConnect ( otherPlug * pOther )
        {
          -- Plug1 () ;
        }

        virtual StrStream1::plug::myEnd & Plug () = 0 ;
        virtual StrStream1::socket::myEnd & Socket () = 0 ;
    } ;


#endif
```

The implementation of the *StrStream2* plug uses a pair of *StrStream1* file plugs. Access is provided to these plugs using virtual functions. *StrStream2Plug* provides a basis for the compound plug but requires definitions for the internal *Plug1* and *Socket1* functions. The *FileStrStream2Source* provides a file interface for both of the internal connections. Support for the file specification is provided through access to the internal support plug and socket. An abstract class could be implemented for *FileStrStream2Source*.

An alternative to defining *FileStrStream2Source* is to define a *StrStream2* plug class that includes a pair of public redirectors, one for each internal connection. The redirectors could then be assigned *FileStrStreamDestination* and *FileStrStreamSource* object references.

```
// File: ActualPB.DOC ConnectionB plug definition
/*
```

StrStream2Plug is the basic compound plug definition. It is an abstract class and cannot be used to declare objects. *FileStrStream2Source* is not an abstract class and can be used to declare objects. The *FilePlug* and *FileSocket* functions provide access to the *StrStream1* plug and socket objects of type *FileStrStreamDestination* and *FileStrStreamSource*.

```
====  Public Interface  ====
   Connection: StrStream2
     Abstract Plug: StrStream2Plug
        none

      Plug: FileStrStream2Source
         FileStrStreamDestination & FilePlug ()
         FileStrStreamSource & FileSocket ()

====  Internal Interface  ====
   Connection: StrStream2
     Plug: StrStream2Plug
        none

      Plug: FileStrStream2Source
         StrStream1::plug::myEnd & Plug1 ()
         StrStream1::socket::myEnd & Socket1 ()
```

The *Plug* and *Socket* functions return the same values as the *FilePlug* and *FileSocket* function, but these additional functions are required because the type of reference returned by the *Plug1* and *Socket1* functions will not allow access to the file-related object functions. The *Plug* and *Socket* functions are needed by the superclass. The function names cannot be overloaded because overloaded C++ functions must differ by the type or number of parameters. The return type is not included in this comparison.

```
*/

// ===================================
// File: ActualPB.HPP  ConnectionB plug definition

#include "BaseB.HPP"

class FileStrStream2Source : public StrStream2Plug
{
  protected:
    FileStrStreamDestination MySocket ;
    FileStrStreamSource MyPlug ;

    virtual StrStream1::plug::myEnd & Plug1 () ;
    virtual StrStream1::socket::myEnd & Socket1 () ;

  public:
    virtual FileStrStreamDestination & FilePlug () ;
    virtual StrStream1::socket::myEnd & FileSocket () ;
} ;


// File: ActualPB.CPP  ConnectionB plug definition

#include "ActualPB.HPP"

StrStream1::plug::myEnd & FileStrStream2Source::Plug ()
{
  return MyPlug ;
}

StrStream1::socket::myEnd & FileStrStream2Source::Socket ()
{
  return MySocket ;
}
```

```
FileStrStreamDestination & FileStrStream2Source::Plug1 ()
{
  return MyPlug ;
}

FileStrStreamSource & FileStrStream2Source::Socket1 ()
{
  return MySocket ;
}
```

The socket side of the *StrStream2* connection looks the same as the plug side. The definitions mirror the ones just presented.

```
// File: ActualSB.DOC  ConnectionB socket definition
/*

see ActualPB.DOC.

====  Public Interface  ====
see ActualPB.DOC.

====  Internal Interface  ====
see ActualPB.DOC.

*/


// ====================================
// File: ActualSB.HPP  ConnectionB socket definition

#include "BaseB.HPP"

class FileStrStream2Destination : public StrStream2Socket
{
  protected:
    FileStrStreamDestination MySocket ;
    FileStrStreamSource MyPlug ;

    virtual StrStream1::plug::myEnd & Plug1 () ;
    virtual StrStream1::socket::myEnd & Socket1 () ;
```

```
    public:
      FileStrStreamDestination & FileSocket () ;
      FileStrStreamSource & FilePlug () ;
  } ;



  // File: ActualSB.CPP ConnectionB socket definition

  #include "ActualSB.HPP"

  StrStream1::plug::myEnd & FileStrStream2Destination::Plug1 ()
  {
    return MyPlug ;
  }


  StrStream1::socket::myEnd & FileStrStream2Destination::Socket1 ()
  {
    return MySocket ;
  }


  FileStrStreamSource & FileStrStream2Destination::FilePlug ()
  {
    return MyPlug ;
  }


  FileStrStreamDestination & FileStrStream2Destination::FileSocket ()
  {
    return MySocket ;
  }
```

Component Definitions

The component header file, *CompC.HPP*, defines both *StrStream1* and *StrStream2* components. These could be broken out into separate definition files, but for the example it is easier to combine them into one. Two distinct implementation file groups are used, one for *StrStream1* components and another for *StrStream2* components. The latter uses *StrStream1* components internally.

```
// File: CompC.DOC      ComponentC interface definition
/*
```

The *CompC.HPP* file defines four abstract component classes. Two are for *StrStream1* connections, with a complementary pair for *StrStream2* connections. The *StrStream1* components include a 2-to-1 merge and a filter component. A tee connector is missing from this group and is defined in the implementation files as a subclass of the filter component. A tee component should actually be defined here.

```
==== Public Interface ====

class StrStream1Merge
    StrStream1::socket::myEnd & Socket1 ()
    StrStream1::socket::myEnd & Socket2 ()
    StrStream1::plug::myEnd & Plug ()

class StrStream1Filter
    StrStream1::socket::myEnd & Socket1 ()
    StrStream1::plug::myEnd & Plug1 ()

class StrStream2Merge
    StrStream2::socket::myEnd & Socket1 ()
    StrStream2::socket::myEnd & Socket2 ()
    StrStream2::plug::myEnd & Plug1 ()

class StrStream2Filter
    StrStream2::socket::myEnd & Socket1 ()
    StrStream2::plug::myEnd & Plug1 ()


==== Internal Interface ====
  none

*/


// ==================================
```

```
// File: CompC.HPP      ComponentC interface definition

#ifndef ( _CompC )
#define _CompC

#include "BaseA.HPP"
#include "BaseB.HPP"

class StrStream1Merge
{
  public:
    virtual StrStream1::socket::myEnd & Socket1 () = 0 ;
    virtual StrStream1::socket::myEnd & Socket2 () = 0 ;

    virtual StrStream1::plug::myEnd & Plug1 () = 0 ;
} ;

class StrStream1Filter
{
  public:
    virtual StrStream1::plug::myEnd & Plug1 () = 0 ;
    virtual StrStream1::socket::myEnd & Socket1 () = 0 ;
} ;

class StrStream1TeeFilter : public StrStream1Filter
{
  public:
    virtual StrStream1::plug::myEnd & CopyPlug () = 0 ;
} ;

class StrStream2Filter
{
  public:
    virtual StrStream2::plug::myEnd & Plug1 () = 0 ;
    virtual StrStream2::socket::myEnd & Socket1 () = 0 ;
} ;

class StrStream2TeeFilter : public StrStream2Filter
{
  public:
```

```
        virtual StrStream1::plug::myEnd & CopyPlug () = 0 ;
        virtual StrStream1::plug::myEnd & CopySocket () = 0 ;
} ;

#endif



// File: CompC.CPP      ComponentC interface definition
//
// nothing to define
```

There is actually no *CompC.CPP* file. It was simply included here for consistency. This file would normally implement any functions defined in the *CompC.HPP* file. This file is empty because all of the functions in the *CompC.HPP* file are pure virtual functions that do not require a definition.

The components defined in *ActualC1* are given in the following listing.

```
// File: ActualC1.DOC ComponentC type 1 definition
/*

====  Public Interface  ====

Component: StrStream1Merge
  Component: StrStream1BasicMerge
    Implements Plug, Socket1, and Socket2 functions.
    Input from Socket1 and Socket2 sent to Plug.

Component: StrStream1Filter
  Component: StrStream1BasicFilter
    Implements Plug1 and Socket1 functions.
    Passes input from Socket1 to Plug1.

  Component: StrStream1BasicTeeFilter
    Implements StrStream1Filter Plug and Socket functions.
    Adds StrStream1::socket & CopyPlug ()
    Input from Socket1 sent to Plug1 and CopyPlug.
```

```
"2nd line, StrStream1Filer/Filter


Component: StrStream2Filter
  Component: StrStream2BaseFilter
    Implements Plug1 and Socket1 functions.


  Component: StrStream2BasicTeeFilter
    Implements Plug1 and Socket1 functions.
    Adds CopyPlug and CopySocket.
    Passes input from Plug's StrStream1::plug to CopyPlug.
    Same for CopySocket.



====  Internal Interface  ====


Connection: StrStream1
  Socket: StrStream1ForwardSocket
    StrStream1ForwardSocket ( Stream1::plug::myPlug & MyPlug )


    Socket: StrStreamForwardSocket2
      StrStream1ForwardSocket
        ( Stream1::plug::myPlug & MyPlug1
        , Stream1::plug::myPlug & MyPlug2
        )


    Plug: StrStream1ForwardPlug
      StrStream1ForwardPlug
        ( Stream1::socket::myPlug & MySocket1
        . Stream1::socket::myPlug & MySocket2
        )


    Plug: StrStream2PlugIndirect
      StrStream2PlugIndirect
        ( StrStream1::plug::myPlug & Plug1
        , StrStream1::socket::myPlug & Socket1
        )


  */
```

```
// ===================================
// File: ActualC1.HPP  ComponentC type 1 definition

#include "CompC.HPP"

class StrStream1ForwardSocket : public StrStream1::socket
{
  protected:
    Stream1::plug::myPlug & Plug ;

  public:
    StrStream1ForwardSocket ( Stream1::plug::myPlug & MyPlug ) ;

    virtual void Process ( const char * buffer ) ;
} ;


class StrStream1ForwardSocket2 : public StrStream1::socket
{
  protected:
    Stream1::plug::myPlug & MyPlug1 ;
    Stream1::plug::myPlug & MyPlug2 ;

    virtual void Process ( const char * buffer ) ;

  public:
    StrStream1ForwardSocket
      ( Stream1::plug::myPlug & Plug1
      , Stream1::plug::myPlug & Plug2
      ) ;
} ;


class StrStream1ForwardPlug : public StrStream1::plug
{
  public:
    Stream1::socket::myPlug & Socket1 ;
    Stream1::socket::myPlug & Socket2 ;
```

```
        StrStream1ForwardPlug
          ( Stream1::socket::myPlug & MySocket1
          . Stream1::socket::myPlug & MySocket2
          ) ;

        virtual void Process ( const char * buffer ) ;
    } ;



class StrStream1BasicMerge : public StrStream1Merge
{
   protected:
     StrStream1::plug::myPlug MyPlug ;
     StrStream1ForwardSocket MySocket1 ;
     StrStream1ForwardSocket MySocket2 ;

   public:
     StrStream1BasicMerge () ;
     virtual StrStream1::socket::myEnd & Socket1 () ;
     virtual StrStream1::socket::myEnd & Socket2 () ;

     virtual StrStream1::plug::myEnd & Plug1 () ;
} ;

class StrStream1BasicFilter : public StrStream1Filter
{
   protected:
     StrStream1::plug::myPlug MyPlug ;
     StrStream1ForwardSocket MySocket ;

   public:
     StrStream1BasicMerge () ;

     virtual StrStream1::plug::myEnd & Plug1 () = 0 ;
     virtual StrStream1::socket::myEnd & Socket1 () = 0 ;
} ;

class StrStream1BasicTeeFilter : public StrStream1TeeFilter
{
```

```
  protected:
    StrStream1ForwardSocket2 MySocket ;
    FileStrStreamSource MyPlug1 ;
    FileStrStreamSource MyPlug2 ;

  public:
    StrStream1BasicTeeFilter () ;
    virtual StrStream1::plug::myEnd & Plug1 () ;
    virtual StrStream1::socket::myEnd & Socket () ;
    virtual StrStream1::socket::myEnd & CopyPlug () ;
} ;

class StrStream2PlugIndirect : public StrStream2:plug
{
  protected:
    StrStream1::plug::myPlug & MyPlug ;
    StrStream1::socket::myPlug & MySocket ;
    StrStream1BasicTeeFilter TeeFilter1 ;
    StrStream1BasicTeeFilter TeeFilter2 ;

  public:
    StrStream2PlugIndirect
      ( StrStream1::plug::myPlug & Plug1
      , StrStream1::socket::myPlug & Socket1
      ) ;
    virtual StrStream1::plug::myEnd & Plug1 () ;
    virtual StrStream1::socket::myEnd & Socket1 () :
} ;


class StrStream2BaseFilter : public StrStream2Filter
{
  protected:
    StrStream1BasicFilter Filter1 ;
    StrStream1BasicFilter Filter2 ;

    StrStream2PlugIndirect MyPlug ;
    StrStream2SocketIndirect MySocket ;

  public:
```

```
      StrStream2BaseFilter ()
      virtual StrStream2::plug::myEnd & Plug1 () ;
      virtual StrStream2::socket::myEnd & Socket1 () ;
  } ;


  class StrStream2BasicTeeFilter : public StrStream2TeeFilter
  {
    protected:
      StrStream1BasicTeeFilter TeeFilter1 ;
      StrStream1BasicTeeFilter TeeFilter2 ;

      StrStream2PlugIndirect MyPlug ;
      StrStream2SocketIndirect MySocket ;

    public:
      StrStream2BasicTeeFilter () ;
      virtual StrStream2::plug::myEnd & Plug1 () ;
      virtual StrStream2::socket::myEnd & Socket1 () ;

      virtual StrStream1::plug::myEnd & CopyPlug () ;
      virtual StrStream1::plug::myEnd & CopySocket () ;
  } ;



// File: ActualC1.CPP  ComponentC type 1 definition

#include "ActualC1.HPP"

StrStream1ForwardSocket::StrStream1ForwardSocket
  ( Stream1::plug::myPlug & MyPlug )
  : Plug1 ( MyPlug )
{}

void StrStream1ForwardSocketProcess ( const char * buffer )
{
  Plug1.Process ( buffer ) ;
}


void StrStream1ForwardSocket2::Process ( const char * buffer )
```

```
{
  MyPlug1.Process ( buffer ) ;
  MyPlug2.Process ( buffer ) ;
}


StrStream1ForwardSocket2::StrStream1ForwardSocket
  ( Stream1::plug::myPlug & Plug1
  , Stream1::plug::myPlug & Plug2
  )
  : MyPlug1 ( Plug1 )
  , MyPlug2 ( Plug2 )
{}



StrStream1ForwardPlug::StrStream1ForwardPlug
  ( Stream1::socket::myPlug & MySocket1
  . Stream1::socket::myPlug & MySocket2
  )
  : Socket1 ( MySocket1 )
  , Socket2 ( MySocket2 )
{}

void StrStream1ForwardPlugProcess ( const char * buffer )
{
  Socket1.Process ( buffer ) ;
  Socket2.Process ( buffer ) ;
}



StrStream1BasicMerge::StrStream1BasicMerge ()
  : MySocket1 ( MyPlug )
  , MySocket2 ( MyPlug )
{}

StrStream1::socket::myEnd & StrStream1BasicMergeSocket1 ()
{
  return MySocket1 ;
}

StrStream1::socket::myEnd & StrStream1BasicMergeSocket2 ()
```

```
  {
    return MySocket2 ;
  }


StrStream1::plug::myEnd & StrStream1BasicMergePlug ()
  {
    return MyPlug ;
  }



StrStream1BasicFilter::StrStream1BasicMerge ()
  : MySocket ( MyPlug )
{}



StrStream1BasicTeeFilter::StrStream1BasicTeeFilter ()
  : StrStream1BasicTeeFilter ( MyPlug1, MyPlug2 )
{}


StrStream1::plug::myEnd & StrStream1BasicTeeFilter::Plug1 ()
  {
    return MyPlug1 ;
  }


StrStream1::socket::myEnd & StrStream1BasicTeeFilter::Socket1 ()
  {
    return MySocket ;
  }


StrStream1::socket::myEnd & StrStream1BasicTeeFilter::CopyPlug ()
  {
    return MyPlug2 ;
  }



StrStream2PlugIndirect::StrStream2PlugIndirect
  ( StrStream1::plug::myPlug & Plug1
  , StrStream1::socket::myPlug & Socket1
  )
  : MyPlug ( Plug1 )
```

```
    , MySocket ( Socket1 )
{ }


StrStream1::plug::myEnd & StrStream2PlugIndirect::Plug1 ()
{
  return MyPlug ;
}


StrStream1::socket::myEnd & StrStream2PlugIndirect::Socket1 ()
{
  return MySocket ;
}



StrStream2BaseFilter::StrStream2BaseFilter ()
  : MyPlug ( Filter1.Plug(), Filter2.Socket())
  , MySocket ( Filter1.Socket1, Filter1.Plug1())
{ }


StrStream2::plug::myEnd & StrStream2BaseFilter::Plug1 ()
{
  return MyPlug ;
}


StrStream2::socket::myEnd & StrStream2BaseFilter::Socket1 ()
{
  return MySocket ;
}



StrStream2BasicTeeFilter::StrStream2BasicTeeFilter ()
  : MyPlug ( TeeFilter1.Plug1(), TeeFilter2.Socket1())
  , MySocket ( TeeFilter1.Socket1, TeeFilter2.Plug1())
{ }


StrStream2::plug::myEnd & StrStream2BasicTeeFilter::Plug1 ()
{
  return MyPlug ;
}
```

```
StrStream2::socket::myEnd & StrStream2BasicTeeFilter::Socket1 ()
{
  return MySocket
}


StrStream1::plug::myEnd & StrStream2BasicTeeFilter::CopyPlug ()
{
  return TeeFilter1.CopyPlug () ;
}


StrStream1::plug::myEnd & StrStream2BasicTeeFilter::CopySocket ()
{
  return TeeFilter2.CopyPlug () ;
}
```

The components defined in *ActualC2* are similar to *ActualC1* except that the filters and tees are annotated. Annotation is accomplished by doing an extra Process call with a prefix string that can be set at any time. This is simpler but possibly less desirable than creating a buffer, adding the prefix string, and appending the original *Process* parameter. Of course, you could define a component that worked this way and use it instead of the ones defined here. That's the nice thing about plugs.

```
// File: ActualC2.DOC ComponentC type 2 definition
/*
```

This set of definitions augments *ActualC1*. The basic filters and tees are presented in a simple annotated form. A *StrStream1* annotated filter includes an annotating string, which can be changed. Every *Process* call to the filter's *Socket* will cause two *Process* calls to its *Plug*. The first uses the annotating string as the parameter, while the second is the parameter to the *Socket Process* call.

Tee filters for *StrStream1* and *StrStream2* tee filters annotates the data coming out of the copy plug(s). The data passing through the filter is not affected.

```
====  Public Interface  ====
```

```
Connection: StrStream1
  Socket: StrStream1AnnotatedSocket
    Adds void Annote ( const char * pPrefix )


Component: StrStream1Filter
  Component: StrStream1AnnotatedFilter
    Adds void Annote ( const char * pPrefix )


Component: StrStream1TeeFilter
  Component: StrStream1AnnotatedTeeFilter
    Adds void Annote ( const char * pPrefix )


Component: StrStream2TeeFilter
  Component: StrStream2AnnotatedTeeFilter
    Includes two public StrStream1AnnotatedFilters:
      AnnotatedFilter1 and AnnotatedFilter2


====  Internal Interface  ====
  none

*/



// ===================================
// File: ActualC2.HPP ComponentC type 2 definition

#include "ActualC1.HPP"

class StrStream1AnnotatedSocket : StrStream1Socket
{
  protected:
    const char * pMyPrefix ;
    StrStream1::plug::myPlug & MyPlug ;

    virtual void Process ( const char * buffer ) ;
```

```
    public:
      StrStream1AnnotatedSocket ( StrStream1::plug::myPlug & Plug1 ) ;

      virtual void Annote ( const char * pPrefix ) ;
  } ;


  class StrStream1AnnotatedFilter : public StrStream1Filter
  {
    public:
      StrStream1::plug::myPlug MyPlug ;
      StrStream1AnnotatedSocket MySocket ;

    public:
      StrStream1AnnotatedFilter () ;

      virtual StrStream1::plug::myEnd & Plug1 () = 0 ;
      virtual StrStream1::socket::myEnd & Socket1 () = 0 ;
      virtual void Annote ( const char * pPrefix ) ;
  } ;

  class  StrStream1AnnotatedTeeFilter : public StrStream1TeeFilter
  {
    protected:
      const char * pMyPrefix ;

    public:
      StrStream1AnnotatedTeeFilter () ;

      virtual StrStream1::socket::myEnd & CopySocket () ;

      virtual void Annote ( const char * pPrefix ) ;
  } ;

  class  StrStream2AnnotatedTeeFilter : public StrStream2TeeFilter
  {
    public:
      StrStream2BaseFilter () ;
```

```
      StrStream1AnnotatedFilter AnnotatedFilter1 ;
      StrStream1AnnotatedFilter AnnotatedFilter2 ;

      virtual StrStream1::plug::myEnd & CopyPlug () ;
      virtual StrStream1::plug::myEnd & CopySocket () ;
} ;


// File: ActualC2.CPP  ComponentC type 2 definition

#include "ActualC2.HPP"

void StrStream1AnnotatedSocket::Process ( const char * buffer )
{
  MyPlug.Process ( pMyPrefix ) ;
  MyPlug.Process ( buffer ) ;
}

StrStream1AnnotatedSocket::StrStream1AnnotatedSocket
  ( StrStream1::plug::myPlug & Plug )
  : MyPlug ( Plug )
{}

void StrStream1AnnotatedSocket::Annote ( const char * pPrefix )
{
  pMyPrefix = pPrefix ;
}


StrStream1AnnotatedFilter::StrStream1AnnotatedFilter ()
  : MySocket ( MyPlug )
{}

void StrStream1AnnotatedFilter::Annote ( const char * pPrefix )
{
  MySocket.Annote ( pPrefix ) ;
}

StrStream1::socket & StrStream1AnnotatedTeeFilter::CopySocket ()
{
```

```
      return AnnotatedFilter.Socket1 () ;
   }


StrStream2AnnotatedTeeFilter::StrStream2AnnotatedTeeFilter ()
   {
      StrStream2TeeFilter::CopyPlug () <= AnnotatedFilter1.Socket1 () ;
      StrStream2TeeFilter::CopySocket () <= AnnotatedFilter2.Socket1 ()
   ;
   }


StrStream1::plug::myEnd & StrStream2AnnotatedTeeFilterCopyPlug ()
   {
      return TeeFilter1.CopyPlug () ;
   }


StrStream1::plug::myEnd & CopySocket ()
   {
      return TeeFilter2.CopyPlug () ;
   }
```

Summary

In general, the design of the documentation, header files, and implementation files for a plug-based library is no different from those of a conventional library. Unlike conventional libraries, plug-based libraries tend to include in their definitions more abstract classes to define common plug and component interfaces, which can be used for subsequent replacement parts. Providing basic utility components like filters, merges, and tees can make the use of major application components easier.

C Plugs and Templates

Although *Plugs.HPP* is implemented in Appendix A using macros, it can also be implemented using templates in conjunction with macros. The file *PlugsT.HPP* is a version of *Plugs.HPP* that is implemented with templates. Templates can also be used when defining base classes or when subclassing existing plug definitions. This appendix addresses all three uses of templates and plugs. The first section presents the C++ template syntax and semantics. The second and third sections address plug base classes and subclassing plugs. The fourth section presents and examines the details of the *PlugsT.HPP* file.

You may be wondering why the use of templates is even an issue and why it has to be discussed separately. After all, templates are a part of the 2.1 C++ specification. The answer is that not all C++ compilers implement templates; hence the macro approach in *Plugs.HPP*. I should mention, too, that it is possible to use the template plug support in the file, *PlugsT.HPP,* without defining classes using templates.

Even so, there are advantages to using the template version. The major advantage is the ability to use a source level debugger to trace through the template code. This is not possible with the macro version in *Plugs.HPP* because all the associated code is hidden by a single macro definition. Also, templates do not have the size limitation found in some C++ compilers with respect to macro expansion, which can limit the length of class names in the plug macros. You will notice in the *Plugs.HPP* file that the macro definitions include no indentation in the class definition, while the definitions in the *PlugsT.HPP* file are indented and significantly easier to read and understand.

Templates

Templates are a lot like macros in that a single definition—template or macro—is used to generate multiple copies of source code. The difference between macros and templates is that macros have no restriction on parameters and simply perform textual substitutions. Templates, on the other hand, are specifically used for class or function definitions and have a rigid syntax and parameter-passing semantics. While a macro can be used to define part of a class or function definition or be imbedded within these, the template must define a complete class or function. This makes macros more flexible, but it makes templates more useful in writing readable, understandable code.

If you need an introduction to or review of macros or templates in C++, see Appendix E. Macros are described there along with other C++ constructs, and a discussion of templates follows. The description is a basic introduction to templates; it does not address all the rules, implications, or compiler-dependent options. That kind of detail can be found in the documentation accompanying your C++ compiler. The coverage in Appendix E should be more than sufficient to allow you to read and understand the examples in the rest of this chapter.

Templates are easy to recognize; they use a distinctive syntax, while macros look just like normal C functions. A template definition starts with the keyword, *template*. The parameter list is surrounded with angle brackets, < and >, instead of parentheses. Like C++ functions (and unlike macros), the template parameter list includes typed parameters. The template parameter list is followed immediately by a class or function definition. The parameters named in the parameter list can occur in this class or function definition. They are substituted just like macro parameters when a template is used.

A sample template-based class definition looks like this:

```
template <class foo, int size>
class vector
{
  protected:
```

```
    foo Data [ size ] ;

  public:
    foo At ( int i ) { return Data [ i ] ; }
    void Set ( int i, foo value ) { Data [ i ] = value ; }
    int Size () { return size ; }
} ;
```

A particular instance of this sample vector class is declared using the following syntax:

```
vector <int, 100> VectorOf100Int ;
vector <char *, 10 > VectorOf10CharPointers ;

vector <char *, 10 > * pVectorOf10CharPointer ;
```

This example declares two arrays and one pointer to an array. *VectorOf10CharPointer* can be referenced by *pVectorOf10CharPointer*. A template class can be used wherever a conventional C++ class can be used. The distinction between a macro and a template is that a single template definition is provided and used automatically when a variable is defined using the template, or when a template function definition is used. A macro definition would require explicit invocations for each class.

Here is a macro definition that does what the previous template definition does:

```
define DECLARE_VECTOR(c,foo,size)\
class c\
{\
  protected:\
    foo Data [ size ] ;\
\
  public:\
    foo At ( int i ) { return Data [ i ] ; }\
    void Set ( int i, foo value ) { Data [ i ] = value ; }\
    int Size () { return size ; }\
} ;
```

And here is what is required to declare the same two arrays and one pointer, as in the template example:

```
DECLARE_VECTOR ( vectorOf100Int, int, 100 )
DECLARE_VECTOR ( vectorOf10CharPointers, char *, 10 )

vectorOf100Int VectorOf100Int ;
vectorOf10CharPointers VectorOf10CharPointers ;

vectorOf10CharPointers * pVectorOf10CharPointer ;
```

The examples should make it clear that the use of templates rather than macros is cleaner. Using templates also has the advantage of being easier to debug when using a symbolic debugger. The code for the macro version is all hidden behind the two *DECLARE_VECTOR* invocations. Templates have the additional advantage of requiring proper parameter types, which may not generate a compile time error when macros are used, but will not generate the desired code.

Note that the template version does not require an explicit definition for each use; the macro version does. In the template version, a single definition suffices for the two different types used. This issue becomes more important if a class definition defines functions but they must be implemented elsewhere. In this case, templates can also be used once for each additional function definition, but macros would have to be called explicitly for each function of each class. The resulting code would be the same, but the number of explicit definitions is higher with macros.

Template parameters can include any type, as is the case with function parameters, and they may also include class names, as shown in the previous examples. There is no support for default parameters, though, as there is in the case of functions. Also, only simple substitution is supported. Conditional substitution is not supported in either templates or macros.

Function templates look just like the class definitions you've examined, except that in the case of function templates, a function definition follows the template parameter list. The substitution rules are the same, and the use of angle brackets for the parameter list is the same. Template functions can be conventional C functions or class functions. Here is an example of a template function definition:

```
template <class a>
a max ( a i, a j )
{
   return ( i > j ) ? i : j ;
}
```

The use of *max* as a function with two identical parameter types will use this function definition. Function overloading is possible, whereby an additional function definition with different parameters is specified. Explicit function definitions can also be used to overload the function name.

Although templates are easy to use and understand, they can be complicated to use in practice if the code is complex. In general, it is best to define a conventional class or function, get it compiled and working properly, and then convert it to a template. Once you are well versed in templates you can forego this step.

Defining Base Classes Using Templates

Template classes can be used as base classes for the plug or socket of a connection definition. There are no restrictions on what the class definition is, either conventional or template, other than the requirement for a default constructor. If you use a template class as a base plug class it must be defined before it is used in the plug connection definition. For example:

```
template <class foo, int size>
class SampleTemplateBase
{
   public:
     foo Array [ size ] ;
```

```
      int Size () { return size ; }
  } ;


DECLARE_CONNECTION
  (
  , SampleTemplateBase <int, 10>
  , emptyBase
  )
```

The connection is defined using one template and one conventional class. Template base plug classes are equally applicable to the *DECLARE_PLUGS* macro, which uses the *DECLARE_CONNECTION* macro.

Subclassing Using Templates

Templates and plug definitions can also be combined at the other end of the inheritance spectrum. In this case, a plug connection is already defined and the associated classes are used to define new classes. These plug classes can be used in template definitions or invocations. The following example shows a plug connection declaration and its use in a template class definition.

```
DECLARE_PLUGS
  ( SampleConnection
  , Plug1, emptyBase
  , Socket1, emptyBase
  )

template <class foo>
class SampleWithFoo : public Plug1
{
  public:
    foo SampleFunction () ;
} ;
```

The *Plug1* class is used in any instance of the class *SampleWithFoo*. *Sample-Function* was included to make use of the parameter class *foo*.

Plugs can be used as parameters to templates in order to use the plug class in the inheritance chain, or to use it within functions or variables used by the template class. The following example shows both uses.

```
template <class plug>
class SampleUsingPlug : public plug
{
   protected:
     plug * pPlug ;

   public:
     void afterConnect ( plug::otherEnd * pSocket )
     {
       pPlug = this ;
     }
     void beforeDisconnect ( plug::otherEnd * pSocket )
     {
       pPlug = 0 ;
     }
} ;
```

The template class *SampleUsingPlug* redefines two plug functions, *afterConnect* and *beforeDisconnect*. An application of the parameter plug class is used to define a pointer of the appropriate type. This value is set in the redefined functions. The pointer essentially tracks the connection status: 0 if it is not connected and a pointer to the plug if there is a connection.

Using plug and template classes in this way is a good idea if you need to extend a set of plugs using a single generic definition. The template class can provide this extension while maintaining type compatibility.

Description of PlugsT.HPP

The file *PlugsT.HPP* is a template implementation of the file, *Plugs.HPP*, in Appendix A. The two files serve exactly the same purpose and can be interchanged freely, with the proviso that the template version can only be used with a C++ compiler that supports templates. I recommend using the template version if possible because it makes source level debugging easier. The source is presented first, with descriptions of portions of the code following it. A functional discussion of the operations is not repeated here, as this information is discussed in Chapter 2 and Appendix A.

```
// ====  PLUGS.HPP  ====
//
// WGW 8-7-93

#if !defined(_PLUGS_HPP)
#define _PLUGS_HPP


// ----  Description of plug interface  ----
//
// Defining a plug class is not covered in these comments.
// A plug class uses the following operations:
//
// A <= B           connects A to B, does -- A and -- B first
// - A              disconnects A, but will not free otherEnd
//                      returns otherEnd
// -- A             disconnects A, will free otherEnd
// A.connected()        returns 0 if A is disconnected
// A.usable()       returns 0 if not usable
//                      (i.e. uninitialized redirector)
//
// A -> V               access a member of the object at
//                  the other end of A, normally assumes there
//                  is something at the other end
//
// R.redirect(A)        change redirector R's reference to A
//                      returns prior reference
//
// A.addBefore(B,C) connects A to B and C to what A was connected to
//                      if A has a redirector then it points to C
// A.addAfter (B,C)  like addBefore
//                      if A has a redirector it does not change
//
// ----  Plug Class Definition Macros  ----
//
```

```
//
// DECLARE_CONNECTION (connection,plugBase,socketBase)
//
// class plugBase : public connection::plug
// {
//   public:
//     DECLARE_PLUG ()
//
//     /* specifics here */
// } ;
//
//
// class plugBase : public connection::plug
// {
//   public:
//     myEnd * getPlug () { return this ; }
//
//     /* specifics here */
// } ;
//
//
// ----  plugCheck alternate definition   ----
//
// Define a check macro if you want to check for invalid access
// using ->.

#if !defined(plugCheck)
#define plugCheck(ptr)
#endif


// ----  Simple plug macro definitions   ----

#if !defined(BOOL)
typedef int BOOL ;
#endif
#if !defined(FALSE)
#define FALSE 0
#endif
#if !defined(TRUE)
```

```
#define TRUE 1
#endif


#define DECLARE_PLUG() myPlug*getPlug(){return this;}

class Plug
{
  public:
    virtual ~Plug () {}
    virtual BOOL usable ()          {return TRUE;}
    virtual BOOL isRedirector () {return FALSE;}
    virtual BOOL connected  () = 0 ;
    virtual void operator --() = 0 ;
    virtual void connectFailed (){}
} ;


class RedirectorNotify
{
  public:
    virtual void connectFailed     () {}
    virtual void disconnected      () {}
    virtual void disconnectedFree () {}
    virtual void afterConnect      () {}
    virtual void beforeDisconnect () {}
} ;



#define DECLARE_CONNECTION(c,bp,bs)\
class bp;class bs;\
typedef connection<bp,bs> c ;



template <class a>
class plugd : public a
{
  public:
```

```
~plugd ()
{
  if (pOther)
--*(otherEnd*)pOther;
  if (pRedirector)
pRedirector->redirect(0);
}
virtual void operator<=(otherEnd&p)
{
  otherEnd*prior=(otherEnd*)-*this;
  if (prior)
    --*prior;
  if (&p)
  {
    otherEnd*pp=(otherEnd*)-p;
    if (pp)
      --*pp;
    myEnd*e1=getEnd();
     if (e1)
     {
       otherEnd*e2=p.getEnd();
       if (e2)
       {
         myPlug*p1=e1->getPlug();
         otherPlug*p2=e2->getPlug();
         e1->connectto(p2);
            e2->connectto(p1);
            e1->afterConnect(p2);
         e2->afterConnect(p1);
       }
       else
         e1->connectFailed();
     }
  }
  else
connectFailed();
}
virtual otherPlug*operator-()
{
  otherPlug*prior=pOther;
```

```
  if (prior)
  {
    myPlug*mp=getPlug();
    beforeDisconnect(prior);
    ((otherEnd*)prior)->beforeDisconnect(mp);
    disconnected(prior);
    ((otherEnd*)prior)->disconnected(mp);
  }
  return prior;
}
void operator--()
{
  otherPlug*prior=-*this;
  if (prior)
    --*(otherEnd*)prior;
  disconnectedFree(prior);
}
virtual void addBefore(otherEnd*inner,myEnd*newEnd)
{
  redirector*old=pRedirector;
  addAfter(inner,newEnd);
  if (old)
  {
    old->reset(this);
    old->redirect(newEnd);
  }
}
virtual void addAfter(otherEnd*inner,myEnd*newEnd)
{
  if (pOther&&newEnd)
    (*newEnd)<=(*(otherEnd*)-*this);
  (*this)<=(*inner);
}
virtual void afterConnect(otherPlug*p)
{
  if (pRedirector)
    pRedirector->afterConnect(p);
}
virtual void beforeDisconnect(otherPlug*p)
{
```

```
      if (pRedirector)
        pRedirector->beforeDisconnect(p);
    }
    virtual void disconnectedFree(otherPlug*p)
    {
      if (pRedirector)
        pRedirector->disconnectedFree(p);
    }
    virtual void disconnected(otherPlug*p)
    {
      if (pRedirector)
        pRedirector->disconnected(p);
    }
    virtual void connectFailed()
    {
      if (pRedirector)
        pRedirector->connectFailed();
    }
} ;




template <class pc>
class redirectora : public pc
{
  protected:
    RedirectorNotify * pNotify ;

  public:
    redirectora()
      : pNotify (0)
      {}
    ~redirectora()
    {
      remove();
    }
    virtual void setNotify (RedirectorNotify*p)
    {
```

```
      pNotify=p;
   }
   virtual void setNotify (RedirectorNotify&p)
   {
      pNotify=&p;
   }
   virtual void reset (myEnd*)
   {
      pMyEnd=0;
   }
   virtual void remove ()
   {
     if (pMyEnd)
       pMyEnd->setRedirector(pRedirector);
    if (pRedirector)
      pRedirector->setMyEnd(pMyEnd);
   }
   virtual void redirect(myEnd&NewPlug)
   {
      redirect(&NewPlug);
   }
   virtual void redirect(myEnd*pNew)
   {
      remove();
      if (pNew)
      {
        pMyEnd=pNew;
        pRedirector=pNew->setRedirector((redirector*)this);
      }
   }
   myPlug*getPlug()
   {
      return pMyEnd?pMyEnd->getPlug():0;
   }
   myEnd*getEnd()
   {
      return pMyEnd?pMyEnd->getEnd():0;
   }
   void operator<=(otherEnd&p)
   {
```

```
  if (pMyEnd)
(*pMyEnd)<=p;
}
otherPlug*operator->()
{
  return&(*(*pMyEnd));
}
otherPlug&operator*()
{
  return(*(*pMyEnd));
}
otherPlug*operator-()
{
  return pMyEnd?-*pMyEnd:0;
}
void operator--()
{

  if (pMyEnd)
--*pMyEnd;
}
void addBefore(otherEnd*inner,myEnd*newEnd)
{
  pMyEnd->addBefore(inner,newEnd);
}
void addAfter(otherEnd*inner,myEnd*newEnd)
{
  pMyEnd->addAfter(inner,newEnd);
}
BOOL connected()
{
  return pMyEnd?pMyEnd->connected():0;
}
BOOL usable()
{
  return pMyEnd?pMyEnd->usable():0;
}
BOOL isRedirector()
{
  return 1;
```

```
        }
        virtual void afterConnect(otherPlug*p)
        {
          if (pRedirector)
            pRedirector->afterConnect(p);
          if (pNotify)
            pNotify->afterConnect();
        }
        virtual void beforeDisconnect(otherPlug*p)
        {
          if (pRedirector)
            pRedirector->beforeDisconnect(p);
          if (pNotify)
            pNotify->beforeDisconnect();
        }
        virtual void disconnectedFree(otherPlug*p)
        {
          if (pRedirector)
            pRedirector->disconnectedFree(p);
          if (pNotify)
            pNotify->disconnectedFree();
        }
        virtual void disconnected(otherPlug*p)
        {
          if (pRedirector)
            pRedirector->disconnected(p);
          if (pNotify)
            pNotify->disconnected();
        }
        virtual void connectFailed()
        {
          if (pRedirector)
            pRedirector->connectFailed();
          if (pNotify)
            pNotify->connectFailed();
        }
    };


    template <class ap,class as, class bp, class bs, class r>
```

```
class pluga : public Plug
{
  public:
    typedef bs otherPlug;
    typedef as otherEnd;
    typedef bp myPlug;
    typedef ap myEnd;
    typedef r redirector;
  protected:
    union
    {
      myEnd*pMyEnd;
      otherEnd*pOtherEnd;
      otherPlug*pOther;
    };
    redirector*pRedirector;
  public:
    pluga()
      :pRedirector(0)
      {pOther=0;}
    virtual myPlug*getPlug()=0;
    virtual myEnd*getEnd()
    {
      return(myEnd*)getPlug();
    }
    virtual void operator<=(otherEnd&)=0;
    virtual otherPlug*operator->()
    {
      plugCheck(pOther);
      return pOther;
    }
    virtual otherPlug&operator*()
    {
      plugCheck(pOther);
      return*pOther;
    }
    virtual otherPlug*operator-()=0;
    virtual void addBefore(otherEnd*,myEnd*)=0;
    virtual void addAfter(otherEnd*,myEnd*)=0;
    virtual BOOL connected(){return pOther!=0;}
```

409

```
    virtual void connectto(otherPlug*p)
    {
      pOther=p;
    }
    virtual redirector*getRedirector()
    {
      return pRedirector;
    }
    virtual redirector*setRedirector(redirector*pR)
    {
      redirector*pOld=pRedirector;
      pRedirector=pR;
      return pOld;
    }
    virtual void disconnectedFree(otherPlug*)=0;
    virtual void disconnected(otherPlug*)=0;
    virtual void setMyEnd(myEnd*p){pMyEnd=p;}
    virtual void afterConnect(otherPlug*p)=0;
    virtual void beforeDisconnect(otherPlug*p)=0;
};
template <class bp,class bs>
class connection
{
  public:
    class plugRedirector;
    class socketRedirector;
    class socketA;
    class plugA ;
    class plugA    :
      public pluga<plugA,socketA,bp,bs,plugRedirector> {} ;
    class socketA :
      public pluga<socketA,plugA,bs,bp,socketRedirector> {} ;
    class plugRedirector   : public redirectora<plugA> {} ;
    class socketRedirector : public redirectora<socketA> {} ;
    class plug   : public plugd <plugA> {} ;
    class socket : public plugd <socketA> {} ;
};
#endif
// ====  End of PLUGS.HPP  ====
```

The differences between *Plugs.HPP* and *PlugsT.HPP* should be readily apparent. Template definitions for classes are used in *PlugsT.HPP*. The template classes, *Connection, CompoundConnection, Plug, PlugRedirector, DeclarePlug*, and *DeclarePlugRedirector* are provided. Each defines the appropriate class. The macros used throughout this book remain, although the internal macros used in *Plugs.HPP* to define the plug and redirector classes have been eliminated through the use of the template classes.

The function definitions in both the template classes and the internal macro generated classes in *Plugs.HPP* are identical.

One aspect of the macro definitions that stands out is that they are very small. For example, the DECLARE_CONNECTION macro simply makes a type definition. The actual code required by a use of this type definition will be included only if a particular instance of the class is required.

D Plugs and Other OOP Languages

The bulk of this book is dedicated to C++ and plugs. But C++ should not be taken as a requirement for using plugs. The plug concept is language-independent. This appendix deals with implementing plugs in two other popular languages: Smalltalk and Pascal; Digitalk Smalltalk/V and Borland Pascal to be more specific. The syntax and semantics of the code in this appendix are different from what you've seen in C++ because of the various features and limitations of the specific languages.

Smalltalk does not support macros or multiple inheritance, but all objects are polymorphic, and Smalltalk includes automatic garbage collection. The features and limitations of Smalltalk require a different implementation of plugs than the C++ version. Use of - and -- is replaced with function names, because Smalltalk does not support prefix operators, but the connection operator <= is retained. Nevertheless, the overall construction and use of plugs and connections remains the same under Smalltalk. In many ways, Smalltalk plugs are actually easier to use and implement than plugs under C++.

Borland has essentially written the Pascal standard with Turbo Pascal. There are DOS and Windows versions, and Borland Pascal also includes object-oriented support. Object-oriented support is limited, but sufficient for this discussion. Like Smalltalk, Borland Pascal does not support macros or multiple inheritance. It also lacks Smalltalk's automatic garbage collection. The Pascal version of plugs is very similar to the Smalltalk version. Unfortunately, Borland Pascal does not support function overloading or class-related operators, so function names only are used for all plug-related functions. This makes the connection operations a bit longer, but that's all. For example, here is how the same code looks in Pascal and C++:

```
Pascal
Plug.connect ( Socket )
C++
Plug <= Socket
```

Each of the following sections addresses the advantages and disadvantages of one language in implementing plugs, as well as the source code for the base implementations. The coverage is not as detailed as in the rest of this book, but it gives enough information to start using plugs in the associated environment.

The one aspect not addressed in this section, or this book, is how to implement plugs in two different languages and interface them within the same program or different programs using interprocess communication methods. This is difficult, and it is beyond the scope of this book. The mechanisms presented here are limited to use within a homogeneous language solution.

Digitalk Smalltalk/V

Digitalk Smalltalk/V is a very extensive implementation of Smalltalk. Versions are currently available for Microsoft Windows, OS/2, and the Apple Macintosh. The implementation provided here works with all three and should work with just about any Smalltalk implementation. Before diving into the description of how plugs are defined and how they work, I'll present a brief introduction to Smalltalk. Although short, it should give you enough of a feel for Smalltalk to at least understand the source code presented here.

Unlike C++, Smalltalk is an object-oriented language from the ground up. Everything in Smalltalk is an object, including numbers, strings, and classes. All operations are implemented by sending messages to an object. Sending a message is essentially the same as calling an object function/method in C++. All messages return a result, so there are no procedures/subroutines, only functions. The syntax for functions is also different from more conventional procedural languages like C++, Pascal, or Basic. The following are some Smalltalk messages:

```
Sample foo
Array at: 1
Multiple add: 'string' after: 4 with: foo
Multiple add: 'string' before: 4 with: foo
```

The object appears to the left and the message name to the right. The first example has no parameters. The message/function name is *foo*.

The second example shows how arrays are accessed. This is similar to *Array [1]* in C++. The advantage with Smalltalk is that the function *at:* looks and operates just like any other function. The colon after the function name indicates that a parameter follows.

The third example shows how multiple parameters are passed. The keyword order is important and essentially allows a form of function overloading. The sample message name would be referred to as *add:after:with:*, while the fourth example is referred to as *add:before:with:*. Smalltalk development environments are very interactive, and message names are normally presented in a list box using this compacted form.

Another difference between Smalltalk and C shows up in the string constants. Smalltalk uses single quotes for strings. Double quotes are reserved for comments. C uses */* and **/* or *//* for comments. Binary operators are supported but not unary operators. This allows you to retain the <= plug connection operator, but you lose the ability to use the - and - - disconnect operators. Luckily, they can be replaced with message names like *disconnect* and *disconnectFree*. It will look a bit different, though, with source code like this:

Smalltalk

```
PlugA disconnect
```

C++

```
- PlugA
```

Making everything an object does turn things a bit topsy-turvy if you are used to a more conventional language like C. Assignments are now messages, and Smalltalk uses the Pascal assignment operator, :=, instead of the C and Basic operator, =. For example:

Smalltalk

```
Symbol := 1
```
C++

```
Symbol = 1
```

All bets are off for program control, too. Smalltalk implements all control structures via block objects. A block is essentially an unnamed function. Blocks are marked using square brackets, []. Blocks, like functions, can take parameters, although zero parameter blocks are the most common. Conditional statements are actually implemented as messages to Boolean objects. In fact, the True and False classes are subclasses to Boolean, and true and false are global instances of these classes. This leads to code that looks like the following:

Smalltalk

```
variable ifTrue:
[
    foo operation
]
```

C++

```
if ( variable )
{
    foo.operation () :
}
```

Smalltalk

```
variable ifTrue:
[
  foo operation1
]
ifFalse:
[
  foo operation2
]
```

C++

```
if ( variable )
{
    foo.operation () ;
}
else
{
    foo.operation () ;
}
```

Smalltalk

```
[ variable ] whileTrue:
[
  foo operation
]
```

C++

```
while ( variable )
{
    foo.operation () ;
}
```

The first example introduces the differences. The variable must respond to the *ifTrue:* message. Boolean values evaluate the block parameter if it is true. The next example shows how Smalltalk elegantly extends its syntax to accommodate two block parameters. Conditional loops require two blocks. The block object responds to the *whileTrue:* message by evaluating itself and then its parameter if the block returns true.

Numeric iterative statements are implemented using messages to numbers, as in the next examples:

Smalltalk

```
1 to: 10 do:
[ :i |
  foo operation: i
]
```

C++

```
for ( int i = 1 ; i < 10 ; ++ i )
{
    foo.operation ( i ) ;
}
```

The Smalltalk block takes one parameter, *:i*. This value changes each time the block is evaluated. The vertical bar separates the parameter list from the statements within the block. The use of blocks has some interesting consequences, which cannot be duplicated easily in most other languages (unless you consider Lisp one of your other languages). For example, the *to:do:* block parameter can be a variable or a function call that evaluates to a block. But you won't get to explore these interesting features, as the Smalltalk implementation of plugs does not require them.

A few more things must be covered before diving into the Smalltalk plug code.

Smalltalk function definitions look a bit different from C or Pascal function definitions. They are usually presented in the context of a class browser window, which includes a list of classes, a list of local variables, a list of message names, and an edit field, which displays the selected message source code. The contents of the edit field change as a message name is selected. Selecting add:after: might show something like this:

```
add: aSocket after: aPlug
        "Comments can go anywhere"
    | x y z |
    ( pOther isNil not ) or: [aPlug isNil not]
       ifTrue: [ self disconnect <= aPlug ].
    self <= aSocket.
    ^self
```

The syntax of the message comes first. A colon is used to indicate when a parameter is required, and the parameter name comes after it. The parameter name can be used in the source code, as in most programming languages. The important thing to note is that there are no type specifications. Smalltalk does not require type definitions on any variables. Any variable can reference any kind of object. Comments can appear anywhere and are strings surrounded with double quotes. The local variables in this function are listed between the vertical bars, |. They are optional, and the bars can be omitted if there are no local variables. The statements are separated using periods. Semicolons can be used as statement separators, but the semantics change. They indicate that another message should be sent to the object used in the prior statement. For example:

```
aTurtle home ; go: 60 ; turn: 10
```

The turtle gets three messages. The results from the first two are ignored.

The code in the previous example shows an interesting aspect of Boolean messages. Note that the (*pOther isNil not*) is an expression that evaluates to a

Boolean value, which is then sent the *or:* message. The message indicates that the block parameter should be evaluated if the message is sent to a false value.

The other thing to note in the previous example is the use of the keyword *self* and the use of the return character, ^. The keyword *self* is analogous to the C++ keyword *this*. The main difference is that *self* does not have to be dereferenced, since Smalltalk does not bring out the use of pointers explicitly, as C++ does. The return character indicates that the expression result is to be the result of the message. It is one syntactic oddity in Smalltalk.

Smalltalk's source listing syntax looks a bit odd as well, but you normally don't see it when working within a Smalltalk environment because all source code is presented using browser windows. The source listing syntax is divided into sections using exclamation points. Each section is compiled individually but in order. A class definition starts with the following:

```
Object subclass: #ClassName
    instanceVariableNames: 'objectVar1 objectVar2'
    classVariableNames:    'classVar'
    poolDictionaries:       ' '
```

This is a message that gets sent to the Object object, which is a class object— actually called a meta class object— which receives the subclass:instance-VariableNames:classvariableNames:poolDictionaries: message. Quite a mouthful. The strings contain lists of symbols, which wind up being the names of variables that can be used in object message definitions. Without getting into too much detail, the instance variables are the same as C++ object variables. The class variables are the same as C++ static class variables. You don't have to worry about what a pool dictionary is unless you really want to learn a lot more about Smalltalk. Also note the pound sign, #, in front of the first parameter. This designates the following text to be a symbol. A symbol is different than a string constant.

The types of methods are separated using one of the following:

```
!Plug class methods !
!Plug methods !
```

Class methods are messages that can be directed to class objects. This is not the same as C++ static functions, but the purpose is similar. Essentially, there

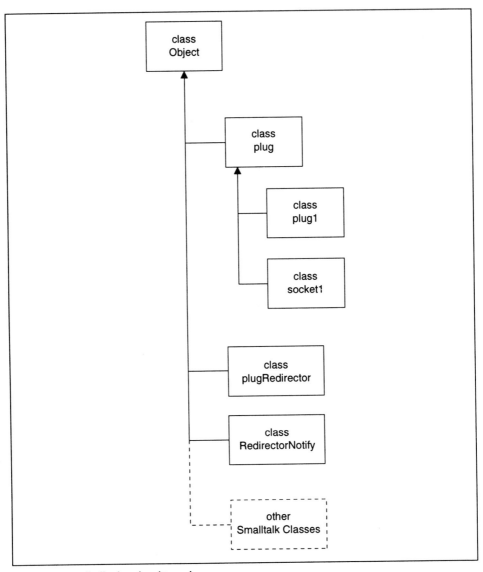

Figure D-1. Smalltalk plug class hierarchy

are functions that can be used with objects of a class and functions that are common to the class. The difference in Smalltalk is that you need to use the class object (meta class object), which is always associated with the global symbol of the same name, in this case *Plug*.

Finally, a few explanations about implementation are in order before presenting the source code. The details are covered after the source code is presented.

First the restrictions: Smalltalk implements only single inheritance. It does not support prefix operators; there is no macro support, no access to object instance variables, and no private or protected methods.

These restrictions force a different approach to implementing plugs. There is now a generic Plug and PlugRedirector class from which all other plugs can be implemented. The - and -- operators have been replaced with the message names *disconnect* and *disconnectFree*, and all definitions must be done explicitly. The latter means that each class must be created using the class browser and functions must be redefined manually. Not having access to object instance variables means that you have to use explicit messages for retrieving and setting an instance variable. This is similar to the approach recommended earlier in this book, with the pure virtual functions in the plug base class. This restriction is somewhat of an advantage when you consider the other restriction of no private or protected members. Functions cannot be hidden, but object variables are. As you will see later, these changes and restrictions are not really all that bad.

Next, Smalltalk capabilities that are not available in C++ include unrestricted polymorphism and automatic garbage collection. Unrestricted polymorphism means that any object can be referenced by any variable and any object can be sent any message. Note that the latter does not mean that an object will know what to do for any message, only that it can be sent any message. An error message is sent to the object if it does not handle the message. What this does mean is that you can define a new class that is not a subclass of Plug and still use an object of that class with a plug. In fact, the PlugRedirector class is *not* a subclass of Plug (more on that later). Automatic garbage collection makes the creation of dynamic objects significantly easier, although it does not completely eliminate the need for this type of specialization, as you will see.

At last, here is the source code for the base plug implementation. The following are the base class definitions for plugs in Smalltalk/V. Figure D-1 shows the Class hierarchy.

```
"File: Plug.cls

"Object subclass: #Plug
  instanceVariableNames:
    'pOther pRedirector '
  classVariableNames: ''
  poolDictionaries: ''     !

!Plug class methods !

new
      "Setup locals"
    ^super new initialize! !

!Plug methods !

<= aPlug
      "Connect to a plug"
    | prior e1 e2 p1 p2|
    prior := self disconnect.
    prior isNil
      ifFalse: [ prior disconnectedFree ].
    e1 := self getEnd.
    e1 isNil
      ifTrue: [ self connectFailed ]
      ifFalse:
      [ e2 := aPlug getEnd.
      e2 isNil
          ifTrue: [ e1 connectFailed ]
          ifFalse:
```

```
        [ p1 := e1 getPlug.
          p2 := e2 getPlug.
          p1 connectto: p2.
          p2 connectto: p1.
          p1 afterConnect: p2.
          p2 afterConnect: p1.
        ]
    ].!


add: aSocket after: aPlug
      "Insert a socket"
   ( pOther isNil not ) or: [aPlug isNil not]
     ifTrue: [ self disconnect <= aPlug ]
   self <= aSocket!


 add: aSocket before: aPlug
      "Insert a socket"
      self add: aSocket after: aPlug.
      pRedirector isNil
        ifFalse: [ pRedirector redirectBefore: aPlug ]!


 afterConnect: aPlug
      "Just connected to aPlug, normally does nothing"
   pRedirector isNil
     ifFalse:
     [ pRedirector afterConnect: self.
     ]!


 beforeDisconnect: aPlug
      "About to disconnect aPlug, normally does nothing"
   pRedirector isNil
     ifFalse:
     [ pRedirector beforeDisconnect: self.
     ]!


connected
      "Indicate if there is a otherEnd"
   ^pOther isNil not!


connectFailed
```

```
        "Connection failed."
    pRedirector isNil
      ifFalse:
      [ pRedirector connectFailed: self.
      ]!


connectto: aPlug
        "Connect to the other end"
    pOther := aPlug!


  disconnect
        "Disconnect from our plug"
    | result |
    result := pOther.
    pOther isNil ifFalse:
    [
      pOther beforeDisconnect: self.
      self beforeDisconnect: pOther.
      pOther disconnected: self.
      self disconnected: pOther.
    ].
    ^result!


  disconnected: aPlug
        "Disconnect from our plug and free if necessary"
    pOther := nil .
    pRedirector isNil
      ifFalse:
      [ pRedirector disconnected: self.
      ]!


disconnectedFree: aPlug
        "Plug is going to be dereferenced.
          Garbage collection takes care of the plug"
    pRedirector isNil
      ifFalse:
      [ pRedirector disconnectedFree: self .
        pRedirector resetRedirection: self .
        pRedirector := nil.
      ]!
```

```
disconnectFree
        "Disconnect from our plug and free"
    | prior |
    prior := self disconnect.
    prior isNil ifFalse:
    [
      prior disconnectedFree: self
    ].
    self disconnectedFree: prior!

  getPlug
        "Just return self for simple plugs"
    ^self!
getEnd
        "Just return self for simple plugs"
    ^self!
getRedirector
        "return our redirector"
     ^pRedirector!

  initialize
        "Allows new to use initialize"!

  isConnected
        "isSomething is a Smalltalk convention"
     ^self connected!

  isRedirector
        "This is a plug"
     ^false!
otherEnd
        "This replaces the -> operator in the C version"
     ^pOther!

setMyEnd: aRedirector
        "Used with redirectors"
    pOther := aRedirector!

setRedirector: aRedirector
```

```
        "setup new redirector"
    pRedirector := aRedirector!

usable
        "Plugs are always usable"
    ^true! !
```

Other than the change of syntax, the Smalltalk source code looks exactly like the class definitions in *PLUGS.HPP*. In fact, with minor exceptions like the use of *disconnect* for -, the source code is operationally identical. There are some interesting ramifications, though. The basic *Plug* class can be used to connect to any other plug subclass. Any connection restrictions must be explicitly built in. This is easily accomplished by redefining the *afterConnect:* operator. This function can check the type of the other plug object and break the connection if it is inappropriate. Another alternative, which changes how this code looks, would require a change to the *getPlug* function so that it takes a type indicator parameter. The function would then return a non-nil value only if it were the right type.

Let's look at the previous code in more detail, even though it is essentially the same as the C++ version described in Appendix A. Note that the Plug class contains two variables, *pOther* and *pRedirector*. The names are kept the same as in the C++ source code to make comparisons easier. The prefix character was used to indicate pointers in C++, but this distinction is irrelevant in Smalltalk, because all variables contain a reference to an object.

One item that is different from the C++ version is the only class method, *new*. This method creates a new object by calling *super new*. The variable *super,* like *self,* is implicitly defined in every method. It sends the message to the superclass of the current object class. This is like the *superclass::function* syntax used in C++. The main difference is that Smalltalk can only pass messages up one level, whereas C++ can, in theory, go up any number of levels in the class hierarchy. On the other hand, Smalltalk does not require you to specify which class handles the message. In general, Smalltalk's implementation is more than adequate. The result of *super new* is our plug object, which is then sent the *initialize* message. This is added to allow the plug to initialize any instance variables. Unlike C++, Smalltalk does not automatically initialize the variables other than fill them all in with the value *nil*. This is comparable to initializing the C++ instance variables to *0* (well, not exactly, but close enough). The Plug class has an initialize function that does nothing. Subclasses can define this function to initialize new objects as necessary.

The connection operator, <=, has a definition that looks almost exactly like the C++ version, with alterations made for Smalltalk syntax. In particular, the assignment operator is now :=, *isNil* is used to check the value of the variables so a Boolean value can be sent the *isTrue:isFalse:* messages, and blocks are marked by square brackets instead of curly brackets as in C++. The Smalltalk version actually reads better than the C++ version, as long as you remember that conditionals require the test value to come before the keywords. Note that there is no return value indicated by ^. In this case, Smalltalk returns *self* because every message must return a result.

The *add:after:* and *add:before:* functions also look like their counterparts, although the *or:* operator is a bit more difficult to get used to. Next come a couple of the empty definitions, such as *afterConnect:*. These must be defined (even though they do nothing) as in C++, because they are called when making or breaking connections. Smalltalk can send any message to any object, unlike C++, which can only call functions explicitly defined for an object. But Smalltalk will also generate an error message if an object does not handle a message. The connected function might look a bit odd, but it is really a straightforward way of returning a Boolean value indicating whether a connection exists. The *isNil* message returns true if there is no connection and the value of *pOther* is nil. The *not* message sent to the returned object converts it into our needed result.

The *disconnect* and *disconnectFree* messages take the place of the - and -- plug operators in C++. The code is almost identical to the C++ counterparts, with a minor change in syntax. The *disconnect* message calls *beforeDisconnect:* and *disconnected:*, if a connection exists, while the *disconnectedFree* method calls the *disconnectedFree:* method. The main difference in implementing *disconnectFree:* in the subclass is that Smalltalk has automatic garbage collection, so this method only needs to break down any internal structures initially created by the object. This is the same as with the C++ version, but, unlike the C++ version, the Smalltalk version does not have to call a delete method. (This is covered further when dynamic plugs in Smalltalk are discussed later in this section.) The rest of the methods are empty or very simple and match the C++ versions, so there is no need to look at them individually.

The Plug class just presented implements a class corresponding to a C++ plug class that is implemented using the *DECLARE_CONNECTION* macro. This means the object contains the *pOther* and *pRedirector* instance variables. Smalltalk is not amenable to abstract classes as C++ is. You could define a Plug superclass that did not contain the instance variables, and define some of the methods, but you cannot require the subclasses to implement the missing methods, as you can in C++. On the other hand, if you want a class that can be used as a plug that implements the internal operations in a different way, then you can define a class that is not a subclass of Plug and still use the plug with other plugs.

There are two important aspects to note about the presentation thus far. The first is the lack of anything comparable to the *DECLARE_CONNECTION* macro. The second is that the additional methods associated with a plug are added after and not before, as in C++ with its base classes. This means that the interface must be described either in the documentation or by looking at a particular implementation of a plug. Likewise, the lack of a comparable connection definition means that the plugs that can be connected together must be specified in the documentation. Smalltalk will not restrict what plugs can be connected to a socket. In many ways, this is a powerful feature, which can be exploited by good programmers and designers. On the downside, having the ability to connect any plug to any other plug, at least initially, can lead to some very insidious bugs. For example, a program could construct a connection structure using plugs and components without any problems, but a bug would appear as soon as it starts up an internal protocol by invoking an external method. That is, the external method sends a message across a connection, and the plug at the other end then indicates that it cannot handle the message. Then again, that is the nature of Smalltalk.

One thing that can be done to help the connection documentation problem is to define plug classes in pairs and include a comment in the class definition section that describes both the other plug example and the internal protocol required. Additional documentation or comments can describe the details, but adding this comment means that it will be seen when someone is using the class browser and initially clicks on the class name. The code might look like the following:

```
Plug subclass: #ASamplePlug
  instanceVariableNames:
     'myData'
  classVariableNames: ''
  poolDictionaries: ''
"
ASamplePlug connects to ASampleSocket object.
ASampleSocket object has access to myData via
getData and setData: methods. These methods are
for the internal protocol. ...
"
```

The class definition for *ASampleSocket* would be similar. The class browser does not lend itself to making extensive notes, but it is adequate to point out what kind of object is to be used at the other end of a connection. Note that you cannot include comments within a string, so you cannot include a comment within the list of instance or class variables. A simple plug definition might look like the following:

```
Plug subclass: #ASamplePlug
  instanceVariableNames:
     'myData'
  classVariableNames: ''
  poolDictionaries: ''
```

```
"
ASamplePlug connects to ASampleSocket object.
ASampleSocket object has access to myData via
getData and setData: methods. These methods are
for the internal protocol. ...
"

!ASamplePlug methods !

initialize
   myData := 'An initial value'  !

getData
   "Internal function"
   ^myData  !

setData: newData
   "Internal function"
   myData := newData ! !
```

The initialize function was included to show how an instance variable might be set up when the object is created. The value could be any object, including a new plug, which would be allocated using the following:

```
!ASamplePlug methods !

initialize
   myData := Plug new
```

The corresponding socket definition might look like this:

```
Plug subclass: #ASampleSocket
   instanceVariableNames: ''
   classVariableNames: ''
   poolDictionaries: ''
"
ASampleSocket connects to ASamplePlug object.
ASamplePlug object provides data via
```

```
getData and setData: methods. These methods are
for the internal protocol. ...
"

!ASampleSocket methods !

getData
  "Internal function"
  ^self otherEnd getData  !

setData: newData
  "Internal function"
  self otherEnd setData: newData ! !
```

Notice how the *otherEnd* function replaces the use of -> found in the C++ version. This is slower than accessing the *pOther* instance variable directly, but it works regardless of how the superclass is implemented. It corresponds to the C++ version, where use of the -> operator or *otherEnd* function is recommended.

Once you get the hang of Smalltalk plugs, it is easy to move on to the more complex compound and dynamic plugs and components. Components must be implemented using methods, since instance variables are not available outside of class methods. This actually follows the C++ component design recommendations, which state that references to the component's plugs should be provided by a function return value. A Smalltalk component object would include one method for each plug it wishes to make available. In fact, this is how compound plugs are done in Smalltalk.

Compound plugs can be implemented from the *Plug* class or any other class that you create that supports the plug protocol functions. The next example presents just one side of a compound connection, but an object of this class can actually be connected to another object of this class. This symmetry is easy to accomplish in Smalltalk but more difficult in C++, which relies on the macros to implement plug classes.

The *SampleCompoundPlug* class shown next uses two *Plug class* objects to form two internal connections. The basic *Plug* objects can also be connected to each other. There is also an additional instance variable that works the same way as the previous plug class definition. The source code listing follows.

```
Plug subclass: #SampleCompoundPlug
   instanceVariableNames:
      'myPlug mySocket myData '
   classVariableNames: ''
   poolDictionaries: ''    !


!SampleCompoundPlug class methods ! !


!SampleCompoundPlug methods !


afterConnect: aPlug
      "Compound connection: assume we are connecting to one of
our own"
    super afterConnect aPlug.
    myPlug <= (aPlug socket).!


beforeDisconnect: aPlug
      "Close down compound connection"
    super beforeDisconnect aPlug.
    myPlug disconnectFree!
getData
      "Return our data value"
    ^myData!


initialize
      "Private method"
    myPlug := Plug new.
    mySocket := Plug new!


setData: newData
      "Set our data value"
    myData := newData!


socket
```

```
        "Allow access to our socket"
    ^mySocket! !
```

Things to note are the addition of the *afterConnect:* and *beforeDisconnect:* methods, the contents of the initialize method, and the socket method. The initialize method creates two *Plug* objects and assigns them to the instance variables. Unlike C++, Smalltalk objects can only contain variables or arrays of variables or bytes. Here, this means that the *Plug* objects must be created out of free space and the pointers to them be stored in the object. Before you object too strongly, remember that this is how Smalltalk works in all cases, not just here. The socket method is necessary to provide access to the *mySocket* variable, which points to the *Plug* object. Only the socket method is included, because the *myPlug* variable is only used internally to create a connection between it and a plug at the other end of a compound connection. This is done in the *afterConnect:* method. The *aPlug* parameter is sent the socket message, which will provide access to its mySocket value, assuming there is another *SampleCompoundPlug* at the other end. One side of the connection makes the *myPlug* to *mySocket* connection, while the other side does the same but for the other two plugs. One side also disconnects its internal connection in the *beforeDisconnect:* method, with both internal connections being broken after both *beforeDisconnect:* methods return.

Moving from this example to more complex versions should be easy if you have taken a look at the C++ examples earlier in the book.

The issue of dynamic plugs is something slightly different in Smalltalk, where everything is allocated from free space—if you haven't guessed it already. However, the main purpose for dynamic plugs still remains and is actually more important in Smalltalk. The purpose of dynamic plugs is to cause themselves and their related components to go away when they are no longer needed. Smalltalk, with its automatic garbage collection, makes objects go away when they are no longer referenced. Unfortunately, the two-way nature of plugs can keep connections around forever. The way to prevent this is the same as in C++; determine when a plug or component no longer provides the necessary connections and then break any that remain. The main difference in Smalltalk is that after this is done the object does not have to call the delete function. It simply lets the function that is doing the cleanup return, and Smalltalk takes care of the rest. In the simplest case, there is nothing to do. For example:

```
aMethodName
    "Dynamic plug example"
    | myPlug |
    myPlug := Plug new.
    myPlug <= Plug new.

    "do something"

    myPlug disconnectFree.

    "myPlug is still usable here but the other is gone"
```

This simple function definition has a single local variable that is initialized to a *Plug object*. It is immediately connected to another unnamed object of the same type. *Unnamed* may be a misnomer—it means that a named object is one that has a symbol that references it. The unnamed plug exists as long as there is a reference to it. In this case, the reference comes from the *myPlug* plug via its connection. This connection is broken when the *disconnectFree* message is sent, at which point the unnamed plug is no longer referenced and will be removed on the next garbage collection. Nothing extra needs to be done for this to occur.

Designers of more complex components or connections must keep the dynamic plug aspect in mind when creating new classes because all plugs are essentially dynamic. Nothing is automatically deleted when a method returns as in C++, which implicitly calls a local plug object's destructor, which in turn calls the disconnect operator. So plugs should be disconnected when a method returns unless they are intended to be dynamic plugs. Likewise, components that contain many external connections need to be careful as to when these must be broken. For example, say you have a component with three external connections. Two are required and one is non-required. The non-required connection should be broken when both required connections are broken. This is normally done by checking when each required connection is broken.

Smalltalk redirectors use the same type of *RedirectorNotify* object as the C++ version. This class accepts the same set of messages and does nothing for each, as in the C++ version. A subclass of *RedirectorNotify* normally redefines one or more of the following functions:

```
Object subclass: #RedirectorNotify
  instanceVariableNames:    ''
  classVariableNames: ''
  poolDictionaries: ''    !

!RedirectorNotify class methods ! !

!RedirectorNotify methods !

connectFailed: aPlug
  "Subclass normally redefines this message"
    !

disconnected: aPlug
    !

disconnectedFree: aPlug
    !

afterConnect: aPlug
    !

beforeDisconnect: aPlug
    ! !
```

Redirectors are actually simpler in Smalltalk than in C++, and often the basic *PlugRedirector* class is all that is needed for any plug. The redirector class definitions look like this:

```
Object subclass: #PlugRedirector
```

```
    instanceVariableNames:
        'pMyEnd pRedirector  pNotify'
    classVariableNames: ''
    poolDictionaries: ''    !


!PlugRedirector class methods ! !


!PlugRedirector methods !


<= aPlug
        "Connect to a plug"
    ^pMyEnd isNil
        ifFalse: [ pMyEnd <= aPlug ]!


add: aSocket after: aPlug
        "Insert a socket"
    ^pMyEnd isNil
        ifFalse: [ pMyEnd add: aSocket after: aPlug ]!


add: aSocket before: aPlug
        "Insert a socket"
    ^pMyEnd isNil
        ifFalse: [ pMyEnd add: aSocket before: aPlug ]!


afterConnect: aPlug
        "Notify chain"
    pNotify isNil
        ifFalse: [ pNotify afterConnect: aPlug ].
    ^pRedirector isNil
        ifFalse: [ pRedirector afterConnect: aPlug ]!


beforeDisconnect: aPlug
        "Notify chain"
    pNotify isNil
        ifFalse: [ pNotify beforeDisconnect: aPlug ].
    ^pRedirector isNil
        ifFalse: [ pRedirector beforeDisconnect: aPlug ]!


connected
        "Indicate if there is a otherEnd"
```

437

```
        ^pMyEnd isNil
            ifTrue: [ nil ]
            ifFalse: [ pMyEnd connected ]!


    connectFailed: aPlug
            "Connection failed."
        pNotify isNil
          ifFalse: [ pNotify connectFailed: aPlug ].
        ^pMyEnd isNil
          ifFalse: [ pMyEnd connectFailed: aPlug ]!


    connectto: aPlug
            "Connect to the other end"
        pMyEnd isNil
            ifFalse: [ pMyEnd connectto: aPlug ]!


    disconnect
            "Disconnect from our plug"
        ^pMyEnd isNil
          ifFalse: [ pMyEnd disconnect ]!


    disconnected: aPlug
            "Notify chain"
        pNotify isNil
          ifFalse: [ pNotify disconnected: aPlug ].
        ^pRedirector isNil
          ifFalse: [ pRedirector disconnected: aPlug ]!


    disconnectedFree: aPlug
            "Notify chain"
        pNotify isNil
          ifFalse: [ pNotify disconnectedFree: aPlug ].
        ^pRedirector isNil
          ifFalse: [ pRedirector disconnectFree: aPlug ]!


    disconnectFree
            "Disconnect from our plug and free"
        ^pMyEnd isNil
          ifFalse: [ pMyEnd disconnectFree ]!
```

```
getEnd
        "Just return self for simple plugs"
    ^pMyEnd getEnd!

getPlug
        "Just return self for simple plugs"
    ^pMyEnd getPlug!

getRedirector
        "return our redirector"
     ^pMyEnd getRedirector!

isConnected
        "isSomething is a Smalltalk convention"
    ^self connected!

isRedirector
        "This is a redirector"
    ^true!

otherEnd
        "This replaces the -> operator in the C version"
    ^pMyEnd otherEnd!

redirect: aPlug
        "Redirect a new plug"
    | pOld |
    self remove.
    aPlug isNil
      ifFalse:
      [ pMyEnd := aPlug.
        pOld := aPlug setRedirector: self.
        pOld isNil
          ifFalse:
          [ pRedirector := pOld.
            pOld setMyEnd: self.
          ]
      ]!

redirectBefore: aPlug
```

```
| pOld |
pOld := pRedirector.
self redirect: pPlug.
pOld isNil
    ifFalse: [ pOld redirectBefore: aPlug. ]!

remove
  pMyEnd isNil
    ifFalse: [ pMyEnd setRedirector: pRedirector ].
  pRedirector isNil
    ifFalse: [ pRedirector setMyEnd: pMyEnd]!

resetRedirector: aPlug
    pRedirector := nil!

setMyEnd: aPlug
    pMyEnd := aPlug!

setRedirector: aRedirector
        "setup new redirector"
    pRedirector := aRedirector!

usable
        "Plugs are always usable"
    ^pMyEnd isNil
      ifTrue: [ nil ]
      ifFalse: [ pMyEnd usable ]! !
```

As in the C++ version, this example essentially forwards all applicable messages to the redirected plug. The exceptions are the methods that set and reset the *pMyEnd* instance variable. The nice thing about Smalltalk and redirectors is the ability to handle any kind of plug using the same redirector class. The redirector is essentially out of the way once a connection is made, so it only needs to implement the redirection and plug methods.

I found working with plugs and Smalltalk to be a lot of fun. In many ways it was the Smalltalk environment that made it enjoyable, but Smalltalk's polymorphism and typeless nature make it easier to implement plugs. I just wish it were easier to make connection specifications more explicit.

Borland Pascal

I am sorry to say that I have not worked extensively with the latest version of Borland Pascal and that this section only presents the groundwork for using plugs. On the other hand, much of the information presented in the previous section is applicable to Pascal because it has many of the same considerations. The main differences between the Pascal implementation and the Smalltalk implementation deal with Pascal's similarity to C++. In particular, Pascal does not support automatic garbage collection, and Pascal is a strongly typed language like C++, whereas Smalltalk is not strongly typed. For example, in Smalltalk, any object can be assigned to a variable, but in C++ and Pascal, the type of data being assigned must match the type of variable being assigned. These differences make it somewhat more difficult to work with plugs in Pascal than in Smalltalk or C++, but it can be done and without too much trouble.

First, here is a quick introduction to Pascal; then onto the program.

Pascal uses an interesting combination of special characters in its syntax. Comments are bracketed by either curly brackets, {}, or parenthesis/asterisk pairs, (* *). Pointers are designated with a leading caret, ^, as in the following:

```
type
  PlugPointer = ^Plug ;
  PlugRedirectorPointer = ^PlugRedirector ;

  anObjectClass = object
    public
      x, y : Integer ;
      procedure foo ; virtual ;
      function bar ( a, b : Integer; var ref : Integer )
          : Integer ;
  end ;
```

This example also introduces Pascal's type definition, which is similar to but uses a different syntax from the *typedef* statement in C++. The type name is to the left of the equal sign, and the type is to the right. The first two definitions are pointers. The last is a class definition.

Notice that in Pascal, sections are marked by keywords such as *type* and *public*. The class contains two variables, *x* and *y*, which are of type *Integer*; one procedure with no parameters; and one function with three parameters. The types come after the variable names, and the type name is preceded by a colon. Multiple variables can be defined at one time by separating them with commas. The keywords *virtual* and *var* are used in the definitions. The *virtual* keyword indicates that the prior procedure or function definition uses the same kind of virtual calling mechanism found in C++. There is no comparative =0 or pure designation. The *var* keyword is analogous to the *&* reference indicator in C++. It means the parameter is a pass-by reference, and any reference to the parameter within the function body will refer to the object itself, not to a copy.

Assignments in Pascal look like Smalltalk's, with the := operator, but they work like C++ assignment statements. Functions, procedures, and statements are the name of the game here, not messages. Calling an object's function or procedure looks like C++ using the dot notation, as in:

```
theObject.otherEnd()^.V
```

The *otherEnd* function associated with *theObject* is called, and the result is used with the rest of the expression. In this case, the result should be a pointer to structure (record or object in Pascal jargon). The pointer is dereferenced via the caret, ^, operator and then a member of the structure, *V*, is referenced. This syntax is actually used in conjunction with plug objects in Pascal to access functions at the other end of a connection.

Control statements work like C++ control statements, but the syntax is a little different. For example:

Pascal

```
if ( variable ) then
begin
  foo operation ;
end ;
```

C++

```
if ( variable )
{
    foo.operation () ;
}
```

Pascal

```
if ( variable ) then
begin
  foo operation1 ;
end
else
begin
  foo operation2 ;
end ;
```

C++

```
if ( variable )
{
    foo.operation () ;
}
else
{
    foo.operation () ;
}
```

Pascal

```
while ( variable ) do
begin
  foo operation ;
end ;
```

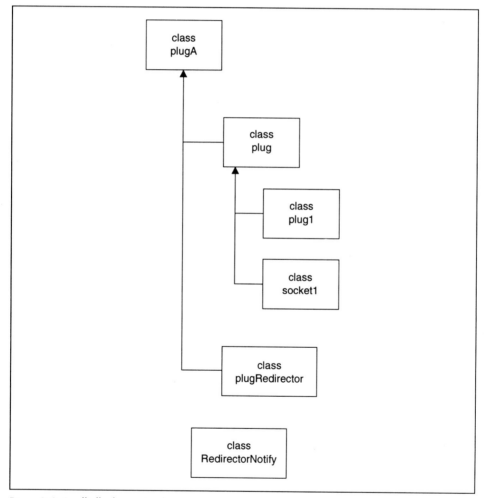

Figure D-2. Smalltalk plug protocol

C++

```
while ( variable )
{
    foo.operation () ;
}
```

Pascal uses begin/end statements instead of the C++ curly brackets to mark a block. Pascal blocks are like C++ blocks, not Smalltalk blocks, which are more flexible. You will need to keep an eye out for when semicolons need to be used in Pascal. In the *if/then/else* example, notice that there is no semicolon between the first *end* and the *else* keywords. Including a semicolon would mark the end of the *if/then* statement, so if you think there is a mistake in the samples, you may want to check it twice. Then again, it might be a misprint.

Borland Pascal does not allow function overloading or definition of operators, so all plug functions use keywords. The connect function replaces the <= connection operator. Procedures are also distinctly noted with the appropriate keyword.

As in Smalltalk, Borland Pascal supports single inheritance. The *Plug* and *PlugRedirector* class is used to define other classes. The redirector class is a subclass of the *Plug* class. In Smalltalk it was not. The two main problems with the plug class definition in Pascal are that plugs must be defined individually, and you must cast the plug reference to the appropriate type. Plugs must be defined individually because there is no macro mechanism as in C++. Casting is the way to convert a pointer of one type to another type. In this case, a generic *Plug* pointer must be changed to a more specific plug subclass pointer. This is necessary so that a plug at the other end of a connection can be referenced properly. Without casting, the only functions and procedures that could be accessed are the basic plug functions and procedures. You will see how this affects subclass definitions after looking at the basic plug and redirector class definitions, as shown in figure D-2.

The basic plug and redirector class definitions follow.

```
{ File: Plugs.PAS
V1.00 January 1993    Original version


—  Description of plug interface  —


Defining a plug class is not covered in these comments.
A plug class uses the following operations:

A.connect(B)         Connects A to B, does - -A and - -B first
A.disconnect()       Disconnects A, but will not free otherEnd;
                     returns otherEnd
A.disconnectFree()   Disconnects A; will free otherEnd
A.connected()     Returns 0 if A is disconnected
A.usable()           Returns 0 if not usable
                     (i.e. uninitialized redirector)
A.otherEnd()^.VAccess a member of the object at the other
                      end of A; normally assumes there is something
                      at the other end
R.redirect(A)        Change redirector R's reference to A; returns
                     prior reference
A.addBefore(B,C)     Connects A to B and C to what A was connected
                     to; if A has a redirector then it points to C
A.addAfter (B,C)     Like addBefore; if A has a redirector it does
                     not change
}


************************************************************
type  EndPointer = ^PlugA ;
  PlugPointer = ^Plug ;
  PlugRedirectorPointer = ^PlugRedirector ;
  RedirectorNotifyPointer = ^RedirectorNotify ;

  RedirectorNotify = object
    public
      procedure disconnected     ( pPlug : PlugPointer ) ; virtual ;
      procedure disconnectedFree ( pPlug : PlugPointer ) ; virtual ;
      procedure connectFailed    ( pPlug : PlugPointer ) ; virtual ;
      procedure afterConnect     ( pPlug : PlugPointer ) ; virtual ;
      procedure beforeDisconnect ( pPlug : PlugPointer ) ; virtual ;
    end ;
```

```
PlugA = object
  private
    pOther      : Pointer ;
    pRedirector : PlugRedirectorPointer ;

  public
    destructor Done           ; virtual ;

    function  otherEnd         : PlugPointer ; virtual ;

    function  isRedirector     : Boolean ; virtual ;
    function  connected        : Boolean ; virtual ;
    function  usable           : Boolean ; virtual ;

    procedure connect          ( var newEnd : PlugA ) ; virtual ;
    function  disconnect       : PlugPointer ; virtual ;
    procedure disconnectFree   ; virtual ;

    procedure addBefore        ( inner, newEnd : EndPointer ) ; virtual ;
    procedure addAfter         ( inner, newEnd : EndPointer ) ; virtual ;

    function  getRedirector    : Pointer ; virtual ;
    function  setRedirector    ( newRedirector :
      PlugRedirectorPointer )
                               : PlugRedirectorPointer ; virtual ;
    procedure setMyEnd         ( newEnd : EndPointer ) ; virtual ;

    function  getPlug          : PlugPointer ; virtual ;
    function  getEnd           : EndPointer ; virtual ;

    procedure connectFailed    ; virtual ;
end ;

Plug = object ( PlugA )
  public
    function  disconnect       : PlugPointer ; virtual ;
    procedure disconnectFree   ; virtual ;

    procedure addBefore        ( inner, newEnd : EndPointer ); virtual ;
```

```
      procedure addAfter              ( inner, newEnd : EndPointer ); virtual ;

      procedure connectto             ( newEnd : PlugPointer ) ;virtual ;
      procedure disconnectedFree ( oldEnd : PlugPointer ) ;virtual ;
      procedure disconnected          ( oldEnd : PlugPointer ) ;virtual ;
      procedure connectFailed         ; virtual ;
      procedure afterConnect          ( newEnd : PlugPointer ) ;virtual ;
      procedure beforeDisconnect ( oldEnd : PlugPointer ) ;virtual ;
  end ;



PlugRedirector = object ( PlugA )
  private
    pNotify : RedirectorNotifyPointer ;

  public
    destructor Done               : virtual ;

    procedure setNotify           ( p : RedirectorNotifyPointer ) ; virtual;

    function  otherEnd            : PlugPointer ; virtual ;

    function  isRedirector        : Boolean ; virtual ;
    function  connected           : Boolean ; virtual ;
    function  usable              : Boolean ; virtual ;

    procedure connect             ( var newEnd : PlugA ) ;virtual ;
    function  disconnect          : PlugPointer ; virtual ;
    procedure disconnectFree      ; virtual ;

    procedure addBefore           ( inner, newEnd : EndPointer ) ; virtual ;
    procedure addAfter            ( inner, newEnd : EndPointer ) ; virtual ;
    function  getPlug             : PlugPointer ; virtual ;
    function  getEnd              : EndPointer ; virtual ;

    procedure disconnectedFree ( oldEnd : PlugPointer ) ;virtual ;
    procedure disconnected        ( oldEnd : PlugPointer ) ;virtual ;
    procedure connectFailedPR     ( myPlug : PlugPointer ) ;virtual ;
    procedure afterConnect        ( newEnd : PlugPointer ) ;virtual ;
```

```
      procedure beforeDisconnect ( oldEnd : PlugPointer ) ;virtual ;

      procedure redirectBefore   ( newEnd : EndPointer ) ;virtual ;
      procedure redirect         ( newEnd : EndPointer ) ;virtual ;
      procedure remove           ; virtual ;
   end ;



{ —   Abstract Plug Class definitions  — }

destructor PlugA.Done ;
begin
  if ( pOther <> nil ) then
     PlugPointer(pOther)^.disconnectedFree ( @ Self ) ;
end ;

function PlugA.otherEnd : PlugPointer ;
begin
  otherEnd := pOther ;
end ;



function PlugA.isRedirector : Boolean ;
begin
  isRedirector := False ;
end ;



function PlugA.connected : Boolean ;
begin
  connected := ( pOther <> nil ) ;
end ;



function PlugA.usable : Boolean ;
begin
  usable := True ;
end ;
```

```
procedure PlugA.connect ( var newEnd : PlugA ) ;
var
  prior1,prior2  : PlugPointer ;
  e1, e2         : EndPointer ;
  p1, p2         : PlugPointer ;
begin
  prior1 := Self.disconnect ;


  if ( prior1 <> nil ) then
    prior1^.disconnectFree ;

  if ( @ newEnd <> nil ) then
  begin
prior2:=PlugA.disconnect;
  if ( prior2 <> nil ) then
    prior2^.disconnectFree ;
    e1 := getEnd ;
    if ( e1 <> nil ) then
    begin
      e2 := newEnd.getEnd ;
      if ( e2 <> nil ) then
      begin
        p1 := e1^.getPlug ;
        p2 := e2^.getPlug ;
        p1^.connectto    ( p2 ) ;
        p2^.connectto    ( p1 ) ;
        p1^.afterConnect ( p2 ) ;
        p2^.afterConnect ( p1 ) ;
      end
      else
    e1^.connectFailed ;
    end
  end else
    connectFailed ;

end ;
```

```
function PlugA.disconnect : PlugPointer ;
begin
  { defined in Plug and PlugRedirector }
end ;


procedure PlugA.disconnectFree ;
begin
  { defined in Plug and PlugRedirector }
end ;


procedure PlugA.addBefore ( inner, newEnd : EndPointer ) ;
begin
  { defined in Plug and PlugRedirector }
end ;


procedure PlugA.addAfter ( inner, newEnd : EndPointer ) ;
begin
  { defined in Plug and PlugRedirector }
end ;


function PlugA.getRedirector : Pointer ;
begin
  getRedirector := pRedirector ;
end ;


function PlugA.setRedirector ( newRedirector :
 PlugRedirectorPointer )
   : PlugRedirectorPointer ;
var
  pOld : PlugRedirectorPointer ;
begin
  pOld          := pRedirector ;
  pRedirector   := newRedirector ;
  setRedirector := pOld ;
end ;
```

```
procedure PlugA.setMyEnd ( newEnd : EndPointer ) ;
begin
  pOther := newEnd ;
end ;


function PlugA.getEnd : EndPointer ;
begin
  getEnd := @ Self ;
end ;


function PlugA.getPlug : PlugPointer ;
begin
  getPlug := @ Self ;
end ;


procedure PlugA.connectFailed ;
begin
end ;


{ —   Plug Class definitions  — }

function Plug.disconnect : PlugPointer ;
var
  prior : PlugPointer ;
begin
  prior := pOther ;

  if ( prior <> nil ) then
  begin
    beforeDisconnect ( prior ) ;
    prior^.beforeDisconnect ( @ Self ) ;
    disconnected ( prior ) ;
    prior^.disconnected ( @ Self ) ;
  end ;
```

```
    disconnect := prior ;
end ;



procedure Plug.disconnectFree ;
var
  prior : PlugPointer ;
begin
  prior := disconnect ;

  if ( prior <> nil ) then
    prior^.disconnectedFree ( @ Self ) ;

  disconnectedFree ( prior ) ;
end ;



procedure Plug.addBefore ( inner, newEnd : EndPointer ) ;
begin
  addAfter ( inner, newEnd ) ;

  if ( pRedirector <> nil ) then
  begin
    pRedirector^.redirectBefore ( newEnd ) ;
  end
end ;



procedure Plug.addAfter ( inner, newEnd : EndPointer ) ;
begin
  if (      ( pOther <> nil )
       and ( newEnd <> nil )
     )
  then
    newEnd^.connect ( disconnect^ ) ;

  Self.connect ( inner^ ) ;
end ;
```

```
procedure Plug.connectto ( newEnd : PlugPointer) ;
begin
  if ( pOther <> nil ) then
    PlugPointer(pOther)^.disconnectFree ;

  pOther := newEnd ;
end ;


procedure Plug.disconnectedFree ( oldEnd : PlugPointer ) ;
begin
  if ( pRedirector <> nil ) then
    pRedirector^.disconnectedFree ( @ Self ) ;
end ;


procedure Plug.disconnected ( oldEnd : PlugPointer ) ;
begin
  pOther := nil ;
  if ( pRedirector <> nil ) then
    pRedirector^.disconnected ( @ Self ) ;
end ;


procedure Plug.connectFailed ;
begin
  if ( pRedirector <> nil ) then
    pRedirector^.connectFailedPR ( @ Self ) ;
end ;


procedure Plug.afterConnect ( newEnd : PlugPointer ) ;
begin
  if ( pRedirector <> nil ) then
    pRedirector^.afterConnect ( @ Self ) ;
end ;
```

```
procedure Plug.beforeDisconnect ( oldEnd : PlugPointer ) ;
begin
  if ( pRedirector <> nil ) then
    pRedirector^.beforeDisconnect ( @ Self ) ;
end ;



{ —    PlugRedirector Class definitions   — }

destructor PlugRedirector.Done ;
begin
  remove ;
end ;



procedure PlugRedirector.setNotify ( p :
 RedirectorNotifyPointer ) ;
begin
  pNotify := p ;
end ;



function PlugRedirector.otherEnd : PlugPointer ;
begin
  otherEnd := EndPointer(pOther)^.otherEnd ;
end ;



function PlugRedirector.isRedirector : Boolean ;
begin
  isRedirector := True ;
end ;



function PlugRedirector.connected : Boolean ;
begin
  if ( pOther <> nil ) then
    connected := False
  else
    connected := EndPointer(pOther)^.connected ;
```

```
end ;


function PlugRedirector.usable : Boolean ;
begin
  if ( pOther <> nil ) then
    usable := False
  else
    usable := EndPointer(pOther)^.usable ;
end ;


procedure PlugRedirector.connect ( var newEnd : PlugA ) ;
begin
  if ( pOther <> nil ) then    EndPointer(pOther)^.connect ( newEnd
) ;
end ;


function PlugRedirector.disconnect : PlugPointer ;
begin
  if ( pOther <> nil ) then
    disconnect := EndPointer(pOther)^.disconnect
  else
    disconnect := nil ;
end ;


procedure PlugRedirector.disconnectFree ;
begin
  if ( pOther <> nil ) then
    EndPointer(pOther)^.disconnectFree ;
end ;


procedure PlugRedirector.addBefore ( inner, newEnd : EndPointer
 ) ;
begin
  if ( pOther <> nil ) then
    EndPointer(pOther)^.addBefore ( inner, newEnd ) ;
```

```
end ;


procedure PlugRedirector.addAfter ( inner, newEnd : EndPointer
  ) ;
begin
  if ( pOther <> nil ) then
    EndPointer(pOther)^.addAfter ( inner, newEnd ) ;
end ;


function PlugRedirector.getPlug : PlugPointer ;
begin
  if ( pOther <> nil ) then
    getPlug := EndPointer(pOther)^.getPlug
  else
    getPlug := nil ;
end ;


function PlugRedirector.getEnd : EndPointer ;
begin
  if ( pOther <> nil ) then
    getEnd := EndPointer(pOther)^.getEnd
  else
    getEnd := nil ;
end ;


procedure PlugRedirector.disconnectedFree ( oldEnd :
PlugPointer ) ;
begin
  if ( pRedirector <> nil ) then
    pRedirector^.disconnectedFree ( oldEnd ) ;
  if ( pNotify <> nil ) then
    pNotify^.disconnectedFree ( oldEnd ) ;
end ;


procedure PlugRedirector.disconnected ( oldEnd : PlugPointer )
```

```
                ;
              begin
                if ( pRedirector <> nil ) then
                  pRedirector^.disconnected ( oldEnd ) ;
                if ( pNotify <> nil ) then
                  pNotify^.disconnected ( oldEnd ) ;
              end ;


              procedure PlugRedirector.connectFailedPR ( myPlug : PlugPointer
              ) ;
              begin
                if ( pRedirector <> nil ) then
                  pRedirector^.connectFailedPR ( myPlug ) ;
                if ( pNotify <> nil ) then
                  pNotify^.connectFailed ( myPlug ) ;
              end ;


              procedure PlugRedirector.afterConnect ( newEnd : PlugPointer )
              ;
              begin
                if ( pRedirector <> nil ) then
                  pRedirector^.afterConnect ( newEnd ) ;
                if ( pNotify <> nil ) then
                  pNotify^.afterConnect ( newEnd ) ;
              end ;


              procedure PlugRedirector.beforeDisconnect ( oldEnd : PlugPointer )
              ;
              begin
                if ( pRedirector <> nil ) then
                  pRedirector^.beforeDisconnect ( oldEnd ) ;
                if ( pNotify <> nil ) then
                  pNotify^.beforeDisconnect ( oldEnd ) ;
              end ;


              procedure PlugRedirector.redirect ( newEnd : EndPointer ) ;
```

```
var
  pOld : PlugRedirectorPointer ;
begin
  remove ;
  if ( newEnd <> nil ) then
  begin
    pOther := newEnd ;
    pOld   := newEnd^.setRedirector ( @ Self ) ;
    if ( pOld <> nil ) then
    begin
      pRedirector := pOld ;
      pOld^.setMyEnd ( @ Self ) ;
    end
  end
end ;


procedure PlugRedirector.remove ;
begin
  if ( pOther <> nil ) then
EndPointer(pOther)^.setRedirector(pRedirector) ;
  if ( pRedirector <> nil ) then
    pRedirector^.setMyEnd ( pOther ) ;
end ;


procedure PlugRedirector.redirectBefore ( newEnd : EndPointer )
;
var
  pOld : PlugRedirectorPointer ;
begin
  pOld := pRedirector ;
  redirect ( newEnd ) ;
  if ( pOld <> nil ) then
    pOld^.redirectBefore ( newEnd ) ;
end ;


{ ====  RedirectorNotify Definitions  ==== }
```

```
procedure RedirectorNotify.disconnected ( pPlug : PlugPointer )
;
begin
end ;


procedure RedirectorNotify.disconnectedFree ( pPlug : PlugPointer
) ;
begin
end ;


procedure RedirectorNotify.connectFailed ( pPlug :PlugPointer
) ;
begin
end ;


procedure RedirectorNotify.afterConnect ( pPlug : PlugPointer )
;
begin
end ;


procedure RedirectorNotify.beforeDisconnect ( pPlug :
PlugPointer ) ;
begin
end ;


begin
end.
```

The comment at the beginning of the code shows how the functions have changed from the C++ operators. Overall, the difference is just a few characters. The semantics remain the same. The two pointer type definitions allow the use of *PlugPointer* and *PlugRedirectorPointer* instead of the more cryptic pointer specification. Actually, it is probably not that cryptic if you are used to Pascal. The PlugA class definition includes a pair of private pointers and a set of public functions and procedures. The bodies for all the functions and procedures must come after the class definition. The same is true of the *Plug* and *PlugRedirector* class, which inherits from the *PlugA* class, hence the *PlugA* keyword in parentheses after the keyword object. The *destructor* keyword indicates a special procedure that is called when an object is destroyed. This does the same things as the *~class* definition in C++.

The body for the *PlugA* destructor procedure appears after the type definitions. Of note in this definition is the use of the keywords *nil, Self,* and the address operator, @. The value *nil* is the same as a *NULL* or *0* pointer in C++. *Self* refers to the object. It is effectively the same as * *this* in C++ or *self* in Smalltalk. The address operator returns a pointer to the respective variable.

The class hierarchy is similar to the C++ version. The difference is that a single *Plug* and *PlugRedirector* class is defined for all connections. There is no differentiation between objects with respect to connections.

There should be no surprises until you get to the connected function. The function return value is set by assigning a value to a variable whose name is the same as the function. In this function, the value assigned is a Boolean result obtained from the comparison between *nil* and the pointer *pOther*.

Moving over a few other functions, to the connect function, you can see how Pascal defines local variables. The *var* keyword marks the section for new variables. Yes, this is the same *var* keyword found in the parameter list, but it has a different meaning depending upon where you find it. (Hey, I didn't write the specs for Pascal, I just write in it.) In any case, the function does the same thing as the C++ and Smalltalk versions. The @ operator is used to obtain the address of the *newEnd* parameter, just in case a nil value is passed to the function. If you have been reading this book from the start you are probably tired of seeing this code.

The *disconnect* and *disconnectFree* functions have nothing new compared to the C++ or Smalltalk versions other than the syntax change. The same holds true for the *addBefore* and *addAfter* procedures and the redirector-related procedures and functions. The *getPlug* and *getEnd* functions return a pointer to the object just as a basic plug does. The rest of the functions and procedures are about as interesting.

The *PlugRedirector* class function and procedure definitions come after the *PlugA* definitions. These are operationally the same as the C++ and Smalltalk versions. Each function that forwards the call to the plug checks to see if *pOther* is not *nil* and then calls the plug function if the plug is referenced.

A pair of plugs can be defined to work with each other, but there must be an additional function added. This is necessary in order for the plug to access the socket at the other end of the connection using the pointer of the appropriate type, so all members can be accessed properly. For example:

```
type
  SamplePlugPointer = ^SamplePlug ;
  SampleSocketPointer = ^ SampleSocket ;

  SamplePlug = object ( Plug )
    public
      function SampleSocket : SampleSocketPointer ; virtual ;

      procedure Procedure1 ; virtual ;
  end ;



  SampleSocket = object ( Plug )
    public
      function SamplePlug : SamplePlugPointer ; virtual ;
      procedure Procedure2 ; virtual ;
  end ;



  function SamplePlug.SampleSocket : SampleSocketPointer ;
```

```
begin
  SampleSocket := SampleSocketPointer ( otherEnd ) ;
end ;



procedure SamplePlug.Procedure1 ;
begin
  SampleSocket^.Procedure2 ;
end ;



function SampleSocket.SamplePlug : SamplePlugPointer ;
begin
  SamplePlug := SamplePlugPointer ( otherEnd ) ;
end ;



procedure SampleSocket.Procedure2 ;
begin
end ;
```

The preceding code shows the necessary additional functions for accessing the other side of a connection as well as functions to access. *Procedure1* uses the *SampleSocket* function, which is also the name of the class socket class, to get the pointer to the socket at the other end of the connection. It hides the cast within itself so *Procedure1* does not have to. This trade-off may seem insignificant in this example, but imagine a dozen procedures that need to access the other end of the connection. Then keeping the cast hidden within a function makes sense. The choice of names is arbitrary. Something like *OtherEnd*, which would not conflict with *otherEnd*, could have been used just as easily.

In any case, calling *Procedure1* causes *SampleSocket* to be called, which in turn calls the *Plug* class *otherEnd* function. The pointer returned is then returned by *SampleSocket*. This pointer is then used to call the *Procedure2* procedure. The *SampleSocket* function can easily be optimized by using *pOther* directly, in which case there is no more overhead than with the *otherEnd* function. It is even possible to use a non-virtual inline function, in which case the access is as efficient as using *pOther* directly. In fact, the code winds up being the same thing because the cast operation does nothing.

Once you have access to functions and procedures at the other end of a connection, you can build any of the plugs or components discussed in this book. Pascal supports dynamically allocated objects, so dynamic plugs can be created in addition to compound plugs. Keep in mind that dynamic plugs operate as they do in C++, not Smalltalk. Plugs must be explicitly deleted if they are allocated from free space. Local plugs are automatically deleted when the function in which they are declared returns.

The main problem with this and with the Smalltalk implementation is that it allows any kind of plug to be connected with another plug. One way around this is to require that each plug class define its own connect procedure and *otherEnd* function. The base *Plug* class could keep the existing procedure and functions but rename them so they could be used by a subclass, as in the following definition:

```
type
  Sample2Plug = object ( Plug )
    public
      procedure connect ( var newEnd : Sample2Socket )  ;
  virtual ;
      function      otherEnd : Sample2SocketPointer ; virtual ;
    end ;


  procedure Sample2Plug.connect ( var newEnd : Sample2Socket ) ;
  begin
    internalConnect ( newEnd ) ;
```

```
    end ;



function Sample2Plug.otherEnd : Sample2SocketPointer ;
begin
    otherEnd := Sample2SocketPointer (pOther) ;
end ;
```

This requires more work but prevents inadvertent connections.

Regardless of the implementation approach taken, plugs can be used with Borland Pascal. It takes a little more typing than with C++ because of the lack of macro support, but the payoff can be well worth the typing time.

C++ Alternative and Other Comments

Although not included here, it is possible to define a *Plug* and *PlugRedirector* class for C++ in the same way as Smalltalk and Pascal. However, you wind up with the same problems and restrictions found in the Pascal implementation. The same comments apply to such a version.

Plugs can be implemented in just about any object-oriented language without too much difficulty. This book shows three different implementations that differ very little from each other semantically. Unfortunately, most object-oriented languages do not work well with each other. Use of functions or procedures in a linked library or dynamic linked library is typically limited to simple function and procedure calls, not the more powerful object-oriented function and procedure calls. Until this type of support is available, mixing plugs across languages is going to be very difficult at best.

E A C++ Primer

C++ is an object-oriented extension for C. This appendix presents some of the syntax and semantics of C++. It is not intended as an overview of the entire C++ language but rather of the portions used in this book.

Class definitions are central to C++. A class definition is similar to a C structure definition with named elements or members. The difference is that C structures can only contain data members, while C++ classes can contain function and data members. Each C++ class member is also either *public, protected,* or *private,* specifying in what context a member of a class can be accessed. The contexts considered include the class member functions, subclass member functions, *friend* functions, and other functions. A *friend* function is not a member function, and it must be explicitly defined as a friend function in a class definition.

Member functions can access any members defined in the same class. A *public* member can be accessed from any context. A *protected* member can be accessed by friend functions and subclass functions (that is, member functions with a superclass that has protected members). A *private* member can only be accessed by member functions of that class definition. The following is a basic class definition:

```
class BasicClass
{
    int ImplicitlyProtected ;

  public:
    void PublicMember1 () ;
    int PublicInt ;
```

```
protected:
  char ExplicitlyProtected ;

private:
  long PrivateMember ;

public:
  void PublicMember2 () {}
  int PublicMember3 ( int i ) { return i +1 ; }


} ;
```

This definition shows a class that uses all three access groups: *public, protected,* and *private.* The members coming after the respective keyword have the associated access controls. The initial default group is *protected.* However, it is good programming practice to explicitly state the initial access group instead of using the initial default. Member functions can be defined in a class definition or after the class definition, in which case the class definition contains a function prototype. *PublicMember1* is a prototype, while the other two public members are defined inline. (The function is the part within the braces.)

The definition for non-inline functions must come after a class definition. However, only one instance of the definition is allowed within all modules that are to be linked together to form a program. This restriction is identical to external function definitions. A class definition often appears in a header file so an object of the class can be used in different modules, which are compiled and include the header file. The public member definition from the previous example requires a definition such as the following:

```
void BasicClass::PublicMember1 ()
{
}
```

The class name precedes the member name and is separated by double colons *(::).* This syntax is used whenever a class member needs to be explicitly referenced to avoid ambiguities. For example, a subclass can explicitly call a superclass function that has been redefined in the subclass by using the superclass name; otherwise, the subclass function would be called.

Members are accessed using the C structure access syntax. For example, if foo is an object of class *BasicClass*, then *foo.PublicInt* will refer to *PublicInt* in *foo*, and *foo.PublicMember1* invokes a function. Member functions have implicit access to the members of their class. Name scope in a member function starts with local definitions, including parameters, followed by object members, and finally, global definitions. A member function also has an implicit hidden parameter included as part of each function call. It is the pointer to the object used to invoke the call, and the pointer can be referred to within the function by the name *this*.

Actually, the member functions may be static or not. A static function has a *static* keyword before the function name in the class function definition or prototype. The function operation described in the previous chapter is for non-static member functions. Static class functions are not invoked in conjunction with an object and do not have the implicit object pointer parameter. Therefore, the *this* variable cannot be used in static member functions. Static member functions can be called by member functions using the name of the static function. Functions outside the scope of the class definition can access the static member, assuming they have the right to; that is, if the static member function is public, it can prefix the invocation by the class name, as in:

```
class StaticClassExample
{

  public:
    static void StaticMemberFunction ()
    {
      StaticMember = 1 ;
    }

    static int StaticMember ;
```

```
    int PublicInt ;
    int PublicFunction ( return StaticMember + PublicInt ; )
} ;
```

The previous definition includes a static member function as well as a static variable. Objects of type *StaticClassExample* include only *PublicInt*. There is also a single instance of *StaticMember*, which is a global variable whose naming scope is the class definition. Non-static member functions, such as *PublicFunction*, can access static and non-static members. Static functions can only access static members. External references to static members are done using the class name prefix, as in *StaticClassExample::StaticMember*.

Non-static class member functions can also be *virtual*. Virtual functions provide polymorphic object support for C++. A virtual function is defined and used in the same way as a non-virtual member function. The additional keyword is the only syntactical difference. However, an object whose class or superclass contains at least one *virtual* function will contain a hidden pointer to a table that contains pointers to the functions. An invocation of the function will use this pointer in the corresponding object to find the corresponding function. The function call then proceeds like a normal member function call, including providing support for the implicit object pointer, *this*. The size of the function pointer table is based upon the number of virtual functions associated with the class.

Virtual functions only become interesting in conjunction with class inheritance. The following example shows the syntax for a class with a single superclass (that is, single inheritance):

```
class SuperClass
{
  public:
    int PublicInt ;
    virtual int VirtualIntFunction () { return PublicInt + 1 ; }

} ;
```

```
class SubClass : public SuperClass
{

   public:
     int SubClassInt;
     virtual int VirtualIntFunction () { return PublicInt + 2 ; }


   } ;
```

The *SuperClass* objects contain both a *PublicInt* integer and the hidden function table pointer. The *SubClass* objects use the same structure but add the *SubClassInt*. The access keywords prefix the superclass name and apply the same access restrictions implied by the keyword to all members of the superclass within the class. A protected superclass has protected members with respect to the subclass. The other difference is that the *SubClass* object's table pointer does not point to the same table as the *SuperClass* function pointer table pointer. The one entry in the *SuperClass* function pointer table points to the *VirtualIntFunction* defined in *SuperClass*. The entry in the *SubClass* function pointer table points to the *VirtualIntFunction* defined in *SubClass*. The *virtual* keyword in the *SubClass* function definition can be omitted, but the function will still be defined as virtual because it is defined that way by its superclass.

An object can be used wherever an object of its superclass can be used. For example, a pointer to a *SuperClass* object can point to a *SuperClass* object or a *SubClass* object. A call to *VirtualIntFunction* will use the appropriate table and function depending upon the type of object.

The body of a virtual function does not have to be defined. Such a member function is called a pure function or pure virtual function. A class that contains a pure function definition is called an abstract class. You can define pointers to an abstract class, but you cannot create an object (instance) of an abstract class. A subclass of an abstract class is also an abstract class if it contains pure function definitions or if it does not provide function definitions for all pure virtual functions. Essentially, an object can only be defined by a class that has all its functions defined.

Any class, including an abstract class, can be defined without any data members. An abstract class is often defined this way, with only function definitions. It is not uncommon to have an abstract class that contains only pure function definitions. This type of class defines a functional interface to polymorphic objects with a superclass of the abstract class. Subclasses of the superclass can implement the functions as needed and include additional data members as needed. These subclasses can be very different from each other in both structure and operation. Plug connection classes are implemented as abstract classes to support the polymorphic requirements for replaceable parts.

C++ supports multiple inheritance, which allows a class to have more than one superclass. The names of the superclasses are listed in the class definition with the appropriate access keyword prefixes, as in:

```
class MultipleSubClass :
  public ClassA,
  protected ClassB,
  private ClassC
{
} ;
```

Objects of type *MultipleSubClass* include the structures of an object of *ClassA*, *ClassB*, and *ClassC*. Objects of type *MultipleSubClass* can be used in place of objects of *ClassA*, *ClassB*, *ClassC*, and *MultipleSubClass*. The *virtual* keyword can also be used as a prefix, which causes a single object of that class to be used in the subclass. Superclasses that are also based on the class will use this one common object. An example that could use multiple inheritance is a bank account class used by two other classes, accounts payable and accounts receivable. The two account classes are based upon the *virtual* bank account class. The two account classes use a single bank account object when they are merged into a single subclass. Plugs do not require multiple inheritance for their support, but multiple inheritance can be used by base classes used with a plug. The details of plug definitions are covered in Chapter 2.

Classes have two functions, called *constructors* and *destructors*. There must be at least one of each, but there may be more than one. A default constructor and destructor for every class that does not define one is included, as in the previous examples. The function name for a constructor is the class name. The destructor is the same, except that a tilde, ~, prefixes the name. Both types of functions return no value and have no type associated with them. A constructor is called when an object is created. It can initialize object variables or perform other application-specific operations. The destructor is called when an object is deleted. Local objects are defined within a function and allocated when the function is entered. The constructor is called after this allocation. The destructor is called just before the function returns. Global objects are initialized when the program starts, and the constructor is then called. Destructors for global objects should be called when a program terminates. A constructor is called for dynamically allocated objects after the space for the object is allocated from the stack using the new function. The destructor is called when the object is deleted, using the delete function. Constructor and destructor functions can have parameters.

Unlike C, C++ allows C operators to be defined as functions for any class. This feature is used with plugs to implement the plug operators, <=, -, and --. Unary and binary operators can be defined using different parameters, and they may return results. The syntax for defining an operator looks like a normal function definition, except that the keyword operator comes before the operator itself, as in:

```
class SampleOperator
{

  public:
    void operator - () ;
    int operator - - () ;
    int operator <= ( int i ) ;
} ;
```

Two unary operators, - and --, and one binary operator, <=, are defined. Note that the - operator does not return a value. The type of result and type of parameters are arbitrary, as with any function definition, with some special exceptions. For example, the -> and * operators must return pointers in order to be used to access a structure or object. The only limitation on operators is the number of explicit parameters, which must be 0 or 1. The implied parameter is an object of the class; in this case *SampleOperator.*

Operators and functions can be overloaded, which means that the same name or operator can be used by more than one function definition. The only requirement is that each function be unique with respect to its parameter list, either by number of parameters or by type of parameter. The following function definitions are valid:

```
class OverloadClass
{

  public:
    OverloadClass () ;
    OverloadClass ( int i ) ;
    int foo () ;
    long foo ( long i ) ;
    int foo ( int i, char c ) ;
    int operator - () ;
    int operator - ( int i ) ;
} ;
```

For any parameter list combination only one function will be valid. Constructor and destructor functions can be overloaded. Note that the return type does not have to be the same for different function definitions. Also, some operators have a binary and unary version. It is not possible to have an operator with more than *1* explicit parameter.

Functions can be defined with default parameter values. These values are used if none is provided. For example:

```
class DefaultSample
{

  public:
    int foo ( int i, int j = 1, int k = 2 ) ;

} ;
```

The function *foo* can be called with *1, 2, or 3* parameters. Calling *foo* with *0* parameters will result in a compiler error because there is no definition for *foo* with *0* parameters. It uses *1* for *j* and *2* for *k* if it is invoked using *1* parameter. All parameters after a parameter defined with a default value must also have default values.

The C++ class system is a very powerful and complicated system. Keep in mind that this appendix only briefly addresses the class system with respect to the features used in this book.

C #define

The C *#define* statement is used to define macros, which are expanded when a program is compiled. Macros are used throughout this book, but their definitions are only found in the appendixes. An understanding of macros, other than how to invoke them, is not required to read and understand this book. Skip this section if you already know about C *#define* statements, or if your interest doesn't extend to the detail of the material in the appendixes.

A *#define* statement can define parameterized and non-parameterized macros. A macro's definition must appear before its keyword is used in the program. The *#define* text replaces the keyword and any parameters in the source code when the program is compiled, and the replacement text is then compiled. This process is usually called *macro expansion*. Replacement is recursive until all macros have been expanded. For example, the following are simple non-parameterized macro definitions:

```
#define TRUE 1
```

#define FALSE 0

Any instance of *TRUE* is replaced by *1* and *FALSE* by *0*. Parameterized definitions include a list of names in parentheses, separated by commas. They are invoked like functions, with a matching parameter list. A parameter can be any string with leading and trailing blanks removed when the macro replacement is made. The left parenthesis of the parameter list in a parameterized *#define* must follow immediately after the keyword. For example:

```
#define SetAdd(a,b,c) a = b + c

SetAdd( i, i, 1+2 ) ;
```

The first statement defines the macro and the second invokes it. The compiler winds up compiling a statement that looks like the following:

```
i = i +1+2 ;
```

One additional macro feature definition used in the appendixes allows text to be joined together.

Index